Slaves, Sugar,
& Colonial Society

Slaves, Sugar, & Colonial Society

Travel Accounts of Cuba, 1801–1899

Edited by Louis A. Pérez, Jr.

A Scholarly Resources Inc. Imprint
Wilmington, Delaware

The paper used in this publication meets the minimum requirements of the American National Standard for permanence of
paper for printed library materials, Z39.48, 1984.

Scholarly Resources Inc.
104 Greenhill Avenue
Wilmington, DE 19805-1897

Library of Congress Cataloging-in-Publication Data

Slaves, sugar, and colonial society : travel accounts of Cuba,
  1801–1899 / edited by Louis A. Pérez, Jr.
      p. cm.
    Includes bibliographical references and index.
    ISBN 0-8420-2354-2. — ISBN 0-8420-2415-8 (pbk.)
    1. Cuba—Social conditions. 2. Visitors, Foreign—Cuba—
Attitudes. 3. Cuba—History—1810–1899. I. Pérez, Louis A.,
1943- .
HN203.S57 1992
306'.097291—dc20   91-44977
                                                              CIP

To the memory of Thomas P. Dilkes (1926–1991):
teacher, colleague, and friend

Louis A. Pérez, Jr., is Distinguished Professor of History at the University of South Florida, Tampa. His previous books include *Cuba between Empires, 1878–1902* (1983), *Cuba: Between Reform and Revolution* (1988), and *Cuba and the United States: Ties of Singular Intimacy* (1990).

Contents

Acknowledgments, ix

Introduction, xi

I Havana, 1

II The Sugar Plantation: Production, Culture, and Economy, 41

III Slaves and Slavery, 97

IV Crime and Punishment, 133

V Church, State, and Religion, 147

VI Health, Education, and Charity, 179

VII Rural Life, 203

VIII Nineteenth-Century Society, 225

List of Sources, 249

Bibliographical Essay: Selected Titles, 251

Index, 257

Acknowledgments

This book would not have been possible without the assistance of many others. The staffs of the Library of Congress, the University of Florida Library, and the Library of the University of South Florida provided many of the more useful narratives. I am especially appreciative of the assistance of the interlibrary loan office of the University of South Florida, and of Sharon K. Epps, Pamela See, and Mary Kay Hartung. I am indebted to Carole Rennick, who over the course of two years worked laboriously and patiently to bring the disparate and fragmentary elements of this book into a unified whole. To Richard M. Hopper is owed a particular acknowledgment of gratitude; his patience and encouragement supported the project from its inception.

Introduction

I

The nineteenth century was a time of change in Cuba, dramatic and visible change, almost everywhere on the island, for almost everyone—men and women of all races, of all ages, of all classes. These were decades in which change produced change, often in rapid succession. Residents learned to live with change as a way of life. It often came in ways that were immediate, and people's lives were instantly modified forever. Other times it arrived slowly, from sources unseen and with effects at the time unknown. Change occurred faster in the cities than in the countryside—fastest in Havana and slowest in Oriente. The rural interior often assumed the appearance of changelessness. Novelty and new ways arrived slowly, if at all.

Change was a recurring phenomenon on the island, or so it seemed after the end of the eighteenth century: It was familiar, a condition around which most Cubans routinely organized their daily lives. During these years market forces transformed sugar production into the dominant economic activity of the island and in the process changed everything else. This was true nowhere more than in the realm of relationships: economic and political relations between the colony and the metropolis and social relations within the colony, between whites and blacks and among whites themselves as cultural and ethnic distinctions between Creoles and *peninsulares* increasingly assumed social, economic, and political implications and eventually were shaped into an ideological vernacular.

Cuba was in transition during much of the nineteenth century. The pace of change varied, to be sure, but transition was constant. The changes were all interrelated, and most were related to sugar. The increase of sugar production, the expansion of trade relations, the emergence of new social classes, and the growth of population—especially among people of color, free and slave—all changed the island in ways permanent and profound.

Many of these changes were apparent, then as well as now. They could be measured and quantified, in a variety of ways, through a variety of means. Increased sugar production was weighed and its value calculated. Rising land values were appraised and assessed. Expanding trade revenues were tallied in the form of customs duties, sales taxes, and import fees. Population growth was enumerated periodically, in the censuses of 1792, 1827, 1841, 1861, and 1889.

Hence change came to Cuba in the form of numbers and invariably, it seemed, by addition, and almost everyone could count. But the implications of the figures were not always apparent immediately, and certainly the consequences never were. Change arrived in Cuba in waves, and as the nineteenth century wore on, the waves increased both in frequency and in reach. By the middle of the century, the issue was not merely change, to which Cubans had already become accustomed. The question had become the pace of change. And it was increasingly clear that the nature of change itself had changed. It was no longer measurable, and in some instances it was not even visible, but it was at work always—inexorably, relentlessly, governing the lives of vast numbers of people in ways not always recognizable or comprehensible. It was discerned, if at all, principally in the form of foreboding, of uncertainty, of apprehension.

Class structures were in transition. The ideological rationale of colonialism was under new challenge, a portent of more change to come. Cultural forms were in flux, and the effects of proximity to the United States and distance from Spain were beginning to take their toll. Geography, economics, and technology combined to change Cuban orientation away from Madrid and Barcelona and toward Washington and New York. The United States represented modernity, progress, and the future, many Cubans were certain, and who could afford to remain in the past?

Change was thus assuming new expressions, principally in the form of attitudes and values, many of which implied discontent and disaffection. But at midcentury this had not yet crystallized sufficiently to propel Cubans to action. Annexationist sentiment crested in the 1850s and waned soon thereafter, but no substitute had yet been devised that met Cuban needs fully. Slave labor was under attack, but an adequate replacement had yet to be developed. Discontent with Spanish rule was on the rise, but satisfactory alternatives to colonialism were not yet evident. New production technologies were becoming available, but it was not clear what they would bring in their wake. It was clear, though, that not all producers could afford them or what would happen to those who could not.

Sugar brought well-being to some, of course, but it brought hardship to many more. Slaves suffered unrelieved exploitation. Small producers were expelled from the land. The cost of living increased, local food supplies declined. Nor was prosperity wholly without adversity for those who were otherwise its principal beneficiaries. Increased profits could not but attract the unwelcome attention of the royal exchequer, always alive to the possibility of obtaining new revenues. New sources of contention brought Creoles into conflict with *peninsulares*, principally with Spanish merchants who sought to monopolize trade and with Spanish bureaucrats who sought to monopolize public office.

Discontent was on the rise and spreading, for different reasons, of course, at different times, among different sectors of the colonial body social. The sugar mill emerged as the source of Cuban prosperity and slavery as the principal source of labor. The population changed not only in size but also in composition, as the number of African slaves increased and as the population of free people of color expanded. The dichotomies in Cuban society became daily more pronounced and sharply defined: between free and slave, black and white, city and countryside, men and women, Cubans and Spaniards, and among social classes and within the colonial polity.

The implications of these developments settled over Cuba during the course of the century, but they were rarely discussed publicly—at least not on the island—in part because to do so was frankly subversive, in part because Cubans were not yet quite able to forge a consensus through which to articulate their brooding disquiet. For some the issues were clear. Cubans who traveled to the United States could not help but compare Havana with New York. North America became the frame of reference for many Cubans, and, inevitably, by this standard of "progress" and "modernity," Havana came up short. Unpaved streets, inadequate education, and disease and recurring epidemics were only some of the more obvious deficiencies of Havana compared to New York. In any case, this comparison added new items to the growing list of Cuban grievances.

Discontent was growing, too, among the vast masses of the population. Abolition sentiment was on the rise, both within the slave population and outside of it. Nor were the growing ranks of ex-slaves and free people of color reconciled to their condition. "Free" in this instance meant only that they were not legally slaves. For many this legal distinction was a moot point, for conditions of slavery persisted after slavery itself had ceased, and no amount of "freedom" offset continuing injustice and inequity. Wageworkers and artisans in the cities, peasants in the countryside, and slaves on the plantations were restless and beginning to contemplate ways to resist their oppression. Many fled: Workers emigrated, peasants migrated to the cities, slaves escaped into the remote interior. Many organized—into unions, into rebellion, as outlaw bands. Before the century ended, Cubans had mobilized in new ways for new change: for political change and social change, for a new world, and for a new place in that world. It was with this dream of change that the nineteenth century came to an end.

II

Slave rebellion in 1791 in St. Domingue (present-day Haiti) set in motion forces of change that reverberated immediately in Cuba and eventually across the Atlantic world. In less than a decade, production in this French Caribbean colony had collapsed, eliminating one of the world's principal sources of sugar, coffee, and cacao.

For producers in Cuba the collapse of St. Domingue presented unexpected but welcome opportunities. World supplies decreased, consumer demands increased, and prices soared. Cuban sugar producers had experienced steady if unspectacular expansion during the latter decades of the eighteenth century, but the sheer productive capacity of St. Domingue and the preponderant presence of French producers on the world market had limited Cuba's ability to expand in ways that were both sustained and substantial.

The decline of St. Domingue production was hence a boon to sugar growers in Cuba. The number of Cuban sugar estates (*ingenios*) increased dramatically, from 529 in 1792 to 1,000 in 1827; to 1,439 in 1846; and to 2,430 in 1862. Cuban production increased steadily from 19,000 tons in 1792 to 73,000 tons in 1829; to 144,000 tons in 1846; and to 446,000 tons in 1861.

These developments themselves caused other changes no less far-reaching in their consequences and permanent in their effects. The expansion of sugar production required a vast increase in the number of African slaves, who were not an unfamiliar presence in Cuba, of course. African slavery had been introduced on the island as early as the sixteenth century and had continued to expand thereafter. Prior to the end of the eighteenth century, however, slave labor was not a central element in Cuban production systems. Slaves in Cuba were used principally in domestic and urban labor and not in agricultural work. Nor did free people of color make up a large portion of the island's population. Census data for 1792 indicate the presence of an estimated 85,000 African slaves and 54,000 free people of color. This more than doubled to 217,000 slaves and 109,000 free people of color in 1810, and doubled again to 437,000 slaves and 153,000 free people of color in 1847. The number of whites increased, too, but not in proportion to the population of people of color. By 1841 the white population (418,000) was a minority. Not until 1861 did whites recover a majority status.

During these years, Havana was transformed from a backwater port town into a flourishing mercantile entrepôt. Havana was a city aswirl with bursts of activity: early morning markets, the arrival of foreign ships, the departure of sugar-laden merchant vessels. The docks swarmed with workers lifting and loading, unloading and unpacking. Teams of pack animals burdened with charcoal, produce, poultry, and wares of all types wended their way single file through narrow city streets to markets. The capital followed its own rhythm. Early morning hours saw brisk business and commercial transactions, street peddlers hawking their wares, buyers and sellers striking deals and bargains. The afternoon hours passed comparatively quietly, as the siesta respite brought calm to the city. And in early evening, usually at 6 or 7 P.M., came the hour of the promenades, when the *paseos* of the city filled with well-dressed pedestrians and distinguished carriages on display, to see and be seen.

The population of the capital increased dramatically, from 51,000 in 1792 to 84,000 in 1817; to 238,000 in 1827; and to 388,000 in 1841. Between 1791 and 1841, the total number of residents of Havana increased from 20 percent of the total island population to 40 percent. Tens of thousands of new residents settled into already-overcrowded urban quarters: slaves and slavers, mendicants, hawkers, and panhandlers, the unemployed and the unemployable, merchants, dockworkers, soldiers, and sailors. The population seemed to be in a perpetual state of transit and transition, coming and going, from abroad into the interior, from the provinces to the capital, en route always to some other place.

Havana during these years was filling with beggars, peddlers, and vagrants, or so it seemed to many at the time. Local officials and foreign observers alike commented on the emergence of begging as a full-time vocation—fully organized and engaging the ingenuity and resourcefulness of entire households. A netherworld of petty criminals formed along the fringes of Havana society. Most, no doubt, would have been honest from the start, if there had been a way at making a living at it. For many who had little to lose, and less opportunity to do anything else, crime was not an altogether bad way to get by. Transients and residents alike complained about theft, extortion, and swindling—and indeed small-time crime had become a way of life in the capital. Occasionally, serious crime—assault, murder, or abduction—scandalized Havana society, and never more so than when such transgressions crossed lines of class and color, and the victims were the otherwise-secure propertied and privileged whites. On these occasions, colonial authorities would mobilize into action and with great publicity mount anticrime campaigns, all to reassure the propertied and privileged whites that colonialism was indeed in their best interest.

And perhaps conditions could not have been otherwise. Havana was the center of a society undergoing rapid and radical change. It was the point of contact, where both the comforts and the degradation of prosperity, the beneficiaries and victims of wealth existed in closest proximity with one another. Here, the social distinctions derived from class, race, and property stood in sharp relief, daily, at every turn. Havana was a city in flux, moving at a frenetic pace in many different directions at once. The fortunate and the fortune seekers, foreigners and residents, with schemes licit and illicit, large and small, plotted to get more or just to get by.

The port of Havana bustled as Cuban foreign trade expanded—from a total of $18 million in 1792 to $32 million in 1827, to $51 million in 1842 and $92 million in 1862, most of which passed through Havana. Trade contacts increased with England and Spain, but most of all with the United States. The number of North American ships arriving at Cuba increased from 150 in 1796 to 606 in 1800; 783 in 1826; 1,702 between 1846 and 1850; and 2,088 between 1851 and 1856. Cuba produced more and more sugar for fewer and fewer markets, and by the middle of the nineteenth century more than half of Cuba's sugar export was destined for the U.S. market. (By this time, too, more than half of the North American supply of sugar originated in Cuba.) By early in the 1880s, Cuba had passed almost entirely into the North American economic orbit. Nearly 94 percent of Cuba's sugar production was exported to the United States. The implications of this connection were clear to all parties concerned. *"De facto,"* commented U.S. Consul Ramon O. Williams from Havana in 1886, "Cuba is already inside the commercial union of the United States. The whole commercial machinery of Cuba depends upon the sugar market of the United States."[1]

III

It happened, too, that prosperity arrived in Cuba at a time of political turmoil and social unrest, and this timing influenced decisively the course of subsequent political and social developments. Spain's New World colonies were in rebellion, and almost everywhere the rebellions were succeeding. By early in the 1820s, Spanish rule on the mainland had come to an end.

The direct political challenge of the colonies was only slightly less ominous than the threat of social change within them. The specter of mobilized masses cast a long shadow over the New World. St. Domingue was first, of course, and the implications of

1. Ramon O. Williams to James N. Porter, December 28, 1886, Dispatches from U.S. Consuls in Havana, General Records of the Department of State, Record Group 59, National Archives, Washington, DC.

the successful slave rebellion in the French colony were clear immediately to all New World plantation societies. Social upheaval engulfed Mexico in 1810, when Indians and mestizos mobilized to challenge the colonial elites, both *peninsulares* and Creoles alike. The stirrings of the *castas* of Venezuela and the Indians in Peru, as well as new slave uprisings—in Jamaica in 1795, 1824, and 1841; in Barbados in 1804 and again in 1824; in Demerara in 1808; and in Antigua in 1831—underscored the potential threat posed by the poor and powerless to the rich and powerful.

Producers in Cuba were especially sensitive to these developments. Political turmoil and social upheaval could not have come at a worse time, and the situation forced producers in Cuba to make decisions they would no doubt have preferred not to make. The implications of slave rebellion were immediate. Slave uprisings in the Caribbean reminded planters in Cuba of the fragile balance of social, political, and military forces necessary to preserve any slave system. The planters' concerns deepened in direct proportion to the increase of the number of people of color, free and slave, on the island.

Slavery, however, was challenged as much from above as it was from below. The Cuban demand for an unimpeded supply of slave labor coincided with the decline of the legal slave trade and came at a time when the very institution of slavery itself was under growing attack both from below, inside the island, and above, from abroad. The expansion of the slave system in Cuba occurred as abolitionist sentiment in Europe and the United States was on the rise. Already the trade in slaves had been outlawed by many European powers—as early as 1792 by Denmark, followed by England in 1808, Sweden in 1813, and Holland in 1814. The United States, too, in 1808, outlawed the slave trade, although it would be many years before the use of slaves in agriculture would itself be banned. World pressure was building on Spain to suppress the slave trade in Cuba. In 1817, England wrested from Spain a treaty commitment to suppress the slave trade. Henceforth all trafficking in slaves from Africa was banned. This did not end the trade, of course. It simply increased risks, raised costs—and increased profits. Indeed, the illicit slave trade continued at a brisk pace, and the introduction of new slaves actually expanded. This vast clandestine trade more than adequately met Cuban labor needs during the decades that followed.

These developments were both products and portents of changes of other kinds, not all of which were either immediately apparent or easily measurable. The rapid expansion of sugar production changed everything else. Economic development moved inexorably toward monoculture. Trade moved increasingly toward the export of one product for one market. These developments, in turn, altered relations between Cuba and Spain, on the one hand, and between Cuba and the United States, on the other. Spanish colonialism was slowly revealing that it was incapable of accommodating Cuban interests, and the United States was demonstrating an increasing ability to do so.

When other New World colonies challenged European rule, Cuba chose to cling to its colonial status. This was not, perhaps, the preferred choice of Cuban elites, but it was not simply a matter of choice. Early in the nineteenth century, many Cubans saw no reasonable alternative to Spanish rule. The planters' demand for slave labor was exceeded only by their need to defend slavery and by the necessity to defend themselves against slaves, and for all three objectives they depended on Spain. The prospects of slave rebellion in Cuba increased in direct proportion to the growing numbers of slaves. Colonialism seemed to guarantee political stability, social order, and economic prosperity while defending local privilege and prevailing property relationships. The Spanish politico-military presence, in sum, served to maintain the Cuban socioeconomic hierarchy.

Not that Cuban producers were entirely reconciled to their colonial status. Given their choice, Cubans would have chosen the best of all worlds—arrangements that would have guaranteed control over production and ownership of property and provided participation in local politics and policy formulation, all the while allowing them to enjoy the stabilizing influence of Spanish rule. Indeed, for the better part of the nineteenth century, creole elites pursued such arrangements: alternatives to restrictive colonialism and uncertain separatism. Between the 1820s and the 1850s some Cubans were drawn to the possibilities of annexation to the United States, an arrangement that offered producers security, local rule, and access to the island's principal market. After the 1850s Cuban efforts centered on political reform as the means to ameliorate the most onerous features of colonial rule without losing the most advantageous elements. Cuban producers sought to create political space in which to protect and promote Cuban interests, in which they could participate in or otherwise influence the formulation and implementation of policy concerning those issues that mattered most to them.

Cuba at midcentury had crossed a threshold into dynamic capitalist development. It had made vital linkages to world markets and employed modern production technologies and transportation facilities, but it was forced to function within antiquated colonial structures, many with origins in the previous century. Cuban producers operated within a restrictive trade system and retrogressive tax structures, producing with limited access to markets and expanding with meager capital resources. Spain could not supply the goods, the shipping, or the markets demanded by Cuban producers but persisted nonetheless in obtruding itself between Cuba and world markets. Spain was becoming increasingly superfluous to the expanding Cuban economy in every way but one: It regulated the terms of the exchange. Colonialism was becoming an obstacle to Cuban development, and increasingly this was a point of contention between Cubans and Spaniards.

These issues found expression in colonial political discourse. The Cuban demand for political participation increased in direct proportion to the expansion of Cuban control of the economy, and inevitably the clash of rival economic interests exacerbated political tensions between the colony and the metropolis. Cubans demanded greater control over resources and over commerce—control, in short, over all those areas of vital importance to their interests. As producers of commercial export crops, Cubans sought direct access to foreign markets and cheap prices for foreign imports. They resented *peninsular* control of overseas trade, they resisted Spanish taxes on foreign commerce, and—increasingly and most of all—they resented Spanish monopolization of political office and exclusive control over policy formulation. Creole property owners demanded not only economic policies to protect and promote their interests but also the positions of political power to implement the policies themselves, according to their needs, on their own terms, as they saw fit. Cubans demanded freedom to promote their own interests, to arrange their own taxes, and to regulate their own economic growth. They demanded freedom to expand, to develop resources according to their needs on their terms, and to earn more by producing more and exporting more. They needed, above all, access to political power to protect their economic interests.

They wanted all this, but they also wanted to retain the security of colonial structures, or at least those structures that served their needs. They wanted, in short, for Spain to guarantee internal security and defend the existing social order while relinquishing control over political power and economic policies.

IV

If the principal threat confronting the colonial status quo came in the form of rapid and radical change, which could be forestalled or otherwise deferred and delayed, it was also true that slow and gradual change was irreversible and could be neither contained nor controlled. Indeed, gradual change often set the stage for eventual radical change, and this was not always either apparent or understood.

Through the early years of the nineteenth century, the issue of slavery continued to loom large over the colonial polity. By midcentury an estimated half million Africans were enslaved in Cuba, most of them engaged in agricultural labor. Abolition had emerged as one of the principal elements of colonial discourse, even as the number of slaves increased. Slaves resisted, in ways large and small, passive and active, and this hastened the end of slavery. Many ran away; many rebelled. In growing numbers, slaves purchased freedom by *coartación*, a practice whereby slaves could buy themselves, or family members, out of bondage by reimbursing the slave owner for the cost of their purchase.

Security from people of color—from free blacks and especially from African slaves—developed into the principal concern of the planter class. The implications of Haiti were never lost on Cuban producers, and as Cuba filled with new slaves old concerns were revived with a new urgency. This affected almost every aspect of colonial life, mostly and most obviously political relationships and security arrangements. It influenced, too, the legal system, transportation modes, and religious patterns, as well as plantation architecture. Planter Edwin Atkins constructed the *vivienda* (dwelling house) at Soledad estate with walls several feet thick, "with a view to defense in case of an uprising of negroes."² Others excavated deep under the *viviendas* to construct basements to shelter and conceal family members in the event of slave rebellion.

Creole elites understood well the anomaly of their position. Political discontent was on the rise in Cuba. A small but growing creole middle class—originating out of the liberal professions, salaried personnel, and small farmers—found Spanish rule increasingly odious. They were joined by urban artisans, rural workers, whites of modest social origins, and the growing numbers of free people of color, all of whom found their conditions in the colony daily less satisfactory. Sugar and slavery had emerged as the principal elements that sustained colonial rule, primarily because they were the central elements of creole ascendancy. Increasingly it was apparent to those disaffected with the colonial regime that Spanish authority originated from within Cuba, from the very sources of creole wealth, privilege, and power. The ranks of free people of color increased, and increased exponentially, as the result of the expansion of sugar and slavery. A vast constituency for change was taking form across the island, slowly but dramatically surpassing a quarter of a million people of color who were free but oppressed. They demanded an end to slavery and discrimination, and most of all they demanded space to pursue a livelihood unmolested, to attain a measure of dignity, and to find a place of security in this order.

Nor was discontent confined to free people of color. Whites, too, were having a difficult time finding a place in nineteenth-century Cuba. The vast numbers of the creole middle class were in danger of becoming superfluous. The problem of race in nineteenth-century Cuba was also a problem for whites. An export economy organized around sugar production, based on African slave labor, and in which public administration and political office were monopolized by Spaniards, left little outlet for the talents and ambitions of the creole middle class. And, indeed, for vast numbers of Cubans, white and black, one source of discontent was the increasing inability of the colonial order to accommodate the interests of the fastest growing sectors of the white population. Many of this population found refuge abroad, and indeed, in the latter decades of the nineteenth century, Cuban emigration assumed the proportions of a diaspora: An estimated 100,000 Cu-

2. Edwin Atkins, *Sixty Years in Cuba* (Cambridge, MA, 1926), 91.

bans, approximately one tenth of the total population, were in transit. Cubans were not in flight for the first time, to be sure, but never before had they fled in such numbers. The emigrants were from all classes, black and white, men, women, and children, sometimes entire families but often as shattered households.

These were difficult times in Cuba, times of dashed hopes and vain expectations. Colonialism was revealing itself incapable of accommodating Cuban interests, and by the 1880s Cubans confronted diminished prospects of economic security and political participation. Such hope and expectation as Cubans retained found increasing sustenance in visions of *Cuba Libre*, a Cuba free and for Cubans.

Separatism thus early acquired an explicitly utilitarian feature. Certainly Cubans invoked the notions of liberty, freedom, and justice, and these were indeed entirely appropriate and relevant invocations. But it was no less clear that independence from Spain was necessary to make a place for Cubans in Cuba. Independence also subsumed elements of class antagonism, ethnic strife, and racial tensions, for only through the resolution of these latter issues could Cubans, in the end, claim a place for themselves in Cuba.

Colonial tensions were futher exacerbated by the virtual absence of mitigating social agencies. Few public institutions in Cuba intervened either in the public life of the community or in the private lives of its residents to offer comfort, or relief, or hope. The church was on the side of power and property; it defended privilege and the propriety of colonial rule. It was very much, first and foremost, a Spanish church, unabashedly on the side of *peninsular* rule as the element central to its intrinsic character in the colony. It was principally an urban church, formal and official. Planters rarely gave priests access to slaves, and most priests were loath to press the issue. The expectation that slave owners would provide religious instruction was rarely fulfilled, requirements of law notwithstanding. Few priests served in the rural interior, and many who did were corrupted by situations in which the church had no compelling purpose.

Government services were execrable. Hospitals, orphanages, and charitable organizations (with several notable exceptions) were insufficient, inadequately funded, and poorly staffed. The criminal justice system worked poorly, when it worked at all. The educational system rarely worked.

Life was difficult in Cuba for many—perhaps most—Cubans. But difficulty was not the principal problem. Hopelessness was. The colonial system offered Cubans little to look forward to, and this was one reason so many Cubans emigrated. Structures had become rigid, *peninsulares* had become uncompromising, and property owners had become intransigent. Positions of self-interest were soon transformed into a grand raison d'être of the colonial status quo, and the specters of race war, political tumult, and economic chaos were freely invoked as justification of this defense of the status quo. Many Cubans were having difficulty incorporating themselves into this world. Their growing antipathy toward Spanish colonial administration was transferred easily enough into antagonism toward the creole elites who defended Spanish rule, and just as easily was generalized into misgivings about the slave system upon which rested the privilege and property of those elites. Increasingly, colonial tensions in nineteenth-century Cuba were assuming class and racial dimensions.

These tensions erupted periodically in creole separatist conspiracies—in 1809, 1812, and again in 1821—and in slave uprisings—in 1826, 1837, and 1843. In 1868 a vast separatist uprising occurred in eastern Cuba, and for the next ten years Cubans mounted the most serious challenge to Spanish rule since the revolutions on the mainland. The Ten Years War ended in 1878 with the Pact of Zanjón—something of a truce, with Cubans suspending military operations and Spain promising political reforms.

During these years, abolition worked its way into the expanding separatist agenda, as the end of slavery was linked to the end of Spanish rule. Property owners, too, understood the mounting pressure for abolition and prepared for what many saw as the inevitable and not-too-distant end of slavery. Many sought alternative sources of labor and looked to increased European migration. Some purchased Indian slaves from the Yucatán. Others turned to China, and Chinese coolies during the latter decades of the nineteenth century arrived in Cuba in increasing numbers.

Slavery ended officially in 1886, but racial discrimination persisted. The issue of race in the colony was slowly transformed from one of abolition to one of social justice. These issues passed directly into the new separatist debate of the 1880s and 1890s. By the time the war for independence erupted in 1895, elements of social justice, economic freedom, and political democracy had become central to the separatist vision. Cubans mobilized for dramatic change in 1895, and that they failed to produce it after 1898 set the stage for a new epoch of slow, gradual change.

V

Cuba in the nineteenth century was a much-visited island. Its location at the middle latitudes of the Western Hemisphere, at the crossroads of the principal sea-lanes of the Caribbean and Gulf of Mexico, made a visit to the island all but obligatory to most travelers to the New World. Cuba was also within easy reach of North American travelers, who with increasing frequency and numbers visited the island through much of the nineteenth century.

The nineteenth century was a time of peak popularity for travel literature, and visitors to Cuba were among the most prolific contributors to this genre. Students and scholars of Cuba are indeed fortunate to have available such rich and diverse contemporary accounts of life on the island during this critical century.

As a genre of literature and a source of historical writing, the nineteenth-century travelogue is, of course, uneven in quality and utility. Many travelogues are frivolous, self-indulgent, and unabashedly racist and sexist. Travelers often failed to observe what was significant or misrepresented the significance of what they observed. Often they were deceived, and purposefully so. Sometimes they erred or were otherwise careless with generalizations. Conditions of slavery, for example, differed from city to countryside, from urban domestic work to rural agriculture, and from one plantation to another. Conditions that travelers observed on one sugar estate were not necessarily similar to or representative of others. Many travelers simply were taken in.

Many others were not, however. They were shrewd observers and faithful chroniclers of the time and the place. Many understood the significance, if perhaps not always the implications, of what they observed. They paid attention to detail and were attentive to nuance and subtlety. They moved freely among Cuban residents and Spanish officials, visited homes and workplaces, walked the city streets and traveled over country roads, observed the local mood and noted national developments, recorded conversations and collected statistics. Anecdotes abound that are rich with implication, and valuable data that might otherwise have been lost have been preserved.

Passing mention should be made about the format of the travel narratives that follow. They are organized within each chapter in chronological order, to capture some of the changes occurring in Cuban society. The excerpts represent some of the better accounts of travelers to Cuba. Accounts that were patently frivolous or otherwise inane have been excluded. Original text, accents, spelling—English and Spanish words—and usage have been preserved. Incorrect spelling and antiquated forms have been retained. Where the narrative is unclear or misleading, corrections appear in the text in brackets. For names and usages that require slightly longer explanation, additional information is provided in brackets in the text.

I

Havana

Alexander von Humboldt
The Island of Cuba
Translated by J. S. Thrasher
(New York: Derby and Jackson, 1801, 1856), 104–7, 110–12,
245–46

The view of Havana from the entrance to the port is one of
the most picturesque and pleasing on the northern equinoctial
shores of America. This view, so justly celebrated by travellers of
all nations, does not possess the luxury of vegetation that adorned
the banks of the Guayaquil, nor the wild majesty of the rocky
coasts of Rio Janeiro, two ports in the southern hemisphere; but
the beauty that in our climate adorns the scenes of cultivated
nature, unites here with the majesty of the vegetable creation,
and with the organic vigor that characterizes the torrid zone. The
European who experiences this union of pleasing impressions,
forgets the danger that menaces him in the midst of the populous
cities of the Antilles, and strives to comprehend the different
elements of so vast a country, gazing upon the fortresses crowning the rocks east of the port, the opening arm of the sea surrounded with villages and farmhouses, the tall palms, and the city
itself half hidden by a forest of spars and sails of shipping.

The entrance to the harbor of Havana passes between the
Morro Castle (*castillo de los Santos Reyes*) and the fort of *San
Salvador de la Punta*; its width is from 360 to 450 yards which it
preserves for three-fifths of a mile, when, leaving on the north the
Castle of *San Carlos de la Cabaña*, and the village of Casa Blanca,
it opens into a large trefoil shaped bay, the greatest width of

which, from N.N.E. to S.S.W. is two miles and a half. The three smaller bays which open from it are called Guanabacoa, Guasabacoa, and Atares, the latter containing several springs of fresh water.

The city of Havana, surrounded by walls, is built upon a promontory, extending from the Navy-yard on the south, to the Punta fort on the north. In the harbor, beyond the remains of some vessels that have been sunk and the little isle of Luz, there are only eight or ten, or, perhaps, more correctly speaking, five or six fathoms of water. The castles Atares and San Carlos del Principe defend the city on the western side inland, one of them being 1,400 and the other 2,630 yards from the wall of the city. The intermediate space comprises the suburbs of Horcon, Jesus Maria, and Salud, which encroach yearly upon the Campo Marte.

The principal edifices of Havana, the Cathedral, the Government House, the residence of the Comandante of Marine, the Navy-yard, the Post-office, and the Royal Tobacco factory, are less notable for their beauty than for the solidity of their construction. The streets are generally narrow, and many of them not paved. As the paving stone is brought from Vera Cruz, and its transportation is costly, the singular idea had been entertained, shortly before my arrival, of supplying its place with great trunks of trees, as is done in Germany and Russia, in the construction of dikes across swampy places. This project was speedily abandoned; but travellers who arrived subsequently to the making of the experiment, were surprised to see beautiful trunks of mahogany buried in the ruts of Havana.

During my residence in Spanish America few of the cities presented a more disgusting appearance than did Havana, from the want of a good police. One walked through the mud to the knees, and the many carriages, or *volantes*, which are the characteristic carriages of this city, and the drays laden with boxes of sugar, their drivers rudely elbowing the passer-by, made walking in the streets both vexatious and humiliating. The offensive odor of the salted meat, or *tasajo*, infected many of the houses, and even some of the ill-ventilated streets. It is said the police have remedied these evils, and that lately there has been a marked improvement in the cleanliness of the streets. The houses are well ventilated, and the street *de los Mercaderes* presents a beautiful view. There, as in many of our older cities in Europe, the adoption of a bad plan when laying out the city can only be slowly remedied.

There are two good promenades; one, the Alameda, inside the walls, between the theatre and the hospice of Paula; and the other outside the walls, running from the Punta fort to the Muralla gate. The first was ornamented with much taste by Peruani, an Italian artist, in 1803; and the second, known as the extra-mural *paseo*, is a delightfully cool resort, and generally after sunset is filled with carriages. Its construction was commenced by the Marquis de la Torre [captain general, 1771–1777], who, of all the governors sent to Cuba, was the first to give an impulse to the improvement of the police and the municipal regimen of Havana. Don Luis de las Casas [1745–1807; captain general, 1790–1796], whose memory is also held in high esteem by the inhabitants of Havana, and the Count de Santa Clara, have both improved these grounds. . . .

From the Punta to San Lazaro, from the Cabaña to Regla, and from thence to Atares, the land is filled with habitations; those which surround the bay being of light and elegant construction. The plan of these houses is drawn, and they are ordered from the United States, as one would order any piece of furniture. When the yellow fever prevails at Havana, the inhabitants retire to these countryhouses, and to the hills between Regla and Guanabacoa, where they breathe a purer air. In the cool nights, when the boats crossing the bay leave behind them a long track of phosphorescent light, the inhabitants, who abandon the populous city, find in these rustic abodes a peaceful and enchanting privacy. . . .

The city of Havana proper is surrounded by walls, and is about 1,900 yards long by 1060 yards wide; and yet there are piled in this narrow space 44,000 people, of which 26,000 are blacks and mulattos. A nearly equal population is gathered in the two suburbs, Jesus Maria and Salud; but the latter does not merit the beautiful name it bears (signifying Health); for, although the temperature of the air is lower than in the city, the streets might have been wider, and better laid out.

The Spanish engineer corps has been for the last thirty years making war upon the inhabitants of the suburbs, complaining to the government that the houses are too near the fortifications, and that an enemy might hold possession of them with impunity. But no one has sufficient firmness to raze the suburbs and eject the inhabitants, of which there are 28,000 in that of Salud alone. . . .

The defence of Havana, on the western side, is of the greatest importance, for while the city proper and the southern side of the bay is held, the Morro and Cabaña castles are impregnable. The first of these requires a garrison of 800 men, and the second 2,000 men for their defence, provisions for which, and reinforcements, should the garrison suffer heavy losses, can be supplied from the city. Several able French engineers have assured me that an enemy should begin by taking the city, and then bombard the Cabaña, which is very strong, but whose garrison, shut up in the casemates, could not long resist the sickly climate. The English took the Morro before they had possession of Havana, but at that time, the Cabaña, which commands the Morro, had not been built. The castles of Principe and Atares, and the battery of Santa Clara, are the most important works on the southern and western sides of the city. . . .

The unequal distribution of the population, the want of inhabitants on a great part of the coasts, together with the great extent of these, make the military defence of the island an impossibility; for, neither the contraband trade, nor the debarcation of an enemy can be prevented. Havana is, undoubtedly, a strongly fortified place, its works rivalling those of the most important cities of Europe; the small towers and forts of Cojimar, Jaruco, Matanzas, Mariel, Bahia Honda, Batabano, Jagua, and Trinidad, may offer a longer or shorter resistance, but nearly two-thirds of the island has no defence whatever; for however active the service of gunboats may be, it could never be of much importance.

Robert Francis Jameson
Letters from the Havana, during the Year 1820
(London: John Miller, 1821), 58–62

On approaching the city by sea, you behold a narrow inlet, on the left of which a high rocky prominence is surmounted by a fortress called, *El Morro*. This is a regular and exceeding strong work, whose majestic spread and elevation of masonry, studded with cannon, flags and military figures, in the full blaze of sunshine, presents a noble and truly imposing sight. On the right point of the inlet stands a small square fort called *La Punta*, very inferior in strength and appearance to the *Morro*. On sailing between them you are hailed by a sentry and required to give your name and port of departure, so *conversable* is the width of the inlet, which, have shot through, you glide into a harbour, or rather bay, extending deep and broad nearly a mile across, and three inland. On the right shore behind *La Punta*, stands the *Havana*, presenting its thickly built edifices of stone, interspersed with numerous spires of churches and convents, behind the walls which surround it. There is an air of solid age which the town presents from the harbour, that gives it a *grand* appearance; the maritime bustle give it *interest*; the idea of wealth and luxury is strongly impressed on you, and, as you listen to the rattling of carriages and the strains of gaiety, and gaze at the peculiar brightness and glitter which distinguish tropical scenes, you forget that the city before you is the banquetting place of *death*. The situation of the *Havana* is but too favourable to the propagation and retention of disease, being, in addition to its fortifications, enclosed on all sides with a circle of rising ground which precludes the free circulation of air and causes a stagnant cloud of fetid vapour, exhaled from a crowded population and the marshy shores of the harbour, to hang continually over it. The direful yellow fever (here called *"El vomito negro"* from the final symptom) is found to be nearly entirely confined in its ravages to the sea shore; at any rate there is not such conflux of human beings in the inland towns, and there is consequently, both a diminished cause of pestilence and food for its maintenance. The foreign vessels which arrive here suffer greatly. Whole crews are swept off within a few weeks of their arrival, and great difficulty is found in procuring hands for the home passage. Indeed there is scarcely a European who escapes an attack, and multitudes of young ardent adventurers are hurried off from their earthly hopes with a rapidity that would appal you; but, here, as in the ranks of battle, the survivors, habituated to the dropping around them, scarcely think of turning to note the victim.

On passing the sea-gate you become sensible of one great cause of disease, from the insufferable stench of the stores of dried beef and fish which are imported for the sustenance of the blacks. A multitude of narrow streets open to your eye, each contributing to the congress of smells, by their want of sewers and paving, the holes, worn in the ground by wheels and horses, being carefully filled up with offal. Add to this the swarm of *black* population, and you have a very fair *olfactory* catalogue.

The narrow streets are formed of large solid houses, usually one story high, the ground floors of which are commonly occupied as shops and warehouses. If it be a merchants, the counting houses are up stairs, and the *patio*, or court yard, in the centre of the building (round which) all the rooms are ranged, opening into balconies is filled with produce and effects. In the passage from the outward gate to the *patio*, sits a *yellow white man* to *eye* and answer strangers. You would think him made by *Maillardet*, so stationary you find him, so perpetually with his cigar in his mouth and so mechanically regular in the three measured puffs and the gradual elevation of his eyelids, which invariably take place before he answers you.

A house of this description, you will be astonished to hear, lets from 8000 to 14,000 dollars per annum. . . . But you will recollect that the Havana is a regular fortification, and that *no more houses than those already in it can be built within its walls*; that the influx of commerce has been sudden and its profits enormous; and that both fashion and trade have localities. Beyond the walls, houses are not so exorbitant, though even there, as that situation is considered as possessing some immunity from the fever, they are very high in rent.

The dwellings of the nobility and gentry are similar in construction to those I have described. To the street they present a plain stone front with a broad passage opening at the side, in which the *volante*, or carriage, stands. If there are apartments on the ground floor, the windows are large and high, barred with iron, without any glazing, and usually have curtains hung within, to prevent curiosity and dust from being too intrusive. Above are similar windows opening into a balcony that runs the breadth of the house. The roof is tiled, and of course, in this tropical region, has no plume of chimneys crowning its top.

Most commonly, even in the houses of the nobility, the ground floor is let out for shops, or at least nooks are opened at the corners of the house for that purpose. This relieves the heaviness which would otherwise characterize the streets. There are many houses and shops that have only a ground floor, which of course have more airyness in their appearance, especially as the latter universally have boards over their doors with signs painted on them, as little indicative, however of what they contain as the pole of a barber is of his suds and razor. Thus one may see the figure of a hero, blazoned forth duly with *mustachia's, whiskers*, a huge cocked hat and a Goliah sword, underneath which to prevent mistake, is inscribed—*"El Heroe Espanol."* On entering the place it designs, you behold a meagre wizen-faced tailor flourishing his shears on a shopboard. Next door is a jeweller, or rather silversmith, whose portal is decorated with an interesting portrait of a *caballero*, with one hand on his heart, extending the other towards another equally well-drest *caballero*. This is the sign of *"El buen amigo"*—the *good friend*, and on seeing it, you might be disposed to enter cordially and purchase without fear of imposition, but alas, one probably finds that here, as in other parts of the world, the *outward profession* is very different from the *internal disposition*!

John George F. Wurdemann
Notes on Cuba
(Boston: James Munroe and Company, 1844), 39–46

Havana, in the condition and order of its streets, presents a strong contrast to the large cities of Europe. While in the latter there is every variety, from the ancient, narrow, muddy lane, in its curves exemplifying Hogarth's line of beauty, to the modern, wide, straight street, with its smoothly-flagged sidewalks, and its cleanly wooden pavement,—those of the metropolis of Cuba are uniform in appearance, cross each other at right angles, and extend in straight lines from one side of the city to the other. In 1584 it had only four, so that the notaries in those days commenced certain deeds with *"la publica en las cuatro calles de esta Villa,"* but in consequence of their regularity, they do not now exceed fifty within the walls. They are all McAdamised, thanks to the energy of Tacon [Miguel Tacón, 1775–1855; captain general, 1834–1838], but their want of width has prevented the formation of sidewalks; unless the narrow row of flag-stones close to the houses, and which are often below the level of the street, may be so named. These are not unfrequently used common by the carts and pedestrians; and in wet weather, forming as they do the inner boundaries of the side gutters, are scarcely preferable to the middle of the street. It is not, therefore, surprising that the ladies of Havana do not promenade in the city; indeed, the absence of the female form in the busy crowds that pass before the eyes of the stranger, constitutes one of its most striking features.

In the more frequented channels of the city, considerable skill is requisite to wend your way safely. Besides a multitude of narrow carts, which, however, are supported on iron wheels so low, that you might easily pass over one, if it obstructed the way, there is a lumbering volante, with its long shafts and ponderous wheels, rolling close by you at every moment. . . . Add to these the heavy oxcart, with its team of well-broke cattle; long trains of pack-horses, with their cumbrous loads of charcoal, green fodder or poultry; mounted horsemen, urging their steeds to their utmost speed, whenever the course is clear for but a short distance; and innumerable negro porters with wheelbarrows, or carrying huge loads on their heads—and some idea may be formed of the principal thoroughfares of the city. When the crops of sugar, molasses, and coffee are brought here for exportation, they are sometimes so blocked up by the laden carts, and the whole place becomes so filled with the accumulated produce, that it is not unusual for the Captain-General to grant permission to labor not only on the Sabbath, but during the whole of each night, which is never otherwise permitted among the warehouses and shipping.

The calle des Mercaderes is the principal street for shopping, and contains many fine and extensive stores, filled with choice dry goods, jewelry, china, glass-ware, etc. These are designated by different names, which, however, have no reference to their contents—as "the bomb," a favorite one, "the stranger," "virtue," etc.; but the name of the owner never appears on the sign-board. The principal commercial houses have neither sign nor name, and can only be distinguished from the larger private dwellings, by the bales of goods, or boxes of sugar and bags of coffee that are piled up in their lower stories; the merchant and his family, and clerks, living in the upper part.

Nearly all the retail shops are owned by Spaniards, and, with very few exceptions, none but men are seen behind counters. The Parisian shop-girl, so celebrated for her skill in selling, might, however, here learn a lesson, not only in overcharging, but also in that assiduity in serving, that will scarcely permit the visitor to leave without purchasing something. Let the novice take care how he offers one-half the price asked for an article, if he does not wish it, for that, not unfrequently, is its real one; in almost every case one fourth will be deducted. . . .

Although the calle des Mercaderes is the Bond-street of Havana, retail shops are scattered all over the city, which in a large part seems to be made up of them, the lower stories of many of the dwelling-houses being thus occupied. The ladies in shopping do not in general leave their volantes, but have the goods brought to them, the strictness of Spanish etiquette forbidding them to deal with a shopman; and it is only when the seller of goods is of their own sex, that they venture into a store. The custom of appearing in public only in a volante is so general, that some of my fellow-boarders, American ladies, who ventured to do their shopping on foot, were greeted in their progress by the half suppressed exclamations of the astonished Habaneros, who seemed as much surprised to see a lady through their streets, as a Persian would to see one unveiled in his.

I have said that Spaniards are chiefly the owners of the stores, the Creoles being seldom engaged in commerce. Those containing dry goods belong generally to Asturians, while the sale of groceries and provisions is monopolized by Catalans. These latter, are an industrious, shrewd, economical class; and have, perhaps in consequence of these qualities, received their sobriquet of Spanish Jews, which can only be construed into a compliment to the Israelite. A large portion of the commerce of the island is in their hands, as well as a very great part of its wealth. In the interior of the island they appear to monopolize every branch of trading, from the pack of the humble pedlar to the country tienda with its varied contents; and in the maritime towns, many a commercial house, whose ships cover the sea, is theirs.

Under the arcades near the markets in Havana may be seen a number of shops not ten feet square, with a show-case in front, before which a restless being is constantly walking; reminding one of a caged wild animal that chafes for a wider range. At night the show-case is carried into his little cabin, which serves him for shop, dormitory and kitchen; and where he may be often seen preparing his frugal meal over a chafing dish of live charcoals. "Five years of privations and a fortune," is his motto; and not a few of the wealthiest Spanish residents in Cuba may date the commencement of their prosperity from as humble a source. The greater part of the trade with old Spain is in their hands, and they

have latterly also extended their correspondence to other countries, and entered into active competition with the resident foreign
merchants. The Catalan, moreover, furnishes the planter with all
the necessaries for his negroes and plantation; advances moneys
for his crops, which he then sells on commission; and often loans
to him the requisite sums to erect his costly sugar works, or
make his less expensive coffee estate, but all at an interest,
ruinous in the present depreciated value of his crops.

There is nothing which more forcibly strikes the attention of
the stranger in Havana, than the substantial manner in which
even the most unimportant building is constructed; every one
seems made to last forever. The walls of a single story house are
seldom less than two feet in thickness; and to witness the erection of those of the larger ones, the masonry might readily be
mistaken for that of some embryo fortification, destined to be
cannon-proof. Many of the private dwellings are immense structures. I was shown one belonging to one of the Gomez, that cost
five hundred thousand dollars; and without the walls, facing the
military parade-ground, another was nearly built, which with its
pillars and arches occupied a front as large as some of the minor
palaces in Europe. The value of real estate is very high in Havana;
a lot about sixty feet square, on which a store was afterwards
built, sold a few years ago for forty thousand dollars. It is true that
this was in the palmy days of the island, before the present
depression of trade had lowered the value of everything. Even
now, however, there are not a few houses which rent for ten or
twelve thousand dollars; and the hotel of my host, that can accommodate from thirty boarders comfortably, to sixty packed
away, as they often are here, commands a rent of six thousand
dollars. With such a value set on the land, but little is appropriated
to yards, and the whole city may be said to be divided into
squares of solid blocks.

The architecture of the larger houses is heavy. They are so
constructed as to form open squares in their centres, their only
yards, where sometimes a few shrubs planted in boxes serve to
relieve the eye, and upon which the lofty arches of the corridors
look down. The lower story is occupied by the store-house, reading-
room, kitchen and stable; while the common entrance is often
half blocked up by the volante, its arched passage serving for a
coach-house. From the side of this latter a wide flight of stone

steps leads to the corridor of the second story, into which all the rooms open, and which forms the common passage to all of them. It opens itself on the central square, and the spaces between its heavy pillars and high-sprung arches, are generally closed with Venetian blinds. An air of rude grandeur reigns throughout the whole structure, the architecture partaking of a mixture of the Saracenic and Gothic styles. The chief hall or parlor is generally from forty to fifty feet long, twenty wide, and as many feet high; while the windows and doors, reaching from the floor to the ceiling, render it cool and pleasant during warm days, but afford little protection against the damp northers. The floors are all stuccoed or tiled, and the walls and ceilings not unfrequently ornamented with fresco; while only here and there, a few panes of glass let into the thick shutters, serve to admit the light when they are closed.

But the striking peculiarity of the town-house in Cuba, is the care taken to render it safe against assaults from without. Every window that is at all accessible, either from the street or the roofs of the neighboring houses, is strongly barricaded with iron bars; while the stout folding-doors, guarding the only entrance to the whole building, would not be unfit to protect that of a fortress. They are castellated palaces; and with their terraced roofs, their galleries and passages, their barricaded windows and ponderous doors, remind one of the olden Saxon strongholds, which Scott has so graphically described.

There is no West End in Havana; the stately mansion of the millionaire is often in juxta-position with the magazine of tasajo, jerked beef, with its sign of a large slice swinging over its door, and its Putrid-like odors tainting the air: or its basement occupied by the tienda, with its stock of lard, garlic and groceries, or the work-shops of the humble artisan. Many of the dwellings are, however, of only one story; and their parlors are completely exposed to the gaze of every one, through their large windows, which open on the street. Two rows of armchairs, facing each other, are placed near these, where, during the evening, the older members of the family may be seen seated with their visitors. The younger ones stand within the windows, looking through the interstices of the iron bars at the pedestrians, and occasionally enjoying the conversation of an acquaintance as he loiters for a moment to pay a passing compliment.

Richard Henry Dana, Jr.
To Cuba and Back: A Vacation Voyage
(Boston: Ticknor and Fields, 1859), 31–37

Instantly we are besieged by boats, some loaded with oranges and bananas, and others coming for passengers and their luggage, all with awnings spread over their sterns, rowed by sallow, attenuated men, in blue and white checks and straw hats, with here and there the familiar lips and teeth, and vacant, easily-pleased face of the negro. Among these boats comes one, from the stern of which floats the red and yellow flag with the crown in its field, and under whose awning reclines a man in a full suit of white linen, with straw hat and red cockade and a cigar. This is the Health Officer. Until he is satisfied, no one can come on board, or leave the vessel. Capt. Bullock salutes, steps down the ladder to the boat, hands his papers, reports all well—and we are pronounced safe. Then comes another boat of similar style, another man reclining under the awning with a cigar, who comes on board, is closeted with the purser, compares the passenger list with the passports, and we are declared fully passed, and general leave is given to land with our luggage at the custom-house wharf.

Now comes the war of cries and gestures and grimaces among the boatmen, in their struggle for passengers, increased manifold by the fact that there is but little language in common between the parties to the bargains, and by the boatmen being required to remain in their boats. How thin these boatmen look! You cannot get it out of your mind that they must all have had the yellow fever last summer, and are not yet fully recovered. Not only their faces, but their hands and arms and legs are thin, and their low-quartered slippers only half cover their thin yellow feet. . . .

Seated under an awning, in the stern of the boat, with my trunk and carpet-bag and an unseasonable bundle of Arctic overcoat and fur cap in the bow, I am pulled by a man with an oar in each hand and a cigar in mouth, to the custom-house pier. Here is a busy scene of trunks, carpet-bags, and bundles; and up and down the pier marches a military grandee of about the rank of a sergeant or sub-lieutenant, with a preposterous strut, so out of keeping with the depressed military character of his country, and not possible to be appreciated without seeing it. If he would give that strut on the boards, in New York, he would draw full houses nightly.

Our passports are kept, and we receive a license to remain and travel in the island, good for three months only, for which a large fee is paid. These officers of the customs are civil and reasonably rapid; and in a short time my luggage is on a dray driven by a Negro, and I am in a volante, managed by a Negro postilion, and am driving through the narrow streets of this surprising city.

The streets are so narrow and the houses built so close upon them, that they seem to be rather spaces between the walls of houses than highways for travel. It appears impossible that two vehicles should pass abreast; yet they do so. There are constant blockings of the way. In some places awnings are stretched over the entire street, from house to house, and we are riding under a long tent. What strange vehicles these volantes are!—A pair of very long, limber shafts, at one end of which is a pair of huge wheels, and the other end a horse with his tail braided and brought forward and tied to the saddle, an open chaise body resting on the shafts, about one third of the way from the axle to the horse; and on the horse is a Negro, in large postilion boots, long spurs, and a bright jacket. It is an easy vehicle to ride in; but it must be a sore burden to the beast. Here and there we pass a private volante, distinguished by rich silver mountings and postilions in livery. Some have two horses, and with the silver and the livery and the long dangling traces and a look of superfluity, have rather an air of high life. In most, a gentleman is reclining, cigar in mouth; while in others, is a great puff of blue or pink muslin or cambric, extending over the sides to the shafts, topped off by a fan, with signs of a face behind it. "Calle de los Oficios," "Calle del Obispo," "Calle de San Ignacio," "Calle de Mercaderes," are on the little corner boards. Every little shop and every big shop has its title; but nowhere does the name of a keeper appear. Almost every shop advertises "por mayor y menor," wholesale and retail. What a Gil Blas, Don Quixote feeling the names of "posada," "tienda," and "cantina" give you!

There are no women walking in the streets, except negresses. Those suits of seersucker, with straw hats and red cockades, are soldiers. It is a sensible dress for the climate. Every third man, perhaps more, and not a few women, are smoking cigars or cigarritos. Here are things moving along, looking like cocks of new mown grass, under way. But presently you see the head of a horse or mule peering out from under the mass, and a tail is visible at the other end, and feet are picking their slow way over the stones. These are the carriers of green fodder, the fresh stalks and blades of corn; and my chance companion in the carriage, a fellow passenger by the "Cahawba," a Frenchman, who has been here before, tells me that they supply all the horses and mules in the city with their daily feed, as no hay is used. There are also mules, asses, and horses with bananas, plantains, oranges and other fruits in panniers reaching almost to the ground.

Here is the Plaza de Armas, with its garden of rich, fragrant flowers in full bloom, in front of the Governor's Palace. At the corner is the chapel erected over the spot where, under the auspices of Columbus, mass was first celebrated on the island. We are driven past a gloomy convent, past innumerable shops, past drinking places, billiard rooms, and the thick, dead walls of houses, with large windows, grated like dungeons, and large gates, showing glimpses of interior court-yards, sometimes with trees and flowers. But horses and carriages and gentlemen and ladies and slaves, all seem to use the same entrance. The windows come to the ground, and, being flush with the street, and mostly without glass, nothing but the grating prevents a passenger from walking into the rooms. And there the ladies and children sit sewing, or lounging, or playing. This is all very strange. There is evidently enough for me to see in the ten or twelve days of my stay.

But there are no costumes among the men, no Spanish hats, or Spanish cloaks, or bright jackets, or waistcoats, or open, slashed trousers, that are so picturesque in other Spanish countries. The men wear black dress coats, long pantaloons, black cravats, and many of them even submit, in this hot sun, to black French hats. The tyranny of systematic, scientific, capable, unpicturesque, unimaginative France, evidently rules over the realm of man's dress. The houses, the vehicles, the vegetation, the animals, are picturesque.

Anthony Trollope
The West Indies and the Spanish Main
(New York: Harper and Brothers, 1860), 147–52

There is nothing attractive about the town of Havana; nothing whatever to my mind, if we except the harbour. The streets are narrow, dirty, and foul. In this respect there is certainly much difference between those within and without the wall. The latter are wider, more airy, and less vile. But even in them there is nothing to justify the praises with which the Havana is generally mentioned in the West Indies. It excels in population, size, and no doubt in wealth any other city there; but this does not imply a great eulogium. The three principal public buildings are the Opera House, the Cathedral, and the palace of the Captain-General. The former has been nearly knocked down by an explosion of gas, and is now closed. I believe it to be an admirable model for a second-rate house. The cathedral is as void of beauty, both externally and internally, as such an edifice can be made. To describe such a building would be an absurd waste of time and patience. We all know what is a large Roman Catholic church, built in the worst taste, and by a combination of the lowest attributes of Gothic and Latin architecture. The palace, having been built for a residence, does not appear so utterly vile, though it is the child of some similar father. It occupies one side of a public square or plaza, and from its position has a moderately-imposing effect. Of pictures in the Havana there are none of which mention should be made.

But the glory of the Havana is the Paseo—the glory so called. This is the public drive and fashionable lounge of the town—the Hyde Park, the Bois de Boulogne, the Cascine, the Corso, the Alameda. It is for their hour on the Paseo that the ladies dress themselves, and the gentlemen prepare their jewelry. It consists of a road running outside a portion of the wall, of the extent perhaps of half a mile, and ornamented with seats and avenues of trees, as are the boulevards at Paris. If it is to be compared with any other resort of the kind in the West Indies, it certainly must be owned there is nothing like it; but a European on first seeing it cannot understand why it is so eulogized. Indeed, it is probable that if he first goes thither alone, as was the case with me, he will pass over it, seeking for some other Paseo.

But then the glory of the Paseo consists in its volantes. As one boasts that one has swum in a gondola, so will one boast of having sat in a volante. It is the pride of Cuban girls to appear on the Paseo in these carriages on the afternoons of holidays and Sundays; and there is certainly enough of the picturesque about the vehicle to make it worthy of some description. It is the most singular of carriages, and its construction is such as to give a flat contradiction of all an Englishman's preconceived notions respecting the power of horses. . . .

The great point in the volante of fashion is the servant's dress. He is always a negro, and generally a large negro. He wears a huge pair—not of boots, for they have no feet to them—of galligaskins I may call them, made of thick stiff leather, but so as to fit the leg exactly. The top of them comes some nine inches above the knee, so that when one of these men is seen seated at his ease, the point of his boot nearly touches his chin. They are fastened down the sides with metal fastenings, and at the bottom there is a huge spur. The usual dress of these men, over and above their boots, consists of white breeches, red jackets ornamented with gold lace, and broad-brimmed straw hats. Nothing can be more awkward, and nothing more barbaric than the whole affair; but nevertheless there is about it a barbaric splendour, which has its effect. The great length of the equipage, and the distance of the horse from his work, is what chiefly strikes an Englishman. . . .

The amusements of the Cubans are not very varied, and are innocent in their nature; for the gambling as carried on there I regard rather as a business than an amusement. They greatly love dancing, and have dances of their own and music of their own, which are peculiar, and difficult to a stranger. Their tunes are striking, and very pretty. They are fond of music generally, and maintain a fairly good opera company at the Havana. In the plaza there—the square, namely, in front of the Captain-General's house—a military band plays from eight to nine every evening. The place is then thronged with people, but by far the majority of them are men.

Rachel Wilson Moore
*The Journal of Rachel Moore Kept during a
Tour to the West Indies and South America in
1863–1864*
(Philadelphia: T. Ellwood Zeil, 1867), 22–25

The bay or harbor is surrounded by hills, and is a complete basin, on one side of which stands the city, forming the segment of a circle. The shipping is arranged along the wharves, bow foremost, so as to occupy the smallest possible space, in front of which is erected a long shed, extending from one end of the town to the other, for the accommodation of loading and unloading vessels, and there merchants meet in the morning to transact business. The hours for business are from six to nine o'clock, after which breakfast and custom-house operations. On these wharves may be seen large numbers of slaves, continually loading and unloading vessels. The city looks quite pretty from the harbor; but on entering it the stranger is struck with its jail-like appearance, every house of much account being guarded with iron-grated doors and windows; also, large massive iron doors, which open into courtyards, that lead to dwellings and stores. The lower stories are chiefly occupied as storehouses or places of business of some kind. The streets are narrow, with foot-pavements from two to three feet wide, mostly of round stone. Some of the streets are paved with square blocks of granite, and mostly kept clean, so that you walk in the middle of the street as common as sidewalks. The lower part of the city is in a wretched condition, scarcely fit for decent people to pass through, being filled with groggeries, gambling places, and filth; for my own part, I felt afraid to pass through any of those miserable streets, which was proved to a demonstration by one of our boarders.

There are a few places in the city somewhat attractive. The Governor's Plaza is an open space, ornamented with trees and shrubbery, that affords a pleasant retreat, where, every evening at eight o'clock, the citizens are entertained with a band of music. Outside of the city proper the houses are more expensive, streets wider, and open areas more numerous. There the *élite* of the city are seen driving every evening, from five o'clock, along the Pasio del Ysabel, Casse del Plado, Campa del Marle, up the Tacon.

These siaras are where the aristocracy of the city reside, and where is found grandeur and squalid poverty intermingled to the greatest extent we ever beheld. Here is seen an elegant mansion, according to their architecture, with its fine garden and beautiful grounds, and alongside a miserable shanty, with groggeries, and squalid poverty, in the greatest filth and degradation; most of the latter native Cubans, who with the Spaniards are always at variance. The Cubans are allowed none of the privileges or rights claimed exclusively by the Spaniards. All the fine buildings here, as well as in the city proper, are barricaded with iron bars, as we concluded, to guard against insurrections, as I was satisfied would eventually come upon the people of that island, if they continued to enslave and oppress both colored and whites.

Samuel Hazard
Cuba with Pen and Pencil
(Hartford: Hartford Publishing Company, 1871), 65–69, 81–85, 160–62, 174–77

One thing will strike the stranger curiously in this old town of Havana, and that seems to be that there is no particular locality specially devoted to the residences of the "best society;" for right alongside a private dwelling, with its trim and neat appearance, may be found some shabby-looking establishment used as a warehouse. Again, you look into a neat hall, on one side of which stands a very handsome gig and carriage, maybe, and you think it is a first-class livery stable or carriage shop; when, in casting your eyes to the other side of the same hall, you see fine large rooms, handsomely furnished, where, perhaps, are seated members of the family who occupy the house.

I was in a constant puzzle, on first visiting Havana, in regard to private residences, for there seems to be no "west end,"—at least in the old town. People of the best class live here, there, everywhere,—some up stairs, and some down, some *in* warehouses, others *over* warehouses and stores. . . .

One cannot help thinking, though, in this queer old town, that the people originally must have lived at daggers' points with each other, or were called upon to resist attacks from some feudal lord, anxious to raise the "tin;" for every house almost is walled like a fort, the doors are thick enough to resist a battering-ram, while every window, even to those on the roof, is barred like a prison, as though the occupants expected to be called on at any moment to resist invasion.

Now let us take a dash outside the walls, to the Paseo Isabel, that stretches outside the old city walls in a wide, handsome street, extending down to the sea, being known as the "Prado" in that part of it lying beyond the Tacon theatre, towards the ocean.

This Paseo is, in some respects, the finest in the city, being wide, well built on both sides, laid out with walks and carriage drives and long rows of trees, and having upon it some of the principal places of amusement; nearly all the gates of the city, when the walls were standing, opened onto it, and it is the general thoroughfare between the old and new town. . . .

Beyond the Paseo Isabel is the fine "Calzada de Galiano," a handsome paved highway, with long rows of well-built, striking looking houses, most of them with pillared fronts.

Leaving this street, crossing on our way the "Paseo Tacon," we pass over into the busy street of "Calzada del Monte," one of the strangest, busiest looking streets in the new city, stretching as it does from the city gates past the "Campo Militar," out beyond the Bridge of Chavez, until it finally brings up in the little village of Jesus del Monte, one of the suburbs of Havana. In the city, it is lined with stores and buildings, some very fine, others small, and as you get out farther, there begin to be seen very pretty rustic retreats or summer-houses.

There is also the "Calzada del Cerro," one of the finest streets in the city; the street of "Belascoin" extending out to the sea, and upon which is situated the "Plaza de Toros," and more than all, the beautiful drive, known by its various names of "Tacon," "Reina," and "Principe."

And now, to-day, notwithstanding the attacks of pirates, of fire and sword, and of hurricanes, Havana is a well built, large city, and very attractive to the stranger. Its streets are mostly paved with stone, but, having no gutters, are very wet during the rainy season, though during the winter, when travelers mostly go there, they are in very good order. Being cleaned at night by a force of negroes, all of the refuse of the city after twelve o'clock is set directly upon the narrow side-walk beside the doorways; it is, therefore, advisable for the benighted traveler to take to the middle of the street to be out of harm's way. The police system, with the military guards, seems to work very well; for, though I have passed through some of the loneliest portions of the city late at night, I was never disturbed, nor did I ever hear of any particular cases of robbery or assault; but since the troubles in the island, this has somewhat changed.

Excepting on the quays, at the water side, the old city was surrounded by stone walls, bastions, and forts, to which are attached a great degree of historical interest, as they date back, portions of them, from the earliest history of the town. The moats in late years were all occupied with vegetable gardens, bath and store-houses, and used for other than military purposes; while the grim, grey old stone walls stood still solid, and, I may say, useless, with their ten bastions and seven entrances on the land side, while on the water side several batteries and bastions looked out upon the bay. Thus, as the city has grown so immensely, it is well they have been mostly pulled down.

In the other, or east side of the bay, there is also a considerable population, under the shelter of the principal series of fortifications which stretch from the entrance to the upper end of the bay, comprising the Cabanas, the Casa Blanca, and the little town of the latter name, as well as the busy place of Regla. This bay of Havana is a noble bay indeed, not so extremely large either, but having good depth of water and being so completely sheltered from the storms. Its channel or entrance is about one thousand four hundred yards long, and about three hundred and twenty-five in width, and the harbor is composed of three almost distinct bays, bearing the names of Triscornia, Marimeleña, and the Fondo, or depth of the bay between Guanabacoa and the castle of Atares. The water is of such depth that vessels of the largest size can be moved to the quays; and it is quite a noble and interesting sight to wander along these well-built wharves, under the shelter of the roofs supported by iron columns, which serve to protect both the merchandise and the merchants from the sun and rain, and see the long line of bowsprits almost touching the walls of the edifices facing and upon the quay.

The situation of the city is such, being in some degree a peninsula extending into the bay, that the streets generally run at right angles to the bay, and would, if it were not for their narrowness, receive the benefits of the different breezes; but this narrowness is an advantage, when in the middle of the day, the sun gets so hot that one is very glad to take shelter on the shady side, the shadow of the building not permitting the sun to penetrate entirely into the street. In addition to this, the awnings can be more easily stretched from house to house, making quite a cool, pleasant promenade. Here, for instance, is a portion of O'Reilly street, looking down which you see the old tower of the venerable church of Santo Domingo, while above one's head nearly all the way are these fancy awnings, bearing the signs of the different stores opposite which they are stretched.

Havana, whose government is confined to its jurisdiction, which extends to all the villages and suburbs with a certain distance, as well also as to the Island of Pines, is the capital of the island, and the headquarters of the jurisdiction of Havana, as also of the governments, political and military, of the Western department. It is the residence of the governor Superior, the Captain-General; of the Superintendent General, the Diocesan Bishop, the General Commandant of the Marine, the Intendente of Royal Property of the whole island, and of the "Royal Audencia Pretorial." It has a literary university, collegiate seminary, preparatory schools, and two meteorological observatories, besides various other public institutions of science and learning, and comprises within its actual limits the little towns of Casa Blanca, Regla, Jesus del Monte, Arroyo Polo y Cerro, while there are a number of small places that pass as the suburbs—as Puentes Grandes, Marianao, Guanabacoa, etc.

The total population, according to best authorities, is one hundred and ninety-seven thousand, a large share of which are blacks and mulattoes, free. The inhabitants, as a general thing, appear to be as polished and well dressed as in the most civilized cities of Europe; yet as a rule, the women are so only in appearance, being, many of them, though the possessors of large means, very illiterate; but of course, it is here, as with the best society everywhere,—there is a higher class exceedingly refined, and well educated either in the United States or abroad.

Generally, the men appear to be intelligent and well informed, though I must confess to being surprised at the want of knowledge of—in fact, the indifference to, the peculiarities and places of the island. Every young man's ambition seems to be to go "north," while the women look upon the United States as a country to be dreamed of as a fairy vision, where life and liberty are to be really enjoyed, or as one sweet innocent inquired, "Every one is free there now, Señor?"

"Oh, yes" I replied; "we have no negro slaves there now."

"No, no! Señor; you don't understand me. I mean the women, too,—are they not free?"

To which I was compelled to reply they were, and only we poor men were their slaves.

"*Es muy bueno, Señor;* it is not so here."

The houses, hardly ever more than one story high,—never more than two,—with their tremendous door and windows; when, if the door is open, you see a handsome flight of stone steps, perhaps, leading to the upper story, the walls all gaily painted in white and blue, or yellow; the entrance probably taken up with a gorgeous quitrin, or perhaps a handsome carriage, according as to whether the family are wealthy, and occupy the whole house, or only well off, and keep the upper stories, renting out the lower ones, which are probably filled with merchandise. Notice, now, this great door to the large and showy mansion. It is shut; but see how resplendent it is with brass decorations, latches, hinges, door-plates, or studded with quaintly shaped, brass-headed bolts, which, with the shining handles to the solid wooden leaves of the door, give it a "(k)nobby" appearance in more senses than one. . . .

Here we are in the ever busy street O'Reilly, which, like Obispo or Ricla, one never gets tired of wandering in. Do not imagine for a moment, if you want to find any particular store, that you must ask for Mr. Smith's or Mr. Jones's establishment; oh, no, *amigo mio,*—these people do not generally travel under their own names; but, like a hotel, stick up something that is unique, expressive, or easily remembered. As a consequence, you have "The Nymphs," "The Looking Glass," "The Little Isabel," the "Green Cross," which you see gets its name from the big Maltese cross, built into the wall of that corner store, and hundreds of other funny, curious, and expressive names.

Just look down that street, this hot February day. See those fancy colored awnings, stretching across all the way down, to keep the warm sun away from our heads; those handsome shop windows, or the stores themselves, in fact, with their shelves almost upon the street, all reminding one of the descriptions of Eastern bazaars, were it not that the well-dressed men that are scattered through the non-coated, cool-looking people, show the presence, in a civilized land, of capital tailor's work. . . .

During the day, as a general thing, the streets are peopled simply by those who are necessitated to go forth upon their special business, and few natives either walk or drive out for pleasure until the evening hour, which must be understood as corresponding to our afternoon. After five o'clock, one may begin to expect to see something of life; for, at that hour, the Paseo begins to teem with life and animation, to be filled with promenaders, and handsome carriages and quitrins, with their beautiful and richly-dressed occupants, who, during the previous portions of the day, have been "killing time," most probably, in dowdy dishabille, listlessly lolling in rocking-chairs, with no other effort made than that of fanning themselves, and assisted in the above occupation, perhaps, by an hour or two's *siesta* in the middle of the day. . . .

It is a lovely sight, indeed, this evening drive out the Paseo Isabel, Reina, and Tacon, when the delights of the tropical evening may be enjoyed to their fullest extent. The beautiful women, dressed with extreme taste in their highly-colored stuffs, the well dressed men, the striking and richly decorated equipages, with their liveried servants—add to which the soft air, fragrant with the rich perfume from the tree mignonette, and the tropical character of the surrounding trees and scenery,—have a particularly pleasant and soothing effect upon one accustomed to continued residence in the north. . . .

The cafés now become resplendent with lights and alive with people; the grand theatre Tacon opens its doors, and is also ablaze with light; the old-fashioned watchmen (*serenos*), with their spear-headed poles and their little lanterns, are posted at the corners of the streets, and everything is life, bustle, and animation. These watchmen are also a *cosa de Cuba*, being originally instituted by Tacon in his sweeping arrangements to establish law and order; and if they were not a better lot in his day than they are now, they could not have been of much use, except for show. They are, many of them, stout, jolly-looking fellows, clad in thick coats, with a belt around the waist, in which is some old-fashioned pistol; and they sensibly select, particularly late at night, the softest piece of curbstone they can find at the corners of the street, until it come time, which it does every half hour, for them to get on their feet, knock their staves upon the pavement, or, perhaps, give a long whistle, and then carol out, at the top of their voices; "Twelve o'clock, and all's well,"—night serene or raining, as the case may be. As their prevailing cry is sereno, from the fact that the nights, year in and year out, are usually clear, they themselves have been dubbed with this name.

George Augustus Henry Sala
Under the Sun
(London: Tinby Brothers, 1872), 71–75

I had begun to study the humours of Havana. The time had worn away, it was ten o'clock, and the city had burst into the full blaze of tropical life. The Anglo-Americans rail at Havana, because the streets are so narrow and so tortuous; but ah! from ten to four p.m., how grateful you are for narrow devious lanes, in lieu of broad staring thoroughfares! You have the inestimable blessing of Shade. Now and then you must take, perforce, a hot bath, and frizzle for a moment in the sunshine as you cross a plaza; or, turning a corner, the sun, suddenly espying you, cleverly shoots a ray at your head, which pierces your brain well-nigh as an arrow would: but you are soon in the shade again. The streets of Havana are perhaps as clean as those of most southern European towns. The principal sanitary inspectors are named Garlic and Tobacco-smoke. They are at least determined to keep the other stenches down. The roadway is littered and untidy, but who should complain of litter composed mainly of orange-peel, the rinds of pine-apples, cocoanut shells, fragments of melons, and exhausted Indian corn-cobs? I must go to Covent-garden again for a comparison.

There is but a ridiculous apology for a foot-pavement in these streets. The average width of the trottoir certainly does not exceed twelve inches. It is a kerbstone with nothing to curb. I have fancied this exiguity of path to be a deliberate device on the part of the municipality to keep up the practice of politeness in Havana, for of course, if you meet any one on the trottoir proceeding in a contrary direction to your own, you naturally step into the kennel to allow him to pass. You don't give him the wall, you give him the totality of the pavement. This hypothesis, I fear, however, is as fantastical as the one suggested, that the narrowness of the streets in Havana is also due to premeditation, and is designed to allow opposite neighbours to light their cigars from each other's weeds. Small as is the space between the houses, they preserve, nevertheless, a tolerably perpendicular elevation; whereas in the town of Algiers, which in the narrowness of its thoroughfares closely resembles Havana, the houses are built on the lean-to principle. Each story seems on the brink of toppling over; and at the roofs, opposite houses nearly kiss each other. I have heard that the Moorish architects adopted this style of construction from notions of economy. You see that all but the very narrowest strip of sky must be shut out. Why? The heavens above are for ten hours out of the twenty-four one blazing basin of burnished copper. The Cubans, however, being wealthy, can afford to leave a wider space between their houses; but while the sun shines they shut him out with vast awnings of particoloured stuffs. This aspect of Havana would delight the heart of an Edgington. The populous part of the city is one huge marquee.

Ah, and how shady the shops are! There are some as dark as the purser's store-room in a cockpit. You enter them, not only to shop, but to bestow yourself in a rocking-chair, to nod, and to take, if you please, forty winks. The shopkeeper never dreams of disturbing you. He puts your nap in the bill; that is to say, he adds fifty percent to the price of the articles you wish to purchase. Of course you beat him down. You bargain for everything in Havana mayor o menor, wholesale or retail. The apothecary who sells you a blue pill expects an amicable little tussle over the price. What matter? It fills up the time; and unless you are concerned in sugar or coffee, you are sure to have plenty of time hanging on your hands. 'Are there no beggars at your gate? are there no poor about your lands?' the Poet Laureate might indignantly ask. Well, the poor are slaves, and are very fat and shiny, and seemingly well cared for (which does not in the least militate against slavery being a stupid, blundering, and accursed anachronism, of which the Spaniards themselves are heartily sick), and as for the beggars, I never saw any in Havana; and, had I met one, I should certainly not have presumed to offer him less than a golden dollar.

The tradespeople seldom, if ever, put their names over their shop-fronts. They adopt signs instead—not painted or plastic ones as the Americans and the Germans do, but simply written inscriptions usually implying some ethical allusion. 'La Rectitud' . . . is much patronised by the mercers; but that tradesman in the

Calle O'Reilly must have had queer ideas of rectitude when he charged me seventy-five dollars for a dress professedly made of pina or pine-apple fibre, but which subsequently turned out to be silk grenadine from Lyons, not worth three guineas. Then you have 'La Probidad,' 'La Integridad,' 'La Buena Fé,' 'La Consciencia'—all special favourites with the gentlemen of the narrow width and ell wand [cloth or clothing merchants]. Their signs are very pretty, but methinks they do profess too much. Some are simply arrogant, 'Todos me elogian'—I am praised by everybody; 'Mi famo per l'Orbo vuela'—my fame is universal: these are over the cigar-shops. The photographer has a flourish about 'El Sol de Madrid' and 'El Rayo de Luz;' one studio went by the name of 'El Relampago'—the flash of lightning; and I never could refrain from laughing at the motto adopted by the proprietor of a shop for the sale of lucifer matches—'La Explosion.'

And now, if you please, picture these thread-my-needle thoroughfares, not one of them a third so wide as Hanway-yard, shady to intensity, but yet rich in tender tints of reflected light, and semitones stealing through the diaphanous awnings overhead, with here and there a burst, a splash, an 'explosion,' of positive light and colour—where the sun had found a joint in the armour of awning, and made play with his diamond dart; picture these lanes thronged from morning till night with sallow Spanish Creoles, in white linen and Panamas, and negroes and negresses gaudy, gaping, and grinning, according to the wont of our African brothers and sisters. Now and then a slouch-hatted, black-cassocked priest, now and then a demure Jesuit father; many soldiers in suits of 'seersucker,' a material resembling thin bed-ticking, straw hats, and red cockades; many itinerant vendors of oranges, lemonade, sugar-plums, and cigars, for though every third shop is a tobacconist's, there is a lively trade in cigars done in the streets. The narrowness of the foot-pavement affects you little. You may walk in the roadway without inconvenience. There is nothing to run over you save the bullock-drays, whose rate of speed rarely exceeds a mile an hour, and the pack-mules, which are so laden with fresh-cut Indian corn-stalks for fodder that only their noses and the tips of their tails are visible beneath their burdens, and they look like animated hayricks—and the volantes, which are so light and springy that they would scarcely crush the legs of a fly if their wheels passed over him.

W.M.L. Jay [Julia Louisa M. Woodruff]
My Winter in Cuba
(New York: E. P. Dutton and Company, 1871), 71–76

Juan and I were soon deep in the intricacies of the narrow streets of the old city—so narrow that a stranger is apt to pass the first hours of his explorations in wondering when he will get out of the lanes and into the streets; but he will find only a few worthy of the name, and those outside the walls. In the older streets, I was often obliged to flatten myself against the walls of the houses, to avoid being swept off the narrow pavement by the furious passage of a *volante*; a vehicle which dashes so recklessly through the streets and round the corners, that, if the wide, high windows were less strongly iron-gated, it would be certain to plunge head-long into a drawing-room now and then, in some of its rash turnings and erratic progressions. Many of the streets were quite roofed with awnings, stretched from side to side; and it was easy to imagine one's self walking under the vast tent of Peri-Benon, of Arabian Nights' fame, if there were only a few turbans and caftans about to help out the illusion. In truth, there is an almost ridiculous incongruity between the quaint, Oriental aspect of Cuban architecture and manners, and the modern French fashions—stove-pipe hats and close-fitting pants. In one sense, certainly, Paris *is* "the world."

The walls of the houses are often two or three feet in thickness, built of an irregular mixture of stones and mortar, and then stuccoed and painted. Although they are seldom of more than one story, the front wall is not less than twenty feet high, the top being ornamented with urns or carvings, and the roof sloping back to an interior court, upon which most of the rooms open. If the house boasts of two stories, the lower part is occupied as a store, or devoted to the kitchens, offices, and stables; and the upper floor is reached by a wide staircase from the court, leading to a corridor above. The entrance is wide and lofty; the doors are double, of exceeding thickness, and further strengthened by bands and knobs of brass or iron till they look fit to resist a battering-ram; and the windows are without glass and iron-grated like a prison. The floors are of marble, tiles, or stucco; the walls whitewashed or frescoed; the ceilings high, and often open to the roof, the beams of which are made presentable by painting, staining, or carving.

But, before the stranger has time to notice all these peculiarities of Cuban dwellings, his eyes are dazzled by their brilliancy and variety of color, where all the hues of the rainbow meet and mingle in odd and bewildering contrasts. One house has walls of a light green, with pink cornices and mouldings; its neighbor is a delicate blue, with salmon trimmings; and next is gray and orange, with some admixture of white,—or lilac and yellow, or pink and blue,—all shimmering and quivering in the hot, glowing air, until it seems like a vast, radiating, dissolving view. Nevertheless, after the first surprise is over, and your eyes are a little wonted to the dazzle, you discover that these vivid tints are in exquisite keeping with their surroundings. The tropics suggest color and demand it. It cannot easily be too profuse nor too gorgeous, albeit a better taste might preside over its use.

You are next made sensible of the peculiar compound odor of the street of Havana, very perceptible to newly-arrived noses, but not so easily resolvable by them into its components. The scientific formula would probably read something like this:—"smoke of tobacco, four parts; steam of garlic, three parts; aroma of negro, two parts; miscellaneous garbage, one part." Nevertheless, Havana is not an unclean city in some senses of the word; it has none of that griminess and stickiness of filth which makes New York an abomination to the eyes and a stench in the nostrils, at certain seasons of the year. The dryness of the atmosphere and the arid sunshine, transform most impurities into a fine, cloudy dust; which is kept down in the city by means of sprinkling, but becomes a sufficient nuisance on country roads,—for during my month's stay in Cuba, there has been no rain.

Strangest thing of all, perhaps, to a foreigner, is the fact that as soon as he appears on the streets of Havana, he is taken into the very heart of its domestic life. The broad doorways are wide open, and the window-gratings do not, in the least, obstruct his observation of what occurs within. As he passes along, so close to the windows that he could easily thrust his arm between the iron bars to its full length, he sees ladies chatting and sewing— rocking, meanwhile, as if their lives depended on the regularity and continuity of the vibratory motion; he sees children playing, and servants dusting and scrubbing, and meals being served and eaten; he even gets glimpses of cooking, washing, and other domestic processes, going on in the courts and kitchens in the rear; and he may possibly find himself involuntarily witnessing the finishing touches of a fair *señorita's* toilet. . . .

The "Calle de Mercaderes" is the Broadway of Havana, though the streets of Obispo and Ricla are scarcely less busy and attractive. Jewelry stores are many and handsome; dry-goods and fancy-goods are everywhere; book-stores are good, though not plentiful. A certain corner store makes a specialty of wax-tapers for the devout, displaying them of every size and color, from an immense waxen pole that might serve as a sign for a barber's shop, to tiny pink, blue, and white tapers, fit for illuminating fairy halls. A certain other is devoted to *abanicos*, otherwise fans, ranging in price from fifty cents to a hundred and fifty dollars; the first of which the shopman tells you is "dumb," that is, incapable of the fan-language wherein the *Cubanas* are so well versed, and consequently not worth a groat for purposes of flirtation; while the latter, he assures you, will lay the whole male population low at your feet. . . . Linens and laces are temptingly cheap; so are palm-leaf hats; so are Spanish books; but having satisfied all reasonable wants in these lines of trade, better shut your ears and your purse. Unless you like to go to *La Dominica*, and lay in a stock of guava jelly and marmalade for the home-table. It is good, it is cheap, it will keep (with proper care) till the end of time. Buy a hundred dollars worth, by all means—if you can afford it!

Maturin Murray Ballou
Due South; or, Cuba Past and Present
(Boston: Houghton Mifflin and Company, 1885), 126–33, 141–43

The city presents a large extent of public buildings, cathedrals, antique and venerable churches. It has been declared in its prosperity to be the richest place for its number of square miles in the world, but this cannot be said of it at the present time. There is nothing grand in its appearance as one enters the harbor and comes to anchor, though Baron [Alexander von] Humboldt pronounced it the gayest and most picturesque sight in America. Its multitude of churches, domes, and steeples are not architecturally remarkable, and are dominated by the colossal prison near the shore. This immense quadrangular edifice flanks the Punta, and is designed to contain five thousand prisoners at a time. The low hills which make up the distant background are not sufficiently high to add much to the general effect. The few palm trees which catch the eye here and there give an Oriental aspect to the scene, quite in harmony with the atmospheric tone of intense sunshine. Unlike Santiago or Matanzas, neither the city nor its immediate environs is elevated, so that the whole impression is that of flatness, requiring some strength of background to form a complete picture. The martial appearance of the Morro and the Cabanas, bristling with cannon, is the most vivid effect of the scene, taken as a whole. It might be a portion of continental Spain broken away from European moorings, and floated hither to find anchorage in the Caribbean Sea. One is also reminded of Malta, in the farther Mediterranean, and yet the city of Valetta, bright, sunny, and elevated, is quite unlike Havana, though Fortress St. Angelo overlooks and guards the place as the Morro does this tropical harbor, and Cuba is the Italy of America.

The waters of the harbor, admittedly one of the finest in the world, are most of the time extremely dirty. Many years ago a canal was commenced which was designed to create a flowage calculated to keep the harbor clear of the constantly accumulating filth, but it was never finished, and there remains an evidence of Spanish inefficiency, while the harbor continues to be a vast cesspool. It would be supposed that in a fever-haunted region, great attention would be bestowed upon the matter of drainage, but this is not the case in Havana, or other cities of the island. Most of the effort made in this direction is surface drainage, the liquid thus exposed quickly evaporating in the hot sunshine, or being partially absorbed by the soil over which it passes. . . .

The low-lying, many-colored city of Havana, called San Cristobal, after the great discoverer, was originally surrounded by a wall, though the population has long since extended its dwellings and business structures far into what was, half a century since, the suburbs. A portion of the old wall is still extant, crumbling and decayed, but it has mostly disappeared. The narrow streets are paved or macadamized, and cross each other at right angles, like those of Philadelphia, but in their dimensions reminding one of continental Toledo, whose Moorish architecture is also duplicated here. There are no sidewalks, unless a narrow line of flagstones can be so called, and in fact the people have less use for them where nearly every one rides in a victoria, and fare being but sixteen cents per mile. A woman of respectability is scarcely ever seen walking in the streets, unless she is a foreigner, or of the lower class, such as sellers of fruit, etc. Those living in close proximity to the churches are sometimes seen proceeding to early mass, accompanied by a negress carrying a portable seat, or a bit of carpet on which to kneel upon the marble floor of the cathedral. But even this is exceptional. Cuban etiquette says that a lady must not be seen on the streets except in a vehicle, and only Americans, English, and other foreigners disregard the rule.

The architecture of the dwelling-houses is exceedingly heavy, giving them the appearance of great age. They are built of the porous stone so abundant upon the island, which, though soft when first worked into suitable blocks, becomes as hard as granite by exposure to the atmosphere. The facades of the town houses are nearly always covered with stucco. Their combination of colors, yellow, green, and blue, harmonizes with the glowing atmosphere of the tropics. This will strike the stranger at first as being very odd; there is no system observed, the tenant of each dwelling following his individual fancy as to the hue he will adopt, a dingy yellow prevailing. Standing upon the Campo de Marte and looking in any direction, the changing colors give a picturesque effect to the range of buildings which surround the broad field. In this vicinity the structures are nearly all of two full stories, and many with rows of lofty pillars supporting broad verandas, including one or two palaces, one fine large club-house, some government offices, and the Telegrafo Hotel. These varying colors are not for fancy alone, they have a raison d'être; namely, to absorb the sharp rays of the constant sunshine. But for some toning down of the glare, one's eyes would hardly be able to sustain the power of vision. The vividness with which each individual building and object stands out in the clear liquid light is one of the first peculiarities which will strike a stranger. . . .

The public vehicle called a victoria is a sort of four-wheeled calash, and it has entirely superseded the volante for city use. There are thousands of them about the town, forming a collection of wretchedly wornout carriages, drawn by horses in a like condition. The drivers occupy an elevated seat, and are composed equally of whites and negroes. The charge for a passage from point to point within the city is forty cents in Cuban paper money, equal to sixteen cents of our currency; three times that sum is

charged if engaged for the hour. The streets are in a very bad
condition and sadly need repairing. The roads leading out to the
suburbs in every direction are full of deep holes, and are badly
gullied by the heavy rains. The streets, even about the paseos, are
so impregnated with filth, here and there, as to be sickening to
the senses of the passer-by. Once in three or four weeks somebody
is awakened to the exigency of the situation, and a gang of men is
put to work to cleanse the principal thoroughfares, but this serves
only a temporary purpose. We were told that the reason for this
neglect was that no one was regularly paid for work; even the
police had not received any pay for seven months, and many
refused to serve longer. The soldiery had not been paid their
small stipend for nearly a year, but enlisted men sent out from
Spain, forming the army, are more easily kept together and
more amenable to discipline than any civil body of officials
could be. . . .

The populace of Havana is eminently a festive one. Men
luxuriate in the cafe, or spend their evenings in worse places. A
brief period of the morning only is given to business, the rest of
the day and night to melting lassitude, smoking, and luxurious
ease. Evidences of satiety, languor, and dullness, the weakened
capacity for enjoyment, are sadly conspicuous, the inevitable
sequence of indolence and vice. The arts and sciences seldom
disturb the thoughts of such people. . . . High and low life are ever
present in strong contrast, and in the best of humor with each
other, affording elements of the picturesque, if not of the beautiful. Neatness must be ignored where such human conglomeration
exists, and as we all know, at certain seasons of the year, like
dear, delightful, dirty Naples, Havana is the hot-bed of pestilence.
The dryness of the atmosphere transforms most of the street offal
into fine powder, which salutes nose, eyes, ears, and mouth
under the influence of the slightest breeze. Though there are
ample bathing facilities in and about the city, the people of either
sex seem to have a prejudice against their free use. In most hot
climates the natives duly appreciate the advantage of an abundance
of water, and luxuriate in its use, but it is not so in Cuba. We were
told of ladies who content themselves with only wiping neck,
face, and hands daily upon a towel saturated with island rum, and,
from what was obvious, it is easy to believe this to be true. . . .

In passing through O'Reilly, Obispo, Obrapia, or any business streets at about eleven o'clock in the forenoon and glancing

into the stores, workshops, business offices, and the like, one is sure to see the master in his shirt-sleeves, surrounded by his family, clerks, and all white employees, sitting in full sight at breakfast, generally in the business room itself. The midday siesta, an hour later, if not a necessity in this climate, is a universal custom. The shopkeeper, even as he sits on duty, drops his head upon his arm and sleeps for an hour, more or less. The negro and his master both succumb to the same influence, catching their forty winks, while the ladies, if not reclining, "lose themselves" with heads resting against the backs of the universal rocking-chairs. One interior seen by the passer-by is as like another as two peas. A Cuban's idea of a well-furnished sitting-room is fully met by a dozen cane-bottom rocking-chairs, and a few poor chromos on the walls. These rocking-chairs are ranged in two even lines, reaching from the window to the rear of the room, with a narrow woollen mat between them on the marble floor, each chair being conspicuously flanked by a cuspidor. This parlor arrangement is so nearly universal as to be absolutely ludicrous.

James McQuade
The Cruise of the Montaukto Bermuda: The West Indies and Florida
(New York: Knox and Company, 1885), 367–69

The Havana of daylight and the city by gaslight are different places to the view. One is dull and dingy, with no symmetrical architecture, and with but few broad streets, stately churches, and magnificent buildings, such as one sees in Europe or America; the other is a magnificent metropolis which myriad lights transform into a splendid panorama. We went to hear the Marine Band play in the Park Isabella the Second (where there is a monument to the former Queen of Spain), and the scene brought to mind the Champs Elysees in Paris, with the *cafes-chantants*, puppet-shows, and naughty, but fascinating, fairy-like Mabille. I plead guilty to Mabille. It was delightful; but some Americans I met there were disappointed; they saw nothing improper; they could do better in New York. I believe it has been abolished. It was a mistake; where will the Brooklyn deacons go now when they visit Paris?

But to come back from Paris to Havana. The Park was filled with handsomely-dressed ladies, many of them wearing bonnets, but the majority appearing in the more tasteful and piquant veil. The bonnet, however, is gradually becoming fashionable. I saw none worn except by travelers when here before, but now the hat is making vigorous inroads on the veil. In this I see evidence of Spanish decadence. The innovation cannot fail to have its effect. Patriotism is sapped by millinery. The *bonnet rouge* was the French revolutionary symbol; who knows but that the American bonnet may become the liberty-cap to emblematize Cuban independence?

We sauntered amid the throng—promenading the walks or gathered in groups on the bordering seats—listening to the excellent music, and admiring the beauties (for the Havanese women are very handsome, with fine features, raven hair, dark eyes, flashing beneath strongly-marked eyebrows, and clear, olive complexions), until, tired, we went across the street to the Louvre, where we took a table and remained some time watching the uninterrupted stream of incoming and outgoing visitors. This is the fashionable *café*, and it was filled with men, women, and children, eating, drinking and smoking. At one table, was a party of gentlemen drinking cognac and smoking cigarettes, at another, some ladies and children eating ices, but all exhibiting an un-American nonchalance and unconcern as to the movements of their neighbors. A favorite beverage here is the *panale*, a sweetened compound which takes the place of the French *cau sucrée*. It is a mixture of egg and sugar, something like a *méringue*, and is served with a large glass of water, into which the wafer is broken and dissolved and then drunk. It would look effeminate for a man to go into Delmonico's and drink a *panale*, but it is common here. Gin is a favorite beverage, but American lager-beer is slowly coming into favor. There is a great deal of mind-your-own business in Havana. The puritan has not yet obtained a foothold. Looking out upon this night exhibition of glare and glitter, I could not but think that it was something like the scenery of a theatre, dusty and unattractive until lighted up. And there is an unreality about the splendor, too, for this gay and festive crowd is the population of an island hopelessly insolvent, on the verge of general bankruptcy and universal poverty.

John Mark
Diary of My Trip to America and Havana, in October and November 1884
(Manchester: A. Ireland and Company, 1885), 66–72

In Havana, life and property are protected by a numerous body of smart, military-looking police, both mounted and foot, who, always two and two, patrol the city and suburbs armed with swords and large pistols, as robberies with violence are frequent and quickly executed. . . .

The Cuban ladies are generally small and genteel, and a great majority are pretty, but nearly all of the same type of beauty: black hair, fine dark eyes, regular features, and pale faces. They dress well, and when out of doors wear a mantilla of black lace loosely over the head and shoulders. The men are generally handsome and slender, smartly dressed, and walk erect with elastic step.

Many of the young negresses and mulattas are tall and handsome, and march along with a jaunty air and heads erect. When I remarked that I did not see any elderly women of the same stamp, I was told "they generally die of consumption."

The few aged black women to be seen in the streets are mostly short, stout, and ugly; but the most miserable objects of human beings I have ever seen are the Chinese cripples and beggars in Cuba. Many of the wretched creatures look like mere skeletons covered with parchment.

Business men, as a rule, take when dressing only a cup of chocolate or *café con leche* (coffee with milk), then go to their offices for three or four hours, and return to breakfast at from eleven to twelve. They rest during the heat of the day, and revisit their business later on. At seven they dine, and after that, say from eight to ten, they sit in the open air or promenade and listen to the fine military bands that play in the fashionable Parque Isabel nearly every evening. There it is you see well-dressed ladies and gentlemen in thousands promenading every evening, or sitting on chairs provided, which are charged for exactly as at Rotten Row. Pretty little dark-eyed children, beautifully dressed in muslins and bright sashes, are also there in hundreds, either walking hand-in-hand with their parents or playing and romping

about until a late hour in charge of a black nurse, having probably
been kept indoors during the heat of the day. To these open-air
concerts many ladies come on the Prado in open carriages and do
not alight, in which case the mantilla is often not worn and the
arrangement of the hair is then a triumph. The coachmen are
nearly always negroes in gorgeous livery.

In the morning ladies are seldom seen out, except occasionally
for shopping, and then the best class are always accompanied by
a negress, who rides side by side in the Victoria, or, if walking,
keeps at a respectful distance behind. In the evenings the grand
cafes, especially the Louvre next to the Hotel Inglaterra, are
thronged with gentlemen smoking and talking with great animation. They take a variety of cooling drinks, which are a *specialité*
in a climate where they have perpetual summer.

The public conveyances are mostly one-horse Victorias for
two persons; they have hoods and curtains to protect from the
sun, and the fare is twenty cents (paper), or equal to fivepence per
single journey; there are also open barouches, with two horses,
for four persons. On a few main routes tramcars and omnibuses,
drawn by miserable-looking horses or Spanish mules, run frequently at cheap rates. The horses and mules in harness are
provided with large tassels about the head to keep off the
troublesome flies.

For shade from the sun the streets of Havana have been
purposely made very narrow, excepting only a few squares of
open spaces, and the grand Prado or wide boulevard that divides
the old part of the city from the more modern. The footpaths on
each side are so narrow that people can walk along them only in
single-file.

There is no *select* residential quarter of the city, the best family
houses being scattered about among the business premises, and
often adjoining very objectionable neighbours. In such situations
it is of course impossible to have nice gardens and pleasure
grounds to the houses, as in our suburbs; the best they can do is
to have handsome palms, &c., in their spacious courtyards. The
flat housetops are also available for plants, and for a cool seat in
the evenings.

Charcoal is used for cooking purposes, and as no house fires
are required there is no smoke, and consequently the city may be
said to be without chimneys.

The grand Prado or Paseo has, in addition to a broad carriage drive which runs right down to the sea, convenient walks and paths among beds of shrubs, palms, and tropical trees.

The ancient city was formerly protected by very thick walls of stone and cement, and guards were mounted at the handsome entrance gates. These old walls have been in course of demolition for thirty years, and a gentleman said to me: "At Havana everything goes slow; we have no money to spare for such work."

The best shops are in the streets Obispo, Ricla, and O'Reilly. They are open to the footpaths and attractively arranged in a bazaar-like fashion; the stocks are comparatively small and not of great value. A gay appearance is imparted to some of these narrow streets, by awnings stretched from side to side to shade from the sun.

The streets are badly paved with stone setts, which have to be imported from America, and consequently are very expensive. The insanitary "modern conveniences" indoors and the drainage outside are very defective, and in a tropical climate one is almost thankful that the germs of zymotic disease are not festering in imperfect sewers. In the more modern portion of the city many of the streets remain year after year in deep holes and ruts, neither paved nor sewered.

The streets are swept by negro scavengers, and domestic refuse of all kinds is set out in tubs in the streets, to be removed during the night. Assisting the scavengers in the removal of offal refuse in the city are hundreds of large carrion-birds, like cormorants, flying about almost tame, and under the special protection of the city authorities.

The markets are well supplied with fruit, vegetables, fish, and poultry, and the banana in great abundance, which may be said to be the bread of the poor of Cuba.

Hawking in the streets is carried on to a great extent. Sometimes the baskets or hampers are carried in hand or on the head, but more generally on the backs of mules, on which men sit swinging lazily along, calling out their speciality just as one hears in London. In this way all kinds of bread, fish, fruit and confectionery, live fowls, quails, etc., are distributed. In many public places Chinamen are standing at tables and stalls on tressels, set out with curious cakes and sweetmeats, over which they instinctively keep waving a light feather plume or common fan, to keep the flies off. I noticed scores of these stalls and never once saw a customer stop to buy anything.

Fresh milk is supplied from cows kept standing on the shady side of streets, here and there, in convenient places all over the city; often half-a-dozen together, and always have with them their pretty fawn-coloured young calves.

In offices, factories, and workrooms, drinking water is kept cool in large brown clay, unglazed, pilgrim jars, with a handle at the top and narrow spout at the side, from which water is poured into the mouth without touching the spout with the lips. I tried it once, and the first part of the refreshing stream was spilt all over my shirt front.

The shoeblack boys of Havana look very sharply after business at all likely places, and particularly at the doors of hotels and restaurants. They are permitted to come into the dining-rooms among the tables, to "shine your boots" as you sit at dinner.

The lottery ticket nuisance, the curse of Cuba, is the worst of all. From the first moment of setting foot on shore until the last before leaving, lottery tickets, lottery tickets, lottery tickets are fluttered before one's eyes at all places, and at all times—morning, noon, and night. Old men, old women, and children, at cigar shops, ticket offices, everywhere, push them under notice, and one cannot escape them. At Matanzas it was just the same; the instant we got out of the railway-car the lottery ticket vendors rushed up to us, confident that we could not possibly have gone there for any other purpose than to buy lottery tickets. I understand these Government lotteries of 25,000 tickets, of forty dollars (paper) each, and subdivided into tickets of one and two dollars, take place about every twelve days all the year round. In the way described, speculators in the tickets dispose of as many as they can, perhaps ten or fifteen thousand. The rest of the chances remain in the hands of the Government, who also take twenty-five per cent of the gross amount of each lottery. The expectation of some day drawing a grand prize is sufficient to keep up the excitement among all classes, down to the poorest workmen who can manage to buy or join in buying a ticket in divided shares.

Havana has natural advantages for commerce in its beautiful large harbour, with water deep enough for the largest vessels, and in a climate of perpetual summer. Of the fertile soil of the Island of Cuba, the chief products are sugar, tobacco, and coffee, and on these industries, directly or indirectly, the population of Havana mainly depend. It also grows a great quantity of fruits, such as bananas, cocoa-nuts, pines, limes, oranges, guavas, and green mangos; but for berry fruits of all kinds the climate is too hot, and they are consequently small and shrivelled. Of vegetables may be mentioned sweet potatoes, cabbages, onions, and garlic; the strong odour of the latter is constantly met with among the working-class and is very offensive.

The food supply is considerably supplemented by a great variety of fish caught at Havana, and all around the coast. Sharks are numerous, and shark-shooting is one of the exciting sports; oil is extracted from them, and the smaller ones are eaten.

II

The Sugar Plantation: Production, Culture, and Economy

Alexander von Humboldt
The Island of Cuba
Translated by J. S. Thrasher
(New York: Derby and Jackson, 1801, 1856), 258–62

During my residence in the plain of Guines, I endeavored to gather some exact data relative to the numerical elements of sugar-cane planting. A large sugar plantation producing from 2,000 to 2,500 boxes, generally has fifty *caballerias* of land (about 1,600 acres), one-half of which is planted in cane, and the other is appointed for alimentary plants and pastures, which latter are called *potreros*. The value of the land naturally varies accordingly to its quality, and vicinity to the ports of Havana, Matanzas, or Mariel. In a radius of twenty-five leagues around Havana, the value of each *caballeria* may be estimated at two or three thousand dollars.

That a plantation may produce 2,000 boxes of sugar, it must have three hundred negroes. An adult male slave, who is acclimated, is worth 450 or 500 dollars, and an unacclimated, newly imported African, 370 to 400 dollars. A negro costs from 45 to 50 dollars a year in food, clothing, and medicine, consequently, including the interest on capital, and throwing off the holidays, the cost of labor is a little more than twenty-five cents a day. The slaves are supplied with jerked beef from Buenos Ayres and

Caracas, and salt fish, when meat is dear; with vegetables, such as plantains, pumpkins, sweet potatoes, and corn. In the year 1804, jerked beef was worth 5 to 6 cents a pound in Guines, and in 1825, its cost is from 7 to 8 cents.

On a sugar plantation such as we are describing, producing 2,000 or 2,500 boxes of sugar, there are required, 1st, three cylinder mills, worked by oxen or water-power; 2nd, eighteen kettles, according to the old Spanish method, which, having a very slow fire, burns much wood; and according to the French method, introduced in 1801, by Bailli, from St. Domingo, under the auspices of Don Nicolas Calvo, three clarifiers, three large kettles, and two boiling trains (each having three boilers), in all, twelve pieces. It is generally said that seventy-five pounds of purged sugar yields one keg (seven gallons) of molasses; and that this, with the refuse sugar, covers the expenses of the plantation; but this can be true only where large quantities of rum are made. Two thousand boxes of sugar give 15,000 kegs of molasses, which will make 500 pipes of rum, worth $25 each. . . .

The profit of a plantation, established some time since, consists in, 1st, the fact that, twenty years since, the cost of making a plantation was much less than now; for, a *caballeria* of good land cost then only $1,200 or $1,600, instead of $2,000 or $2,500, as now; and an adult negro $300, instead of $450 to $500; and, 2nd, the variable returns—the prices of sugar having been at times very low, and at others very high. The prices of sugar have varied so much, during a period of ten years, that the return on the capital invested has varied from five to fifteen percent.

David Turnbull
Travels in the West: Cuba, with Notices of Porto Rico and the Slave Trade
(London: Longman, Orme, Brown, Greens, and Longman, 1840), 47–49

Between the planters of Cuba and those of the British colonies, there is this remarkable difference, that when an Englishman does not reside on his estate, he is an absentee from the island altogether, and is willing to remain in England, or at least in Europe, until he has run so far ahead of his resources, that he is compelled to return to the tropics for the sake of retrenchment .... Unlike the British planter, the Cuba proprietor has no desire to return to the mother country, between which and the colony the ties of affection are becoming daily more relaxed, leaving nothing in their stead but the iron grasp of power, which some unforeseen accident may burst suddenly, at once and for ever.

The Spanish planter, although he does not leave the island, scarcely ever resides on his estate; where there is rarely any mansion house fit for his reception. The great majority of them live constantly at the Havana, and a few have taken up their residence at Santiago and Matanzas, and the minor cities of the island. They may possibly be separated from their estates by a distance of hundreds of miles, without the advantage of any thing in the shape of roads that are either safe or practicable. Finding nothing on his plantation to repay the fatigue of his journey, or supply the place of the luxuries of the colonial capital, he visits it so seldom that he may be considered quite as much an absentee from his estate as the Jamaica planter who has taken up his residence at Rome or Naples. . . .

When a stranger visits the town residence of a Cuba proprietor, he finds the family surrounded by a little colony of slaves of every variety of complexion from ebony to alabaster. Most of them have been born in the house, have grown with growth of the family, and are, perhaps, the foster brothers or foster sisters of the master or his children. In such circumstances, it would be surprising if an uncivilised barbarian were to treat them harshly; and for a Spanish, and much more for a Creole, master to do so, imbued as he is with all the warmth of the social affections, is totally out of the question. These long retinues of domestics are kept up by some from an idle love of pageantry, but, by others, from the more honourable desire of not parting with those born under their roof, and for that reason, bearing their name; as it is the practice in Cuba, and in other slave countries into which Africans are imported, for the first proprietor, whether his title be acquired by purchase or inheritance, to bestow his own patronymic, together with a Christian name, on his slave, whether an imported Bozal or an infant Creole, at the time when the indispensable ceremony of baptism is performed.

John George F. Wurdemann
Notes on Cuba
(Boston: James Munroe and Company, 1844), 149–58

The sugar-estate spreads out its solitary but extensive field of cane, with nothing to vary the prospect but the isolated royal palms scattered irregularly over the whole. While the coffee-planter's chief care is to unite in his estate beauty with profit, the only object of the sugar-planter is money, often regardless if it be attained at the expense of the welfare of his laborers. In society he holds a higher rank than the other. . . . When, however, we recollect, that in the palmy days of sugar, the incomes of not a few of them were each more than two hundred thousand dollars, and that even now the crops of many sell for more than one hundred thousand dollars, they might well be considered the natural princes of the land. The capital invested in a sugar estate is also so large, that it alone gives a certain degree of importance to the planter, if he even be, as is often the case, inextricably involved in debt.

A visit to a sugar district will soon dispel from the mind of the traveller all doubts of creole enterprise. It is true that some estates still grind the cane by ox-power, and have but rude contrivances for preparing the sugar; but on many of them the most perfect machinery is employed, and steam, labor-saving steam, has taken the place of manual labor. There is considerable rivalry among the planters to produce the best sugar and the greatest quantity; and so great was the enterprise of one of my neighbors, that, in the midst of the grinding-season, he removed his steam-engine for the erection of another on the plan of those used in France for making beet sugar. The syrup, clarified by animal charcoal, was boiled by steam, and the sugar prepared in a vacuum; the whole cost forty thousand dollars, some said more. As the cutting of the cane ceases when the rains commence, the saccharine matter being greatly diminished by its regrowth, he ran a risk of losing half his crop by the costly experiment. . . .

A sugar-plantation, during the manufacture of sugar, presents a picture not only of active industry but of unremitting labor. The oxen are reduced towards the end of the season to mere skeletons, many of them dying from over-labor; the negroes are allowed but five hours sleep, but although subjected to this inordinate tasking of their physical powers, in general, preserve their good looks.

Before the introduction of the steam-engine, and the example of a milder treatment of the negro by foreign residents in Cuba, the annual loss by death was fully ten per cent, including, however, new slaves, many of whom died from the change of climate. At present the annual loss in Limonar, I was informed by an intelligent English physician, does not exceed two and a half per cent, even including the old. On some plantations, on the south side of the island, the custom still prevails of excluding all female slaves, and even on those where the two sexes are well proportioned in number they do not increase. On a sugar estate employing two hundred slaves, I have seen only three or four children. That this arises from mismanagement is proved by the rapid increase on a few estates where the negroes are well cared for. The Saratoga sugar estate, which with the Carlotta belongs to a highly intelligent merchant of Havana, is noted for the great number of children born on it; while several coffee estates, where the slaves are deprived of sufficient rest, are also unproductive.

It cannot be denied that the slave's life, while employed in the manufacture of sugar, is a very laborious one; from November until the end of May his physical powers are tasked to the utmost, still his peculiar frame of mind, that dwells only on the present, sustains him under it. The weightiest cares cannot drive sleep from his eyelids, or deprive him of his appetite; and so well do the negroes appear even at the end of the grinding-season, that one would be tempted to doubt the amount of labor they have performed. During the rest of the year their daily tasks are comparatively light, consisting chiefly in removing the weeds from the fields, and cutting fuel for the next winter.

The greater portion, during the grinding-season, are employed in cutting the cane. This is done by a short, sword-like cleaver, one stroke sufficing to cut the stalk close to the ground, and another to remove the unripe tops, which with their leaves are thrown in one long heap, while the rest, divided into two or more sticks, are thrown in another. The latter are removed in carts to the mill, and the tops are left for the cattle to feed on. In the best constructed mills a revolving platform conveys the canes to the rollers, through which they pass, and which express from them all the juice. The crushed stalks fall on another revolving way, and are carried off to a spot where a number of negroes are waiting with baskets to convey them into the yard. They are there exposed to the sun until quite dry, when they are packed under large sheds, and used as fuel for boiling the cane-juice.

The juice flows from the rollers through a gutter into a large reservoir, in which it is gently heated, and where it deposits the dirt and portions of cane that have escaped with it from the rollers. From this it is drawn off into a large cauldron, where it undergoes a rapid boiling, and has its acidity corrected by the admixture of more or less lime. When reduced to a certain degree, it is dipped out by ladles into another cauldron, where it is suffered to boil until it reaches the granulating point. It is now removed by large ladles into a long wooden trough, and stirred by long paddles until cold.

The mass now consists of the granulated sugar and its molasses, and when it is intended simply to remove the latter and make the quality called muscovado, it is conveyed into wooden cisterns twelve feet square and two deep, and thence into the hogsheads, where it undergoes its final draining, the molasses escaping through a hold into gutters, which carry it to a general reservoir.

To make the white Havana quality, it is removed from the trough into earthern or tin conical pans, each capable of holding about 80 lbs. of the mass, having at their apices openings closed with a few dried cane leaves, through which the molasses percolates, and fall into gutters below. Clay, made into a soft paste by being well mixed with water, is next spread over the sugar about three inches thick. The water, separating slowing from it passes through the brown sugar below, and washes off the molasses from each grain, converting it into the quality known by the name of Havana white. After a certain time the mass becomes consolidated, and the loaf is removed from the pan, and carried to the driers, large wooden frames fixed on rail-ways, on which they can be readily rolled under cover of the shed when it rains. The base of the conical loaf is the whitest, while the apex is of a dirty-brown hue, and the intervening portion of a light brown. It is divided into these three kinds by the negroes, who with their cleavers walk over the sugar with their bare feet, cutting the masses into small lumps. To a stranger the sight of two or three dozen half-naked negroes thus employed under a broiling sun, and sweating over their task, is far from being pleasant; and I have known more than one who have been afterwards very sparing in the use of clayed sugar. A machine has however, been lately invented for crushing the loaves, and the present unclean method will probably be generally abandoned.

In well constructed furnaces the dried cane stalks, called *bagassa*, are found sufficient for boiling the juice, but wood is required to produce steam for the engine. This is brought to the mill at the expense of great labor; and in consequence of its great consumption, large tracts of land are now bare of forests, and the difficulty of procuring fuel increases every year. Much labor is also expended in raising water from the deep wells to supply the engine boiler, the amount of which may be imagined by the reader, when he learns that they are from one to four hundred feet deep, and that the water is generally drawn up by single buckets. During the dry season the sugar-planter is also in constant dread of his fields being fired by some malicious neighbor, when in a few hours the whole crop and perhaps all his buildings might be destroyed. The canes are so thickly planted, and their numerous dead leaves form such a closely interwoven mass, that when ignited while the wind is fresh, the flames spread with inconceivable rapidity over the whole field. Although the prince of agriculturists, the sugar-planter, is now at the mercy of any of the canaille he may have offended, and an opportunity is not unfrequently taken at this season to revenge some past slight or injury.

As soon as the fire is discovered the large bell of the estate, which can be heard several miles, is rapidly tolled, and the neighboring estates at the summons disgorge their troops of slaves, who hasten to the spot. Alleys are cut through the field to the leeward of the burning portion and counter-fires ignited, and a large quantity of cane is often thus saved. In some cases the alley is cut too close to the fire, which sweeping across it surrounds the workers, some of whom are not unfrequently suffocated by the dense clouds of smoke. I was present on one occasion, and the scene was most exciting. The roaring of the flames, the sharp crackling of the burning cane, the volumes of smoke that now and then swept along the ground, enveloping everything in its dark cloud, the gang of half naked negroes, numbering more than five hundred, with their sword-like *machetes*, hewing down the canes, while others with torches were setting fire to the windward edge of the road, the mounted mayorals with long swords and holsters galloping about, and shouting out orders and counter-orders, and a certain vague sense of danger, combined to render the whole a most animating sight. . . .

To encourage the cultivation of the cane, the Spanish government has granted many privileges to the sugar-planter, some of which are at the expense of justice. The island government has, however, never been remarkably over-scrupulous in the choice of means to increase its revenue. His slaves cannot be seized for debt, nor can his plantation be sold for less than its value adjudged by arbitration; he pays not tithes on his sugar, and late laws have so well protected him, that the creditor is literally compelled to wait until it suits him to pay his debt. All that he can do, is to place an agent on the estate, who secures the crops, from which, however, the planter can deduct sufficient to support himself and workmen, and to pay all the other necessary expenses of the estate.

Richard Robert Madden
The Island of Cuba
(London: C. Gilpin, 1849), 156–68

Guines is a town of about 4,000 souls. The vicinity is thickly studded with sugar estates. . . . We visited two sugar estates within a league of Guines, the first called Olanda, Senhor Montalvo, proprietor. We were permitted to enter without any employer of the estate, which was desirable for the purpose of making inquiries of those we found on the spot. On going into the mill-house we found three persons in a dark corner, in the stocks— two negroes and one mulatto boy, all nearly naked, having nothing on but tattered shirts. We asked them how long they had been in the stocks. They said,—"two months." They were not constantly kept there, however, but were taken out to work in the day; and at meal-time, and during the night, they were kept in the stocks. The crime of the two negro men was vagrancy, wandering at night beyond the precincts of the slave-pen—that of the boy, stealing eggs. The latter belonged to a doctor at Guines, who sent him to the overseer of the Olanda estate, to have him punished there. The nights at this time were not only cool, but extremely cold; and in this damp, dismal place, in the depth of winter, every night, for two months, had these unfortunate wretches been kept in the stocks, without a rug to cover them. We had brought a negro servant with us from Guines, and the poor boy in the stocks begged the former, in the most piteous terms, to intercede with his master for him.

We next visited the mayoral. He told us the estate was in *pleito* (the subject of law), the management and receipts had passed from the hands of the owner to that of the money-lenders of the Havana. There were now ninety-six slaves on the estate, and forty only fit for hard work. They made 1,000 boxes of sugar a year. The soil was a good deal worn out. I spoke to him about the people in the stocks. He said, "Two of them are runaways; the other is a thief." I said, two months' confinement in the stocks every night, in that cold, damp place in winter, without a blanket to put round them, or even straw under them, was a hard punishment. "The sooner they were let out, the better it would be for the estate,"—I did not venture to say for them; for I might as well have spoken to a savage of New Zealand of humanity, as to that Spanish mayoral of any interests that were likely to be served by abridging the sufferings of a slave. He was an unreasoning, unfeeling man, of a brutal mind, and yet he was remarkably good looking, had fine, delicately-formed, nobly-outlined Spanish features, with something of softness in them, and his manners were courteous—naturally so—and pleasing, when he was communicating with us white men. But an awful change I observed come over his countenance and whole demeanour, when once or twice he had occasion to give some orders to the slaves, as we passed along. . . .

The Spanish mayoral, I have little doubt, had been brutalized by his calling—had no energy of character, nor sense of religion, nor enlightenment, to resist the debasing influence of slavery. Had he been placed in a more fortunate position, he might have been a harmless and good-natured, and perhaps even disposed to be a good man.

The time of sleep in the crop time, the mayoral told us, was about four hours, a little more or less. Those who worked at night in the boiling-house worked also next day in the field. They had two meals a day. They had tassajo for one meal, and six plantains and some Indian corn for the other.

On our return, our negro guide told us "that Ingenio (sugar estate) was a very bad one. They were very bad to the negroes

there. Four months ago, the mayoral had a man flogged, and the
flogging went on till the poor slave died." He further informed us
that the authorities at Guines made a judicial investigation, ordered
the body of the murdered negro to be disinterred, and examined
by medical men (the planters' doctors of the district), who found,
of course, no traces of injury to any vital organ, from the scourg-
ing under which the slave died, and no further proceedings
consequently were taken against the mayoral. It was only one
more murder of a slave, committed with impunity, to be added to
the long list of Spanish atrocities registered elsewhere, and, as
surely as the sun shines at noon-day, destined to bring down the
wrath of heaven on the nation whose Government suffers and
sanctions such violations of all law divine and human.

On the estate of Olanda crop time lasted four months; it
began in January, and ended in May. The mill was moved by
water-power. The proprietor was an absentee—like most of his
class, an embarrassed man; the property was mortgaged; involved
in law proceedings, the produce went chiefly to the lawyers; the
management was bad; and treatment of the slaves inhuman, the
sole object of the *administrador* being, to get the utmost amount
of labour in a given time out of the greatest number of slaves that
could be worked day and night, without reference to their health
or strength, age or sex, or to the future interests of the possessor
of the property.

The appearance of the negroes on this estate was wretched in
the extreme; they looked jaded to death, listless, stupified, hag-
gard, and emaciated: how different from the looks of the pampered,
petted, well-fed, idle, domestic slaves of the Dons of the Havana!
The clothing of the Olanda negroes was old and ragged,—of the
coarsest sacking stuff. They lived here in huts, near the Ingenio,
but very miserable places, unfit for the habitation of wild
beasts that it might be thought desirable to keep in health or
comfort. . . .

On the 23rd of December, 1838, I set out for Bejucal, by
railroad six leagues from the Havana and took a volante to St.
Antonio, the same day, a distance of three leagues from Bejucal.
The country between those towns is tolerably cultivated, the
products are chiefly maize, yams, yuccas, and edible fruits.

At St. Antonio, the population is about 3,000—they say there,
5,000; there are two schools. In the summer it is a place of resort
for the Havana people, on account of its baths; the river disap-

pears by a subterranean channel close to the town—at a short distance a deep well, about sixty or seventy feet deep, has been cut down upon its current, where it flows rapidly—it appears again about three leagues off. The nearest sugar property is about a league off the coffee property; there the river also makes its appearance. The country about St. Antonio is picturesque; in the neighbourhood of the town there is nothing remarkable. I could not procure horses to go on to St. Marco; the distance from St. Marco to St. Antonio is six leagues. I returned to Bejucal, and slept there, and the next day proceeded to visit three sugar estates, about a league from the town.

The first is that of Don Francisco de la Luz, called St. Anna; there were ninety negroes, in which number there were thirty women—they made on that property 700 cases of sugar, eighty bucoyes of molasses; the negroes were allowed *three meals* a day. No rum was made on any of the six sugar estates I visited—no distillation was carried on. The mayoral said he was thirty years in the family the Senhor de la Luz; he seemed a very good, humane man, and the negroes looked well, and were well clothed in thick flannel shirts; he said, that on no other estate was there three meals a day, but here the negroes were well taken care of, and Sra. de la Luz was very particular about the negroes hearing mass on Sundays and fete days, and had a chaplain frequently there to make the negroes say prayers. This was the second estate only in the island that I heard of having a chaplain. The priest of Bejucal confirmed this to me; he said that Senhor de la Luz's was the only estate he knew of having a chaplain—that in crop time, if they were near a town where there was a church, they might go there on a Sunday, but not out of crop time. He told us that they were baptised: my companion said—"What! does it end there?" The priest laughed. The food here consisted of Indian corn, salt fish, and tassajo, alternately, and plantains at night. The time for sleep, he said, in crop time was three hours. We remonstrated about the insufficiency of sleep, he said they could not carry on the work with less labour. Subsequently, after we left this Quinta, Mr. T. and I differed about the three hours' sleep. I determined on going back, and returned with Mr. T.: we again put the question as to the time of sleep the negroes were allowed, and our informant then said that four hours was the usual time of rest. The time of crop on this estate was from three to three-and-a-half months. We saw here one man in the stocks, his head was in a broken piece of pottery—the stocks are in the boiling house; there was another man going about heavily laden with chains.

The sugar estate of La Pita, belonging to the Marquis San Felipe, we visited the same day, 24th December. There was on this property 161 negroes, of which forty-eight were women. 757 boxes of sugar were made last year; this year they expect to make 1000 boxes, on account of a new steam engine put up for the purpose of grinding the cane, of eighteen horse power. The engineer, an Irishman, said, that with the steam engine they could grind as much cane in twelve hours, as they could without it in twenty-four hours, but it could not supersede night-work. We saw the mayoral, and from him got the above numbers; he told us, that the last year there had been five deaths and only one birth. Here they had but two meals a day allowed. The time of sleep in crop time was from four to four-and-a-half hours. . . .

We visited a sugar estate of Senor Joakim Cardenas. The mayoral was a surly, savage looking fellow, with the implement of office in hand, "the cart whip." He said there were a hundred negroes on the property; they made last year 600 boxes of sugar. Deaths last year two, and there was not one birth. Four hours were allowed for sleep during crop time. The system in the boiling house was far more imperfect, in point of mechanical contrivance, than any I had seen in Jamaica. The mill was moved by water-power. The negroes resided in huts. Of the slaves thirty were females.

The total number of females on the three estates we visited amounted to 108; the total number of men, 243.

We visited the sugar estate of the Conde de O'Reilly, Alexandria. The Conde, who lives in the Havana, is an absentee from his property, like the owner of Olanda.

Here the works are splendid, and on an immense scale; the power of the mill, water, like that of the Olanda, the aqueduct one thousand varas long. The mayoral was accompanied by another person, apparently a mayoral of some adjacent property; he was an extremely civil, well-informed, frank, rational man, far superior to his class in Jamaica. It is fit to remember that the mayoral, though generally called and regarded by us as an overseer, is more in the light of the resident attorney on the estate, who keeps the accounts, records the produce, orders the supplies from the owners at Havana—while the head driver, or supervisor, the nearest approach to our Jamaica "book-keeper" (who keeps no books), superintends the labour of the field, and in the boiling house. On each estate there is generally one mayoral. The crop time lasted, on this estate, four months—from the 10th January to the 10th of May, at Alexandria. There was one death here the last year.

The mayorals are all Spaniards, the Creoles of the same rank and class being generally so uneducated, even in the first elements of knowledge, as to be incapable of filling this office. Alexandria has 102 negroes, about thirty-five only fit for hard work; in crop time they hire thirty more; the soil is worn out. They make 1,000 boxes of sugar, formerly considerably more. The reason given for this falling off, was want of hands. I asked if the Conde sold off the negroes? My informant said, "No, the Conde was in debt; he did not sell any off, but he bought no new ones."

Now this property formerly produced more than double the amount of sugar, and here was a plain proof, not only that there was no increase by births, but a very great decrease by deaths; yet the mayoral said that last year there was only one death. Here, too, the negroes were in huts, not in an enclosed yard. About the labour he said, the negroes in crop time did not get much sleep. I asked if that did not shorten their lives? The answer was, "sin duda," without doubt.

The Conde paid little attention to his estate, and seldom came there. The alcalde at Guines told me the same thing, and said, these gentlemen think of nothing but their pleasures, gambling, etc. "This would be the richest district in the island if the owners would live on their properties and attend to them; they do neither."

John Glanville Taylor
The United States and Cuba
(London: Richard Bentley, 1851), 180–88

As I propose to devote a few lines to a description of one of the principal sugar estates, or "Ingenios," I may begin by saying that it was formed on a grant direct from the Government. The cleared land amounts indeed to more in extent than any other estate in the district, but the whole is a *league square* (Spanish). Now this enormous quantity of land, if measured off in that neighbourhood, would include several large and small villages and scores of separate holdings. For a long time, a good many such were included in the fence, but they all had to yield, one after another, to the devouring appetite of the *ingenio grande*. . . .

The sugar estate Santa L— was commenced in 1834, but very extensive clearings were not made till two or three years after that date. The care of the part proprietor and resident manager, was very properly directed for a long time, in anticipation of the increase of the estate to what it was when I knew it, to the establishment of large tracts of provision grounds, planted with all sorts of useful vegetables, at the head of which we must place the plantain, that great staff of life in Cuba; and second the cassave, or "yuca," from which is made the nutritious cakes so well known. A small mill was used for the first few years, but when fresh purchases of slaves were made and the estate became extensive, a powerful steam engine, with all its accompaniments of copper pans, steam clarifiers, saw mill, grain mill, etc. were put up; and that that work was done in earnest there can be little doubt, when I say, that the average produce during the four months or so of crop, was about thirty hogsheads (fourteen cwt., more or less, each) per week. The manager's residence was beautifully situated on an eminence of about fifty feet high, and only one in the clearing, and from the verandah up stairs was certainly a view hardly to be equalled, I dare say, any where else. In front, the sea; at a distance of two miles, but between it and the hill, and extending wide on either hand, more than a square mile of canes, all divided into smaller partitions, by neatly kept roads, cultivated, except in crop time, with peas, corn, sweet potatoes and other smaller crops. A sight of this enormous extent of canes, of the brightest verdure (except during the fatal drought, when much was lost) and the whole gracefully waving to the force of the North-east trade wind, is a sight, which *once* seen, could surely never be forgotten. . . .

The "bujios" [*bohios*] or huts of the negroes were all on the same hill also, and formed quite a little village of themselves. A day's proceedings on this estate is soon described, as things went on beneath the strict yet merciful sway of my good friend. Bitterly, I make no doubt, do the negroes, poor creatures, feel his loss! The head overseer's berth, on an estate like this, is verily no sinecure. He must be watchful and wakeful as a cat; for if he slept, who would think himself called on to wake? Accordingly, when the morning star indicates the near approach of dawn, he rises and generally rings a great bell himself. This is called the "Ave Maria," and it is pleasant to hear the hour struck by a number of bells, when many estates join. That no one may mistake the exact moment, they publish it in the journals, and overseers near Havana make a point of being exact to a second. The negroes, who are however already up, are allowed some little time to get ready, and, in effect, *they* chiefly make good use of their minutes by warming a cup of coffee for themselves, and a cake of maize, or roasting a plantain or two, before encountering the hard morning's work. When now the dawn is plainly declared, two or three taps more are given on the bell, and the whole sally forth. In crop time, however, those who are engaged in the boiling are exempt from this rule, they being divided into *watches* of twelve hours turn generally, and in the same way hands are retained to feed the mill. Sometimes, when hard pressed from time, they retain the same hands to feed the mill, which work has not to be continued always; but four rests of two hours each are allowed in the twenty-four hours, which it must be confessed is certainly a full proportion of *work*. All arrived at the overseer's quarter, he reads the names, to which all must answer. They are generally fully informed of their work for the day, on the preceding evening; of course in crop time the only work is cutting and carting canes. Before the last name on the roll is called, they all file off down the hill; the second overseer, already mounted on his pony, brings up the rear. In a few minutes more, the oxen are taken out of the pens and stalls, and yoked, and soon a long string of carts rattle down after the negroes. When certain descriptions of work are going on, they are done by task work; cane cutting is one. According to the growth of the canes, four or five cart loads may be cut by a slave, and they generally finish their task by two o'clock, and spend the rest of the day in their "cunucus." But who is the negro that is not blessed with a sweetheart or a wife? Alas for him, the lady sometimes lags; and as they are the pink of gallantry, he must finish her task for her also, that they may spend the evening together.

The bell again sounds at twelve, and generally an hour and a half's recess is allowed for dinner. This is cooked for some by the owner (for as many as so ask it), or else is served out raw once a week to men with wives, to cook as they please. They are not all bound to present themselves at noon, for most prefer to hold out till they finish the task. In weeding also, and work of that kind, the overseer leaves it optional with them whether they will take a certain piece of work as a task, or "stick it out" the whole day. They generally prefer the former, and it is surprising to see how hard they will labour. The overseer watches them as does a cat a mouse; he is "up to" every "dodge" in the negro calendar of schemes, and detects in a second the quickest possibly executed movement, of covering a tough root with a weed or by a little earth, with the *toe* or the *hoe*.

After the sun has set about a quarter of an hour, the bell is again sounded; this is called "La Oracion," or the hour of prayer. The negroes may now go where they please for the next two hours. At the end of that time the bell is smartly struck three or four times, and all repair to the front of the mill house. They are now expected to work an hour by the light of a large fire of cane trash, which is kept burning in the middle of the yard, when there is no moon. This work is called *"La fagina,"* because performed at the light of a faggot. The negroes, so far from making any objection to this, would not miss it on any account. During the *fagina*, the overseers never get angry, and the negroes take many liberties they would not dare to do at other times. In crop time the *fagina* is taken advantage of, to get into the house the "bagass" (dried squeezed canes) used for fuel, and which have not all been stored up during the day, after which every one seizes a broom, and sweeps the whole yard as clean as possible. All loose canes are collected and piled near the mill. If masons are at work, bricks are placed ready for the next day, and large logs are rolled for carpenters or the saw mill. At nine, the bell sounds a stroke, and the fagina being over, all come together; the roll is called, and the people file off one by one repeating "Buenas noches, mi amo" (good night my master). At half past nine, two very light strokes of the bell are heard, the signal for silence and sleep.

William Henry Hurlbert
Gan-Eden; or, Picture of Cuba
(Boston: John P. Jewett and Company, 1854), 139–45

The great sugar estates of Cuba lie in the Vuelta Arriba, the "upper district," the region of the famous "red earth." The face of this region smiles with prosperity. In every direction the traveller rides astonished through a garden of plenty, equally impressed by the magnificent extent, and the profuse fertility of the estates whose palm avenues, plantain orchards, and cane fields succeed each other in almost unbroken succession. Many of these properties yield princely revenues, and are worked by "gangs" of slaves, much larger than are common in the American States. The original outlay upon such an estate is very large, although land can be procured cheaply enough, and the expenses of management are very heavy. The salaries of engineers upon estates worked in the old-fashioned manner, average about one hundred and twenty dollars a month, during the grinding season. But the French machinery is conducted by persons of superior capacity, who are tempted hither from Europe or America by the offer of permanent situations at much higher salaries. Four or five such persons must be maintained upon a large estate. To the amount thus expended, must be added the wages of white sub-ordinates, the expenses of five hundred or of a thousand negroes, the value of cattle annually destroyed, the incidental outlay, and in the majority of cases, the interest upon the large sums which the planter has borrowed in a country where money has an extraordinary value. Yet so productive are the estates, and so steady is the demand for the planter's crop, that the great sugar planters of Cuba are in truth princes of agriculture. Cholera, sweeping away troops of his slaves, the match of an envious, or the cigar of a careless montero kindling a flame that nothing can arrest, are alike powerless to interrupt seriously the prosperous career of an intelligent and enterprising hacendado. The ruinous practice of absenteeism, which prepared for the British West Indies that sudden ruin, so often and so unjustly charged upon emancipation, is comparatively unknown in Cuba. The *administradores* of the Cuban estates are frequently members of the proprietor's family. And the proprietors themselves generally pass a part of the year on their estates. The master's eye keeps watch over those admirable arrangements and tasteful decorations, which make a great sugar estate so delightful to the stranger. Particularly beautiful are the estates to which a *cafetal* is attached. The coffee culture was introduced by the French refugees from Hayti, men of taste and refinement, who in laying out the grounds of their new homes, took thought for the beautiful as well as for the useful. The Spaniards generally . . . seem to have done but little for the advance of landscape gardening, and the glorious opportunities offered by Cuba to the art, have been little improved excepting in the *cafetales*. Although Brazil has quite broken down the Cuban coffee trade, these coffee estates are still numerous in the Vuelta Arriba, where they are kept up on the French models, chiefly as ornaments to the sugar estates, vegetable farms, and homes for the younger or the decrepit negroes. The imposing scale of the operations on a great *ingenio*, imparts a character of barbaric regal state to the life one leads there. The *baracon* becomes a town, the planter a feudal lord, administering hospitalities as lavish as the bounty of the climate and the soil. Living in such a region, one soon enters into the spirit of that eastern munificence and profusion which disdains limits and calculations. The singular number falls into disrepute. A kind of gorgeous superfluity seems only fit and becoming. Your thought is all "of Africa and golden joys." The luxurious seductions of the land persuade you into a new charity towards men so superbly tempted. . . .

Looking at them simply as an entertainment, the mills of these great sugar estates are not incongruous with the easy delight of the place. Everything is open and airy, and the processes of the beautiful steam machinery go on without the odors as without the noises that make most manufactories odious. Many ingenious applications of chemical and mechanical science lend an interest to De Rosny trains, which were invented by a Frenchman who had never seen a sugar estate, and who on coming to the West Indies, could not work profitably his own machinery. The most interesting to me of these arrangements was the centrifugal process. The molasses, which on the old-fashioned estates eventually distils into diamond drops of aguardiente is converted by this process into sugar. It passes into a large vat, by the side of which is a row of double cylinders, the outer one of solid metal, the inner of wire gauze. These cylinders revolve each on an axis attached by a horizontal wheel and band to a shaft which communicates with the central engine. The molasses is ladled out into the spaces between the external and internal cylinders, and the axes are set in motion at the rate of nineteen hundred revolutions a minute. For three minutes you see only a white indistinct whirling; then the motion is arrested; slowly and more slowly the cylinders revolve, then stop, and behold! the whole inner surface of the inner cylinder is covered with beautiful crystallizations of a light yellow sugar! Watching this ingenious process, I used to fancy that somewhat in this wise, might the nebulae of space be slowly fashioning into worlds.

Richard Henry Dana, Jr.
To Cuba and Back: A Vacation Voyage
(Boston: Ticknor and Fields, 1859), 121–28, 130–38

The sugar plantation is no grove, or garden, or orchard. It is not the home of the pride and affections of the planter's family. It is not a coveted, indeed, hardly a desirable residence. Such families as would like to remain on these plantations are driven off for want of neighboring society. Thus the estates, largely abandoned by the families of the planters, suffer the evils of absenteeism, while the owners live in the suburbs of Havana and Matanzas, and in the Fifth Avenue of New York. The slave system loses its patriarchal character. The master is not the head of a great family, its judge, its governor, its physician, its priest and its father, as the fond dream of the advocates of slavery, and sometimes, doubtless, the reality, made him. Middlemen, in the shape of administradores, stand between the owner and the slaves. The slave is little else than an item of labor raised or bought. The sympathies of common home, common childhood, long and intimate relation and many kind offices, common attachments to house, to land, to dogs, to cattle, to trees, to birds—the knowledge of birth, sicknesses, and deaths, and the duties and sympathies of a common religion—all those things that may ameliorate the legal relations of the master and slave, and often give to the face of servitude itself precarious but interesting features of beauty and strength—these they must not look to have.

This change has had some effect already, and will produce much more, on the social system of Cuba.

There are still plantations on which the families of the wealthy and educated planters reside. And in some cases the administrador is a younger member or a relative of the family, holding the same social position: and the permanent administrador will have his family with him. Yet, it is enough to say that the same causes which render the ingenio no longer a desirable residence for the owner make it probable that the administrador will be either a dependent or an adventurer; a person from whom the owner will expect a great deal, and the slaves but little, and from whom none will get all they expect, and perhaps none all they are entitled to.

In the afternoon we went to the sugar-house, and I was initiated into the mysteries of the work. There are four agents: steam, fire, cane juice, and negroes. The results are sugar and molasses. At this ingenio, they make only the Muscovado, or brown sugar. The processes are easily described, but it is difficult to give an idea of the scene. It is one of condensed and determined labor.

To begin at the beginning, the cane is cut from the fields by companies of men and women, working together, who use an instrument called a machete, which is something between a sword and a cleaver. Two blows with this slash off the long leaves, and a third blow cuts off the stalk, near to the ground. At this work, the laborers move like reapers, in even lines, at stated instances. Before them is a field of dense, high-waving cane; and behind them, strewn wrecks of stalks and leaves. Near, and in charge of the party, stands a driver, or more grandiloquently, a contramayoral, with the short, limber plantation whip, the badge of his office, under his arm.

Ox-carts pass over the field, and are loaded with the cane, which they carry to the mill. The oxen are worked in the Spanish fashion, the yoke being strapped upon the head, close to the horns, instead of being hung round the neck, as with us, and are guided by goads, and by a rope attached to a ring through the nostrils. At the mill, the cane is tipped from the carts into large piles, by the side of the platform. From these piles, it is placed carefully, by hand, lengthwise, in a long trough, it is carried between heavy, horizontal, cylindrical rollers, where it is crushed, its juice falling into receivers below, and the crushed cane passing off and falling into a pile on the other side.

This crushed cane, (bagazo), falling from between the rollers, is gathered into baskets by men and women, who carry it on their heads into the fields and spread it for drying. There it is watched and tended as carefully as new-mown grass in haymaking, and raked into cocks or windrows, on an alarm of rain. When dry, it is placed under sheds for protection against wet. From the sheds and from the fields, it is loaded into carts and drawn to the furnace doors, into which it is thrown by Negroes, who crowd it in by the armful, and rake it about with long poles. Here it feeds the perpetual fires by which the steam is made, the machinery moved, the cane-juice boiled. The care of the bagazo is an important part of the system; for if that becomes wet and fails, the fires must stop, or resort be had to wood, which is scarce and expensive.

Thus, on one side of the rollers is the ceaseless current of fresh, full, juicy cane-stalks, just cut from the open field; and on the other side, is the crushed, mangled, juiceless mass, drifting out at the draught, and fit only to be cast into the oven and burned. This is the way of the world, as it is the course of art. The cane is made to destroy itself. The ruined and corrupted furnish the fuel and fan the flame that lures on and draws in and crushes the fresh and wholesome; and the operation seems about as mechanical and unceasing in the one case as in the other.

From the rollers, the juice falls below into a large receiver, from which it flows into great, open vats, called defecators. These defecators are heated by the exhaust steam of the engine, led through them in pipes. All the steam condensed forms water, which is returned warm into the boiler of the engine. In the defecators, as their name denotes, the scum of the juice is purged off, so far as heat alone will do it. From the last defecator, the juice is passed through the trough into the first caldron. Of the caldrons, there is a series, or, as they call it, a train, through all which the juice must go. Each caldron is a large, deep copper vat, heated very hot, in which the juice seethes and boils. At each, stands a strong Negro, with long, heavy skimmer in hand, stirring the juice and skimming off the surface. This scum is collected and given to the gods, or thrown upon the muck heap, and is said to be very fructifying. The juice is ladled from one caldron to the next, as fast as the office of each is finished. From the last caldron, where its complete crystallization is effected, it is transferred to coolers, which are large, shallow pans. When fully cooled, it looks like brown sugar and molasses mixed. It is then shovelled from the coolers into hogsheads. These hogsheads have holes gored in their bottoms; and, to facilitate the drainage, strips of cane are placed in the hogshead, with their ends in these holes, and the hogshead is filled. The hogsheads are set on open frames, under which are copper receivers, on an inclined plane, to catch and carry off the drippings from the hogsheads. These drippings are the molasses, which is collected and put into tight casks.

I believe I have given the entire process. When it is remembered that all this, in every stage, is going on at once, within the limits of the mill, it may well be supposed to present a busy scene.

The smell of juice and of sugar-vapor, in all its stages, is intense. The Negroes fatten on it. The clank of the engine, the steady grind of the machines, and the high, wild cry of the Negroes at the caldrons to the stokers at the furnace doors, as they chant out their directions or wants—now for more fire, and now to scatter the fire—which must be heard above the din, "A-a-b'la! A-a-b'la!" "E-e-cha candela!" "Pu-er-ta!", and the barbaric African chant and chorus of the gang at work filling the cane-troughs—all these make the first visit at the sugarhouse a strange experience. But after one or two visits, the monotony is as tiresome as the first view is exciting. There is, literally, no change in the work. There are the same noises of the machines, the same cries from Negroes at the same spots, the same intensely sweet smell, the same state of the work in all its stages, at whatever hour you visit it, whether in the morning, or evening, at midnight, or at the dawn of the day. If you wake up at night, you hear the "A-a-b'la! A-a-b'la!" "E-e-cha! E-e-cha!" of the caldron-men crying to the stokers, and the high, monotonous chant of the gangs filling the wagons or the trough, a short, improvisated stave, and then the chorus—not a tune, like the song of sailors at the tackle and falls, but a barbaric, tuneless intonation. . . .

This plantation is a favorable specimen, both for skill and humanity, and is managed on principles of science and justice, and yields a large return. On many plantations—on most, I suspect, from all I can learn—the Negroes, during the sugar season, are allowed but four hours of sleep in the twenty-four, with one for dinner, and a half hour for breakfast, the night being divided into three watches, of four hours each, the laborers taking their turns. On this plantation, the laborers are in two watches, and divide the night equally between them, which gives them six hours of sleep. In the day, they have half an hour for breakfast and one hour for dinner. Here, too, the very young and the very old are excused from the sugar-house, and the nursing mothers have lighter duties and frequent intervals of rest. The women worked at cutting the cane, feeding the mill, carrying the bagazo in baskets, spreading and drying it, and filling the wagons; but not in the sugar-house itself, or at the furnace doors. I saw that no boys or girls were in the mill—none but full-grown persons. The very small children do absolutely nothing all day, and the older children tend the cattle and run errands. And the engineer tells me that in the long run this liberal system of treatment, as to hours and duties, yields a better return than a more stringent rule.

The crop this year, which has been a favorable one, will yield, in well-managed plantation a net interest of from fifteen to twenty-five per cent on the investment; making no allowance, of course, for the time and skill of the master. This will be a clear return to planters like Mr. Chartrand, who do not eat up their profits by interest on advances, and have no mortgages, and require no advances from the merchants.

But the risks of the investment are great. The cane-fields are liable to fires, and these spread with great rapidity, and are difficult to extinguish. Last year Mr. Chartrand lost $7,000 in a few hours by fire. In the cholera season he lost $12,000 in a few days by deaths among the negroes.

According to the usual mode of calculation, I suppose the value of the investment of Mr. Chartrand to be between $125,000 and $150,000. On well-managed estates of this size, the expenses should not exceed $10,000. The gross receipts, in sugar and molasses, at a fair rate of the markets, cannot average less than between $35,000 and $40,000. This should leave a profit of between eighteen and twenty-two per cent. Still, the worth of an estimate depends on the principle on which the capital is appraised. The number of acres laid down to cane, on this plantation, is about three hundred. The whole number of negroes is one hundred, and of these not more than half, at any time, are capable of efficient labor; and there are twenty-two children below the age of five years, out of a total of one hundred negroes.

Beside the engineer, some large plantations have one or more white assistants; but here an intelligent negro has been taught enough to take charge of the engine when the engineer is off duty. This is the highest post a negro can reach in the mill, and this negro was mightily pleased when I addressed him as maquinista. There are, also, two or three white men employed, during the season, as sugar masters. Their post is beside the caldrons and defecators, where they are to watch the work in all its stages, regulate the heat and the time for each removal, and oversee the men. These, with the engineer, make the force of white men who are employed for the season.

The regular and permanent officers of a plantation are a mayoral and mayordomo. The mayoral is, under the master of his administrador, chief mate or first lieutenant of the ship. He has the general oversight of the Negroes, at their work or in their houses, and has the duty of exacting labor and enforcing discipline. Much depends on his character, as to the comfort of master and slaves. If he is faithful and just, there may be ease and comfort; but if he is not, the slaves are never sure of justice, and the master is sure of nothing. The mayoral comes, of necessity, from the middle class of whites, and is usually a native Cuban, and it is not often that a satisfactory one can be found or kept. The day before I arrived, in the height of the season, Mr. Chartrand had been obliged to dismiss his mayoral, on account of his conduct to the women, which was producing the worst results with them and with the men; and not long before, one was dismissed for conniving with the Negroes in a wholesale system of theft, of which he got the lion's share.

The mayordomo is the purser, and has the immediate charge of the stores, produce, materials for labor, and provisions for consumption, and keeps the accounts. On well regulated plantations, he is charged with all the articles of use or consumption, and with the products as soon as they are in condition to be numbered, weighed, or counted, and renders his accounts of what is consumed or destroyed, and of the produce sent away.

There is also a boyero, who is the herdsman, and has charge of all the cattle. He is sometimes a negro.

Under the mayoral, are a number of contramayorales, who are the boatswain's mates of the ship, and correspond to the "drivers" of our southern plantations. One of them goes with every gang when set to work, whether in the field or elsewhere, and whether men or women, and watches and directs them, and enforces labor from them. The drivers carry under the arm, at all times, the short limber plantation whip, the badge of their office and their means of compulsion. They are almost always negroes; and it is generally thought that negroes are not more humane in this office than the low whites. On this plantation, it is three years since any slave has been whipped; and that punishment is never inflicted here on a woman. Near the negro quarters, is a penitentiary, which is of stone, with three cells for solitary confinement, each dark, but well ventilated. Confinement in these, on bread and water, is the extreme punishment that has been found necessary for the last three years. The negro fears solitude and darkness, and covets his food, fire, and companionship.

With all the corps of hired white labor, the master must still be the real power, and on his character the comfort and success of the plantation depend. If he has skill as a chemist, a geologist, or a machinist, it is not lost; but, except as to the engineer, who may usually be relied upon, the master must be capable of overseeing the whole economy of the plantation, or all will go wrong. His chief duty is to oversee the overseers, to watch his officers, the mayoral, the mayordomo, the boyero, and the sugar masters. These are mere hirelings, and of a low sort, such as a slave system reduces them to; and if they are lazy, the work slackens; and if they are ill-natured, somebody suffers. The mere personal presence of the master operates as a stimulus to the work. This afternoon young Mr. Chartrand and I took horses and rode out to the cane-field, where the people were cutting. They had been at work a half hour. He stopped his horse where they were when we came to them, and the next half hour, without a word from him, they had made double the distance of the first. It seems to me that the work of a plantation is what a clock would be that always required a man's hand pressing on the main spring. With the slave, the ultimate sanction is force. The motives of pride, shame, interest, ambition, and affection may be appealed to, and the minor punishments of degradation in duties, deprivation of food and sleep, and solitary confinement may be resorted to; but the whip, which the driver always carries, reminds the slave that if all else fails, the infliction of painful bodily punishment lies behind, and will be brought to bear, rather than that the question be left unsettled. Whether this extreme be reached, and how often it be reached depends on the personal qualities of the master. If he is lacking in self-control, he will fall into violence. If he has not the faculty of ruling by moral and intellectual power—be he ever so humane, if he is not firm and intelligent, the bad among the slaves will get the upper hand; and he will be in danger of trying to recover his position by force. Such is the reasoning a *priori*.

Julia Ward Howe
A Trip to Cuba
(Boston: Ticknor and Fields, 1860), 74–77

We take the Sunday to visit the nearest Sugar-plantation, belonging to Don Jacinto Gonzales. Sun, not shade, being the

desideratum in sugar-planting, there are few trees or shrubs
bordering the sugar-fields, which resemble at a distance our own
fields of Indian corn, the green of the leaves being lighter, and a
pale blue blossom appearing here and there. The points of interest here are the machinery, the negroes, and the work. Entering
the sugar-house, we find the *Maquinista* (engineer) superintending some repairs in the machinery, aided by another white man, a
Cooly, and an imp of a black boy, who begged of all the party, and
revenged himself with clever impertinence on those who refused
him. The *Maquinista* was a fine-looking man, from the Pyrenees,
very kind and obliging. He told us that Don Jacinto was very old,
and came rarely to the plantation. We asked him how the extreme
heat of his occupation suited him, and for an answer he opened
the bosom of his shirt, and showed us the marks of innumerable
leeches. The machinery is not very complicated. It consists of a
wheel and band, to throw the canes under the powerful rollers
which crush them, and these rollers, three in number, all moved
by the steam-engine. The juice flows into large copper caldrons,
where it is boiled and skimmed. As they were not at work, we did
not see the actual process. Leaving the sugar-house, we went in
pursuit of the *Mayoral*, or Overseer, who seemed to inhabit comfortable quarters, in a long, low house, shielded from the sun by a
thick screen of matting. We found him a powerful, thick-set man,
of surly and uncivil manners, girded with a sword, and a stout
whip. He was much too important a person to waste his words
upon us, but signified that the major-domo would wait on us,
which he presently did. We now entered the Negro quarter, a
solid range of low buildings, formed around a hollow square,
whose strong entrance is closed at nightfall, and its inmates kept
in strict confinement till the morning hour of work comes round.
Just within the doorway we encountered the trader, who visits
the plantations every Sunday, to tempt the stray cash of the
negroes by various commodities, of which the chief seemed to be
white bread, calicoes, muslins, and bright cotton handkerchiefs.
He told us that their usual weekly expenditure amounted to about
twenty-five dollars. Bargaining with him stood the Negro-Driver,
a tattooed African, armed with a whip. All within the court swarmed
the black bees of the hive,—the men with little clothing, the small
children naked, the women decent. All had their little charcoal
fires, with pots boiling over them; the rooms within looked dis-
mally dark, close, and dirty; there are no windows, no air and

light save through the ever-open door. The beds are sometimes partitioned off by a screen of dried palm-leaf, but I saw no better sleeping-privilege than a board with a blanket or coverlet. From this we turned to the Nursery, where all the children incapable of work are kept. The babies are quite naked, and sometimes very handsome in their way, black and shining, with bright eyes and well-formed limbs. No great provision is made for their amusement, but the little girls nurse them tenderly enough, and now and then the elders fling them a bit of orange or chaimito, for which they scramble like so many monkeys. Appeals are constantly made to the pockets of visitors, by open hands stretched out in all directions. To these "Nada"—"Nothing"—is the safe reply; for, if you give to one, the others close about you with frantic gesticulation, and you have to break your way through them with some violence, which hurts your own feelings more than it does theirs. On strict plantations this is not allowed; but Don Jacinto, like Lord Ashburton at the time of the Maine treaty, is an old man,—a very old man; and where discipline cannot be maintained, peace must be secured on any terms.

Anthony Trollope
The West Indies and the Spanish Main
(New York: Harper and Brothers, 1860), 133–36

My first object after landing was to see a slave sugar estate. I had been told in Jamaica that to effect this required some little management; that the owners of the slaves were not usually willing to allow strangers to see them at work; and that the manufacture of sugar in Cuba was as a rule kept sacred from profane eyes. But I found no such difficulty. I made my request to an English merchant at Cienfuegos, and he gave me a letter of introduction to the proprietor of an estate some fifteen miles from the town; and by their joint courtesy I saw all that I wished.

On this property, which consisted altogether of eighteen hundred acres—the greater portion of which was not yet under cultivation—there were six hundred acres of cane pieces. The average year's produce was eighteen hundred hogsheads, or three hogsheads to the acre. The hogshead was intended to represent a ton of sugar when it reached the market, but judging from all that I could learn it usually fell short of it by more than a hundred-weight. The value of such a hogshead at Cienfuegos was about twenty-five pounds. There were one hundred and fifty negro men on the estate, the average cash value of each being three hundred and fifty pounds; most of the men had their wives. In stating this it must not be supposed that either I or my informant insist much on the validity of their marriage ceremony; any such ceremony was probably of rare occurrence. During the crop time, at which period my visit was made, and which lasts generally from November till May, the negroes sleep during six hours out of the twenty-four, have two for their meals, and work for sixteen! No difference is made on Sunday. Their food is very plentiful, and of good and strong description. They are sleek and fat and large, like well-preserved brewers' horses; and with reference to them, as also with reference to the brewers' horses, it has probably been ascertained what amount of work may be exacted so as to give the greatest profit. During the remainder of the year the labour of the negroes averages twelve hours a day, and one day of rest in the week is usually allowed to them. . . .

The slaves throughout the island are always as a rule baptized. Those who are employed in the town and as household servants appear to be educated in compliance with, at any rate the outward doctrines of, the Roman Catholic church. But with the great mass of the negroes—those who work on the sugar-canes—all attention to religion ends with their baptism. They have the advantage, whatever it may be, of that ceremony in infancy; and from that time forth they are treated as the beasts of the stall.

From all that I could hear, as well as from what I could see, I have reason to think that, regarding them as beasts, they are well treated. Their hours of labour are certainly very long—so long as to appear almost impossible to a European workman. But under the system, such as it is, the men do not apparently lose their health, though, no doubt, they become prematurely old, and as a rule die early. The property is too valuable to be neglected or ill used. The object of course is to make that property pay; and therefore a present healthy condition is cared for, but long life is not regarded. It is exactly the same with horses in this country.

When all has been said that can be said in favour of the slave-owner in Cuba, it comes to this—that he treats his slaves as beasts of burden, and so treating them, does it skillfully and with prudence. The point which most shocks an Englishman is the absence of all religion, the ignoring of the black man's soul. But this, perhaps, may be taken as an excuse, that the white men here ignore their own souls also. The Roman Catholic worship seems to be at a lower ebb in Cuba than almost any country in which I have seen it.

It is singular that no priest should even make any effort on the subject with regard to the negroes; but I am assured that such is the fact. They do not wish to do so; nor will they allow of any one asking them to make the experiment. One would think that had there been any truth or any courage in them, they would have declared the inutility of baptism, and have proclaimed that negroes have no souls. But there is no truth in them; neither is there any courage.

W.M.L. Jay [Julia Louisa M. Woodruff]
My Winter in Cuba
(New York: E. P. Dutton and Company, 1871), 221–22, 227–34

During my stay at Santa Sofía, the sugar-house exerted a curious fascination over me, and whenever other sources of amusement failed, I was sure to be drawn thither, and to be found hanging over the roller, watching the cane slowly tending toward its hard fate, and listening to the wild chant of the Africans there at work; or inhaling the faint, sweet vapor from the caldrons, or seated silently by the centrifugal wheel, harvesting the abundant crop of analogies growing out of all. It was impossible not to notice, for example, how the cane became the agent of its own destruction,—how the bruised mass from the rollers was made the instrument of drawing in a continual succession of fresh, sweet cane, to be likewise crushed, mangled, and cast out, fit only for burning,—a thing which has its mournful counterparts in the social world. The negroes grew, after a time, to signalize my comings and goings with a smile, and were assiduous in doing me small services; but I do not remember that I ever elicited the slightest mark of interest or attention from the Chinese. These men appeared to be in a state of chronic sullenness; they persistently avoided meeting my eye, and emulated the hardness, inflexibility, and soullessness of the implements with which they labored. As they feel the weight and shame of bondage more than the negroes, it is a comfort to think that they can look forward to a day of emancipation; for the coolies are bound for a term of eight years only during which time their servitude is severe enough, but at the end of which they are their own masters. It is also a comfort to know that their propensity to suicide operates as some check upon the worst forms of cruelty,—one so often has to be glad, in this world, of things which, in happier circumstances, were fitter subjects for tears. . . .

A sugar plantation is a little village within itself, containing church, dwellings, hospital, workshops, storehouses, water-works, and whatever is necessary to its daily economy. That of Santa Sofía numbers about four hundred souls, of whom not more than a dozen or fifteen are contained in white skins; a disproportion which seems to justify, in a measure, the firearms, whips, chains, locks, gratings, etc., which are so prominent a part of its system. How justly these fifteen have acquired the right to dominate over the three hundred and seventy-five, is a question for moralists; but while they exercise it, it behooves them to take measures for their personal safety. The negroes are said to be, in gross, coarse and brutal, the Chinese sly and cruel; if it were not for those same locks, pistols, and other safeguards, I can well understand that my first night at Santa Sofía might have been memorable for worse horrors than the lurid phantasmagoria of my dreams.

Day broke over the plantation as freshly fair as if whips and slave gangs wearisome toil were also but visions of the night;— and other days followed, full of mellow sunshine and a subtle sweetness of luminous air, wherein to bask and breathe was quite enough for happiness. A half-dozen of such days, in our climate, are counted sufficient atonement for the atmospheric delinquencies of a whole season; here, they were the rule—slowly ripening from golden morn to fervid noon, and thenceforward growing ever sweeter and sweeter, until they departed through the gorgeous sunset arch, crowned with gladness, and leaving on the mind a beatific impression of rare concords of lustrous color, and calm floods of iridescent light, but no distinct record of individuality. Possibly their very eventlessness was their subtlest charm; in such an air, at such a temperature, the mind craved neither the excitement of stirring events, not the labor of thought—only the calm enjoyment of observation, and the soft play of fancy. Sufficient unto each day was the evil of that dark shadow of bondage and forced labor, brooding over the cane-fields and under the vast roof of the sugar-house; sufficient for its joy to watch the slow-moving panorama of radiant dawns, and prismatic sunsets, and moon-silvered eves, seen across a billowy luxuriance of rustling cane, and through green arches of great boughs of ceiba, palm, and tamarind.

On this pleasant background, the quiet incidents of the dreamy, leisurely plantation-life were softly pencilled;—among them a few scenes stand out sharply in my memory, as more brilliantly or sombrely tinted than the rest, of which I give faint sketches.

First, the *barracon*, or negro-quarter. A quadrangular structure, whose exterior presents to view only a high wall, without other opening than a massive and sombre archway, closed by an iron gate. The *mayoral* turns key, draws bolt, and ushers us into a large court, covered with a scanty growth of coarse, wiry grass. In the middle is a stone fire-place and huge boiler, wherein certain kinds of cookery are done, in the lump, for the entire tenantry. Around us is a hollow square of two-story dwellings, in as close contiguity as the cells of a honeycomb; the second floor being reached by means of exterior galleries and staircases, and each room serving for home to a limited family. The place is wholly deserted and silent; the adult occupants are at work, and the children are cared for elsewhere, during their absence. We look into some of the rooms, and wonder if life is worth living at such a scanty measure of comfort or attainment. There is a bed of rude plank with a blanket on it, a stool or two, a few pots and pans, two or three coarse garments hanging on the wall, occasionally a little crucifix or an image of the Virgin,—and that is all! No pleasantness within, no verdure without, no breadth of scope, no wholesome retirement—merely a place for eating and sleeping, where the slaves and coolies are driven nightly, like sheep to a pen, and locked in, until the morning's call to labor. Over the gateway is the apartment of the *mayoral*, with the door in the side of the arch, anterior to the gate, and a window opening on the court. It has grim provision of firearms, and is evidently a small fortress, commanding the whole interior, from which it would be easy to shoot down the leaders in any disturbance, and reduce insurgents to terms.

Secondly, the hospital. Its exterior and approach are similar to those of the *barracon*. Entering the court, we find forty or fifty naked negro children at play, who undergo a sudden transformation into so many staring ebony statues, at sight of strange visitors; and are immediately ordered off by Doña Angela, with injunctions not to reappear until they have found somewhat wherewith to cover their nakedness. The gentlemen enter a good-natured plea for the "negritos," so summarily dismissed to retirement or the unwonted thraldom of garments; but the mistress, scandalized by their appearance—vicariously, I imagine—maintains that it is *"una cosa indecenta,"* and carries her point. One side of the court is occupied by the nursery, where all the babes of the plantation are gathered, in charge of girls eight years old and upwards, overseen by two or three superannuated negro women, too old to be of use elsewhere. Some are wrapped in old shawls, or a bit of ragged blanket, others are muffled in all sorts of non-descript garments, and one small morsel of femininity lies curled up on the floor, quite nude, but with a dingy muslin cap on her tiny, woolly head, which gives her an indescribably elfin and wizened aspect. They are all preternaturally quiet and docile, as I have found slave babies to be everywhere. Is it that they come thus early to a perception of their lot in life, or because they are not indulged and pampered into ill-humor and exaction?

In an adjacent room, we found the small people just banished from the court, all tangled and snarled together in a rapid process of toilet-making, and a chaotic confusion of ill-assorted and impromptu raiment. A few, who were already dressed, came forward, and knelt down around me, with crossed hands and bended heads, waiting for something—what? *"Una benedicion, señora,"* said the kindly-eyed woman who was superintending their operations, seeing my perplexity. Somewhat taken aback by so unusual a request, I yet managed to give them the desired "blessing," according to the sweet Spanish formula, *"Dios os haga bueno!"* and went on my way wondering. I learned, later, that it is an African superstition that the benediction of a stranger, from over the ocean, has a Divine efficacy to brighten the future of the recipient,—a relic, doubtless, of those remote times when all such visitors were welcomed as messengers from the gods. But it needs more of that faith which is potent to remove mountains than I possess, to believe that any one's blessing can work much temporal good to these outcasts of civilization, whose place in the world is so vexing a problem. . . .

The remainder of the building is the hospital proper, divided into a dispensary, male and female wards, and lying-in room. The

apartments were all large and lofty, even grand in their proportions, like almost everything else on the estate. They were scrupulously clean also, but their extreme barrenness, the absence of
all adornment, or of aught to stimulate thought or gratify taste,
made them undelightful enough. There was no furniture whatever,
except a row of beds on either side; and these were merely
oblong forms of thick, heavy plank, about the size and height of
an ordinary cot. On these lay the patients, in their usual working
garments, with a blanket over them if they liked. At first, it gave
me a shock to notice the comfortlessness of the whole; it seemed
actual cruelty to put sick people on such beds—tables, rather,
where, I thought, the poor, worn-out body might have been
dissected as soon as the breath was out of it, without any very
harsh violation of the decencies of the place. But I was self-
convicted of unreasonableness, after a little, since the idolized
darling of the wealthiest Cuban house is scarcely more luxuriously
lodged,—the degree of comfort between the side of a plank and a
piece of canvas stretched tightly over an iron frame being much
too nice to be appreciable to any one not born to it.

But the blank, stolid, utterly unilluminated faces on those
beds were pitiful to behold! Perhaps the African face, by reason of
its coarse, heavy traits, and sombre coloring, is always more
profoundly and haggardly melancholy, in sickness, than any other;
and here, that expression seemed intensified by the meagreness
and unloveliness of the surroundings. The patients scarcely noticed me, as I paused to look at them; though one or two made a
faint attempt at a smile, in response to some kind words from the
mistress of the estate. One was already beyond the reach of all
sublunary interests; the stupor of death was settling on her face,
the fixed, glazed eye might even now catch some bewildering
glimpses of the "glory that shall be revealed," even to this hapless,
benighted soul. I noted the fact with something very like gladness;
the door of death seemed the only effectual escape from a life of
such hard and hopeless limitations. What possible happiness or
improvement was there in store for any of these forlorn wretches,
even if they should manage to struggle through this present
misery of sickness? which, to do them justice, not one of them
seemed trying for. They had not found life so good or glad as to
be unwilling to give it up; they just lay quietly on their hard
couches, passive and uncomplaining, and let God and their masters do with them as they would. There was neither light, nor

hope, nor desire, in their hard-lined faces, nothing but a flaccid and dejected helplessness, in lieu of resignation; as if they were conscious that they were born into the world for this and nothing else, and blindly accepted their hard lot, without being able to understand it. Even in the little children, this characteristic seemed as perfectly developed as in their elders, oppressing one with a sense of something dolefully amiss and out-of-joint in all the conditions of humanity.

Here and there, in strong contrast with these depressed and nerveless Africans, a Chinese glowered like a spark of fire amid gray ashes; his usual expression of sullen insubordination being sharpened by the pressure of physical suffering. One of these sat on the edge of his bed, with a swollen and bandaged limb drawn up beside him—the very incarnation of impotent hate and rage. The mayoral laid a firm, detaining grasp on his shoulder, under which I could see the man wince and shiver, while the official told me how he had run away weeks ago, and hidden in the woods, leading a sort of highwayman's life, and baffling all pursuit, until he cut his foot badly on a sharp stone, in jumping a stream; which wound festered and gangrened, and so disabled him that he could no longer procure food, nor drag his wasted body from one hiding-place to another; when he was found—half-dead, but untamed in spirit—and brought back to prison. Since which time, he had twice attempted suicide. The Chinese meanwhile regarded us with a look that would have stabbed us both to the heart, if looks were available for such a purpose. Plainly, he felt himself at war with the whole tyrannous universe; and especially resented the indignity of being exhibited and commented upon as if he had been a wild beast.

Samuel Hazard
Cuba with Pen and Pencil
(Hartford: Hartford Publishing Company, 1871), 351–58

To the cultivation of the cane is also added, on the same place where the cane is raised, and by the same proprietor, the manufacture of sugar, such places being called in the Cuban dialect "*ingenios*," or sugar estates, the carrying on of which requires a large amount of capital, a great degree of intelligence, and much mechanical skill.

These *ingenios* vary in size from five hundred to ten thousand acres, though the results of their crops are not always in proportion to the number of their acres, that depending more particularly upon the nature of the soil of the particular locality in which they are situated, and the degree of intelligence and amount of labor with which they are worked. Each one of the *ingenios* is, in some degree, like a small village, or, as with the larger ones, quite a town, in which are substantial edifices, numerous dwellings, and expensive machinery, together with a large number of inhabitants, the different officials necessary for their government and management representing the civil officers, except with, perhaps, greater power.

The buildings upon a first-class sugar estate are generally a dwelling-house (*casa de vivienda*), which, from its size, style, and cost, might sometimes be called a palace, some of them having, in addition to numerous other conveniences, small chapels in which to celebrate the religious services of the estate, the dwelling being occupied by the owner and his family, if living on the estate; if not, by the *administrador*, who is charged with the care and management of the estate in the absence of the owner, and who, in fact, may be said to be the man of the place. There is also the house occupied by the *"mayoral,"* as he is called the chief of the negro laborers, whose business it is to follow the laborers to the field to see that they do their work properly, and that sufficient amount of cane is cut to keep the mill constantly supplied with material to grind; in fact, he has a general supervision of all the agricultural duties of the estate, receiving his orders only from the owner or *administrador*, as the case may be. The *mayorals* are generally very ordinary men, of no education, the intelligence they possess being simply that gained by long experience in this kind of business.

The *maquinista*, or engineer, is really the most important man upon the place, as upon him depend the grinding of the cane and the care of the mill and its machinery—that it is kept in good and running order, so that no delay may take place in the grinding season. His quarters are generally in some part of the mill, where he manages to be pretty comfortable. These engineers are mostly young Americans, with now and [again] an Englishman or a German; but the Americans, I found, were much preferred on account of their superior intelligence and assiduous attention to their business. Their pay is from one thousand two hundred to two thousand five hundred dollars for the grinding season, which begins about December and ends nearly always in or before June, most of the engineers going over to the States to pass the summer or, as they express it, "to have good time."

The hospital is always an important building on these places, as it is the only place where the sick can be treated and properly taken care of. It is usually arranged with a great deal of care and neatness, the building being divided off into different wards for men and women, and also for contagious diseases; it is generally in charge of a hospital steward, who has quite an apothecary shop in his charge, and who receives his instructions from the attending physician, who also attends a number of estates in the same locality, visiting each one generally every day, and receiving compensation at so much per year. As a matter of simple economy, to say nothing of charity, the invalids get the best of treatment, and are not sent back to work until they are completely restored, though while convalescing they are required to do light work, such as making baskets, hats, etc.

The Nursery is also quite an important place, and is highly amusing to visit, for here the future hopes of the plantation are cared for. These little black, naked sinners, running and tumbling over each other in great glee, are generally kept in a large room, with rows of cradles or cribs on each side, in which each little one is kept at night, the old women who are too feeble to work any longer being retained as nurses in charge, while the mothers of the little ones are out at work in the fields, being allowed, two or three times a day, to return and suckle such infants as need the mother's milk. It is very amusing to enter one of these nurseries when the children are being fed, and see their gambols and antics, and the expression of the little ones' eyes as they see the white master, as he is called, and with whom they keep on friendly terms, enter their quarters. They all appear to be happy and jolly, and make as much noise and have as much fun as would satisfy any "radical" in the States. Poor things, they happily know nothing of the hard lot in store for them.

But the most important of all the buildings is, of course, the sugar-mill, which generally consists of the engine-house, where is all machinery and power for grinding, boiling, and working the cane and juice, and the purging and drying houses. The engine-house is generally an extremely large roof, supported by pillars and posts, and entirely open on all sides,—in fact, nothing more than a very well constructed shed to keep off the sun and rain, the floor being mostly paved with brick, and the stairways leading from one portion of the building to another being of solid stone. In fact, one of these mills of the first class is a very handsome affair—everything about it, the engines and the machinery, being kept in the most scrupulously clean order, equal to a man-of-war.

On the larger places, there are generally what are called barracoons, or quarters for the slaves. They are large buildings, constructed of stone, in the form of a quadrangle, on the inner side of which are the rooms for the negroes, to which there is only one main entrance; this is shut at night when the hands are all in. On the outside, and much better built, there are rooms occupied by the different white men connected with the place and not otherwise provided for; probably, also, a long row of stables for the many horses usually kept upon places of this kind, and of which there is no lack, either for work or play.

On other places, again, the negroes live in *bohios*, or huts,— some few constructed of stone, but most of them simply log or cane huts, of the most ordinary description, thatched with palm-leaf or grass, and making no attempt at comfort, but simply serving as shelters from the rain. I thought, in my journeyings through the Southern States, that the miserable habitations called cabins were bad enough; but I must confess that these were worse; though, to be sure, in a climate like this, it does not matter much about shelter,—all one wants is shade.

The Purging-house (*casa de purga*) is generally of very great extent, being two stories high, and of great length. The floor of the upper story is simply a series of strong frames, with apertures for placing in them the *hormas*, funnel-shaped cylinders of tin or sheet-iron, into which is put the molasses to drain into troughs beneath. One side of this house is open, in order to permit the *gavetas*, or large boxes upon wheels, into which are put the forms of sugar, to be run in and out conveniently. In these boxes, which are immensely large, the sugar in forms is broken up and ex-posed to the air and sun, for the purpose of thoroughly drying it. The number of these *hormas* is something wonderful, there being in some of the houses as many as twenty thousand. Beneath the upper floor are a number of troughs, each trough having a slant to a main trough. Over the minor through are the mouths of the aforesaid funnels, which permit the molasses draining from the pans of sugar above to run into the troughs, which again convey it

to large vats or hogsheads, called *bocoyes*, each of which holds
from twelve to fifteen hundred gallons. It is in this process that
they make the distinction of the different sugars,—*blanco*, or white;
quebrado, or broken; and the common, dark-colored sugar called
cucurucho. In making these three qualities of sugar, a layer of
moist earth or clay is placed upon the top of the pans of crystallized
syrup, from which the moisture, draining constantly through,
carries off all the imperfections, leaving the pans full of dry sugar
in the form of solid cases, and generally of three colors; that
nearest the top, pure white; next below that, the discolored; and
at the bottom of that, the moist or dark colored. If, however, it is
desired to make only a *mascabodo* sugar, which is of a rich brown
color, and does not require the same time or pains of the finer
qualities, the syrup is simply put in the large hogsheads, before
described, and allowed to drain off in the natural way without the
process of "claying" it, as it is called. This, of course, makes more
sugar of an average inferior grade, which weighs more, having
the molasses in it; and this is the sugar generally preferred, I
believe, by sugar refiners.

Antonio C. N. Gallenga
The Pearl of the Antilles
(London: Chapman and Hall, 1873), 91–106

I had brought with me a large bundle of letters of introduction, and, upon first landing in Havannah, I hired a messenger
by whose aid I sent them, with my card and compliments, to their
destination. It happened with them as with the seed in the parable;
some fell upon stony places, some by the wayside, and some
among thorns; but a few fell into good ground and in due time
brought forth fruit. Among those who took notice of the stranger
who, as a friend's friend claimed their hospitality, were two of the
wealthiest land and slave owners, Don Julian de Zulueta and Don
Juan Poey, the men who are universally acknowledged to have
raised the cultivation of sugar to the greatest perfection, and to
have turned it to the utmost advantage for themselves and for
their country. These gentlemen did not call upon me in person,
but sent their ambassadors, in the shape of some junior partners,
or upper clerks in their counting-houses, with many apologies for

their inevitable absence, the most liberal tender of their services, and an especial invitation to visit their country estates. I did not suffer many days to pass before I availed myself of their kind offers, and, according to the Spanish phase, went to the "houses which from the moment I honoured them with my presence became my own."

The traveler who wishes to be on good terms with Cuba should make his best haste to get out of Havannah. The smells and noises of that pestilential town had nearly killed me. The quiet and fragrance of the country revived me. I left Havannah, with a friend on a Monday, the 3rd of March, and crossing the bay to Regla went by the direct Eastern Railway Line to Matanzas—a distance of about forty-three miles. On the following morning we took the train to Bemba and Perico, thirty-seven miles further, and at the last-named station we met Don Julian de Zulueta who was waiting for us with two volantes. He bade me get into one with him and, as a volante can not accommodate more than two persons, pointed to the other as the conveyance of my friend. A drive of less than an hour brought us to the *Batey*—the central establishment of the Ingenio, or sugar estate of España. On one side of the vast quadrangle constituting the *Batey*, and flanked by the crushing and boiling-house, the refining-house, the Negro quarters, school, hospital, etc., was the master's dwelling-house; at the door of which the volantes pulled up; and where on alighting a very large tumbler of *bul*, or bowl, a refreshing beverage of which beer and lemonade are the main ingredients, was handed to us.

The country we had crossed is not destitute of beauty though denuded of trees; as it generally is throughout the island; for even what is called *monte* or forest, consists chiefly of very dense but low brush-wood. As we advanced from Havannah to Matanzas however, the eye was relieved by the sight of wooded hilly ridges gradually rising till they reach the Pan de Matanzas, a conspicuous object, as seen from the sea, to those who come from the north or east to Havannah, but which attains a height of little more than 1200 feet. Matanzas is a place of great beauty. It is situated, like Havannah, at the entrance of a bay—a larger bay— and at the meeting of two rivers, the Yumurri and the San Juan, the two valleys of which, studded with country houses to the hilltops, form a charming background to the city. Not a little liveliness also characterizes the scenery along the road from Matanzas to

Bemba, but, beyond this, and as I afterwards found out, all the way to the south coast as far as Cienfuegos, to the north as far as Sagua and Cardenas, and to the east as far as and beyond Villa Clara, the hills are everywhere lost to sight; and the country becomes a flat, here and there cut up into sugar estates, but a vast part of it still covered with the native forest and unreclaimed savannah. Of large timber there is nothing to be seen save the ubiquitous and monotonous Royal Palm, and here and there a Ceiba or cotton-tree, seemingly forgotten in the general destruction, all decayed with age, and at this time of year stripped of its foliage, looking dry and hoary as a spectre tree. Not many birds in sight; hardly any warbler's note—only everywhere the 'jack crow,' or Turkey buzzard, a foul and unwieldy vulture lazily flapping its wings and clinging to the earth to which the scent of carrion attracts it.

The journey from Havannah to Las Canas, the great *Finca*, or sugar plantation of Don Juan Poey, is reached by another and somewhat more round-about route. We left the capital by the South-Western Line at the Villanueva Station, and travelled by rail over Guines, to a station called Union, sixty-three miles off. Hence the *volante*, or *quitrin*, conveyed us to Don Juan's estate, over a sandy and stony road, or track, in two hours. The roads are everywhere detestable, and the country not interesting. You have either the low forest, or the bare pasture, or the endless cane-fields to the right and left of you; everything is flat; and out of the vast level only the tall chimneys of the steam-engine at the *Batey* in the centre of the plantations enliven the landscape. These *Bateys*, with their various buildings, are all on one model; though some of them are on a larger scale, and in better order than others. The Cubans, like the Spaniards and other Latin races, have no love for the country. They have at their plantations only a *pied-à-terre*; plain and common-place houses, all on one and the same plan, with the scantiest apology for a garden round them. They are not intended for permanent residences, but only for the accommodation of the master on his occasional inspection of his property. All the utilitarian landowner thinks of is sugar, and he grudges half a rood of land for mere cool shade or pleasure-ground. I have seen several of Senor Zulueta's houses, which are among the most comfortable, but are no exception to the rule. But Don Juan Poey's possesses a library and a large collection of good books; and he took us across his two-acre garden, where, among other botanic wonders, he showed us as many as twenty-six different species of orange-trees.

I must not be expected to enter into any discussion respecting the merits of the various mechanical and chemical contrivances which fully justify the name of *Ingenio*, but which the Cubans invariably designate both a sugar house and a sugar estate. My object in going through these establishments was merely the solution of the great social problem—how free labour may be here substituted for the present slave system, without materially affecting the production of these estates, and consequently without causing even the temporary ruin of the Island. I allowed myself to be led about from one building of the batey to the other, examined crushing-machines, steam-engines, vats, vacuum pans, centrifugals, and the like; but kept steadily to my subject, and found in my host the utmost readiness to enlighten me about it.

The slave-owners in Cuba are convinced of the necessity of manumitting their slaves; but readily as they acknowledge the evils of the slave system, they are not persuaded of the wisdom of any measure by which it may be brought to an end. The case they make out for themselves is by no means weak. They found in the Island a system of cultivation thoroughly sanctioned and even encouraged by the laws of their country for more than three centuries, the results of which were, on the whole, beneficial both to the landowner and to the labourer; and they so far improved upon the primitive system by the means of machinery as very greatly to lighten the labourer's toil, at the same time that they heightened and extended the productiveness of their estates. They are compelled now to give in to the philanthropic spirit of the age; but they wish to do so in some manner less injurious to themselves, and less fatal to the helpless beings whom so many years of slavery have unfitted for self-dependence than by sudden abolition. The slaves in the estates I have visited are hard worked; at least, at this season; and I have heard the cane-crushing machine grinding and groaning till two or three o'clock after midnight. Still their lot is far less miserable than is generally imagined. The production of sugar consists of two very distinct proceedings. There is the field work—the cultivation of the cane which can be and is actually done to a great extent by free labour, as in many instances by white men, and which may eventually be altogether made over to them; and secondly there is the work in the sugar-house, which crushes the cane and turns its juice into sugar; and

that is done in a very great measure by machinery; a very complicated and ingenious machinery, which daily receives new improvements, and which leaves men little more to do than to watch
and guide it. It is the pride of such slave-owners as Zulueta and
Poey that they have ransacked all the industrial marts of Europe
and American to make iron, coal, charcoal and steam do the work
which was formerly done by slave; reducing the number of their
"hands" by hundreds and thousands, and leaving for the remaining ones a task by no means heavier than that of the operatives of
Manchester, Sheffield or Newcastle. Señor Zulueta, in his estate
España, which he values at $1,500,000 (£300,000), only employs
500 manual and skilled labourers, both in the field and the sugar-
house. The greatest hardship, so far as I could see, consists in the
atmosphere of some parts of the sugar-house, where the heat is
intense, though by no means so fierce as in certain departments
of English ironworks. . . .

The Negro in a state of slavery is as efficient and willing a
labourer as the master can desire. I have seen crowds of them
clustering round Señor Zulueta, on their knees, joyously crying,
"*El Amo! El Amo!*" as if the master were a demigod to them and
his presence among them an angel's visit, decanting on the extra
work they had voluntarily accomplished, and soliciting a reward;
grinning all the time they were doing obeisance, pocketing the
bounty that was handed to them, as if it were their due, and going
off in great glee without a word of thanks or a mark of respect to
the donor. And yet far above the overseer's whip, the mere flash
of that master's eye, the mere ring of his voice, strike awe and
submission into the whole establishment, and seem to set the
very engines to work in double-quick time. We have here moral
influence and discipline at work. A man of Zulueta's temper rules
his sugar-house pretty much as a general of the Wellington school
would lead an Anglo-Irish army, by expecting every man to do his
duty. And I can understand him when he says he would willingly
give 10,000 dollars a year, instead of 2,000, to a good *Administrator*,
manager or steward of one of his estates, but that such a man as
he wants is not to be had at any price. As well could Napoleon
have expected Austerlitz or Wagram to be won by one of his
marshals. Don Julian de Zulueta is a born king of men. He is, by
his own account, a *Hijo de Labrador* (labourer's son), from Alva,
in the Basque Provinces; he came to this Island without a farthing,
without education, and he remembers the time when the height

of his ambition was to scrape together a sum of 25,000 dollars with which to go back a rich man to his native village. And now the estate *España*, in which he entered with me into all these particulars, is worth $1,500,000; and he has three others of equal value—all of which I have seen—*Alava, Billaya* and *Havannah*, adjoining one another, and connected by a private railway of his own devising. He is daily purchasing and enlarging new ones; he has a large mercantile establishment in town; and he has a hand in almost every industrial and commercial speculation in his own country or out of it, carrying on an immense amount of work, not so much, perhaps, for the great wealth it brings him, as for the absorbing pleasure he finds in the work itself. So indefatigable a labourer is well fitted by nature to set labourers their task. But it is not merely in his private capacity that Zulueta has made himself remarkable. He is the heart and soul of every public institution, political or social, in Havannah. He is president of the *Casino Español*, that *Imperium in imperio*, which as I have often said rules the Island in the interest of the Peninsular and slave-holding party, and holds the 60,000 or 70,000 armed volunteers under control. In the City Corporation, in the Chamber of Commerce, the Exchange, the Bank, the Hospitals and all other establishments, the will of Don Julian de Zulueta is supreme; and in great emergencies the Captain-General would as little venture upon any measure without consulting him, as the *Priori* of the Republic of Florence would have dreamt of issuing a decree without the sanction of the Elder Cosmo de Medici. Zulueta, an illiterate man in youth, has given himself all the education his ruling position required. He both speaks and writes his own language, not only with perfect correctness but with a certain stout eloquence; and his extensive journeys have made him acquainted with the languages as well as with the civilization of other countries.

Differing from him in many respects, but equally striking in mind and character, is Don Juan Poey. He is the son of a Frenchman and a Cuban lady, and by right of his mother calls himself a "Creole," and evinces the greatest interest in the welfare of the Island, apart from its connection with Spain. He is a little slight man, above 70, with an intensely French countenance, beaming with something of the liveliness and intelligence of the late President of the French Republic. A man of extensive scientific acquirements, he converses most agreeably on almost all subjects. If Zulueta is by nature a rough sort of king, Poey seems intended

for a very consummate statesman and diplomatist. In the opinion
of all men Don Juan Poey is the one who best understands the
real position of affairs in this country, and who has always the
keenest insight into the intricacy of the grave questions which
await a speedy solution. Zulueta rules by strength of will, but
Poey leans to circumstances, which he acknowledges to be
stronger than any man's will. Zulueta only asks how long it may
still be possible to fight on; Poey considers how soon and with
what good grace it may be advisable to give in. Zulueta has all the
sanguineness of a man who has known no failure; Poey is, or calls
himself, by instinct a croaker, and can see no issue out of present
evil except in evils incommensurably greater.

Both these gentlemen have signed their names to a manifesto
which has lately been put forth in the name of the Cuban slave-
owners. Judging from its tone, it is evidently intended as an
ultimatum. It is addressed to the whole world, but published as a
Report to the Proprietors and Slave-owners (*Hacendados y
Dueños de Esclavos*) of the Island of Cuba, and bears the names of
the members of a Special Committee (*Junta Delegada*) elected at
a meeting held on the 11th of July, 1870, with the sanction of the
Captain-General, and appointed to consider the question of slavery
and free labour. The Report was drawn up by Senor Zulueta as
chairman of the committee, and first read in the *Casino Español*
over which he also presides.

Don Julian de Zulueta, his colleagues in the Committee, and
all the members of the Association are aware that the cause of
slavery is lost; that the system has become indefensible, and that
its downfall is only a question of time. They have, they say, never
pretended to perpetuate slavery in its present condition, and they
are now more than ever prepared to proceed to its modification,
as the Spanish Government has deemed it expedient to decree
the immediate abolition of slavery in the island of Porto Rico.
Immediate abolition, even if practicable in Porto Rico, where the
slaves do not exceed the number of 30,000, in the midst of a free
population of more than 600,000, would be utter ruin to Cuba,
which possesses more than 300,000 slaves, estimated at a value of
$300,000,000, or about £60,000,000. The Cuban proprietors and
slave-owners profess to be actuated, not by personal interests but
by considerations of patriotism. Thanks to their intelligence, industry and energy, they say, this western part of the Island has
been in a few years raised to a state of prosperity unexampled in

the West Indies; a flourishing condition which enables it to export produce to the amount of $100,000,000, or about £20,000,000 a year, notwithstanding the cruel Civil War which since 1868 has been ravaging the other departments of the Island, reducing the production there absolutely to nothing. The Cuban proprietors and slave-owners cannot consent to any measure likely either to destroy or even to imperil their present well-being. They would oppose any such measure for their own sake, for that of their Negro slaves, for that of their country, and for that of the world; for the sudden collapse of an industry which supplies mankind with one-fifth of its sugar would not fail to affect even the remotest regions. The immediate abolition of slavery, they think and not unreasonably, would have the effect of throwing out of employment and leaving to their own devices an enormous mass of slaves, indolent by temperament, placed above all want by their habits and by the nature of the country, who could never be made to acknowledge God's law which "bids man work that he may live," and never be made to abide in settled homes or to show any regard for family ties. The immediate emancipation of the Negroes would soon bring back the whole black race to the instincts of its native African savagery; the worst horrors which afflicted San Domingo and which threatened Jamaica and the Southern States of the American Union would be reproduced in this Island, where they would be aggravated by the evils inflicted by the Insurrection—a movement which already, in a great measure, relies on Negro sympathies, and reckons many Negroes among its most determined and efficient combatants. It is therefore necessary in the opinion of Don Julian de Zulueta and his associates, so to proceed towards abolition as not to interfere with production—to provide for the elimination of slavery by the substitution of free labour; and, with that view, all the proprietors and slave-owners are invited to tax themselves yearly to the amount of 10 dollars, or £2, for each of the slaves now in their possession, so as to constitute a fund of $3,000,000, or £600,000, to be annually devoted to the importation of free labour from Europe, India, China, Egypt and all other regions of both hemispheres. The presence and the gradual introduction of these free labourers in the plantations, the high wages, the settled life and the well-being they would enjoy, would it is reckoned rouse the emulation and stimulate the energy of the indolent Negroes; and at the same time these would, by stringent and provident laws against vagrancy and their habits of petty thieving and squatting, be prevented from becoming an incumbrance and a nuisance in the island. It is thus expected that in a few years the whole nature and system of labour in the sugar and tobacco estates would be completely transformed, that slavery would disappear, and that production, far from falling off in the Western Department where it now gives such splendid results, would be easily extended to the centre and east of the Island, so as to raise the population of Cuba to 8,000,000 or 10,000,000.

Frederick T. Townshend
Wild Life in Florida with a Visit to Cuba
(London: Hurt and Blackett, 1875), 192–97

At Marianao we engaged carriages to convey us to the plantation, about two miles distant, over the usual abominable stony track which is made to do duty for a carriage road throughout Cuba. At the gate of the plantation we were stopped by an old negro armed with a musket, who examined our pass before allowing us to proceed. We then drove on through immense fields of cane on either hand, until we reached the "ingenio," or sugar manufactory, where we were received by the overseer and his wife, both English.

Outside the crushing-house some fifty or sixty negro children, apparently from six to twelve years old, of both sexes, were occupied piling the canes on the elevator which conveyed them to the crushing wheel, fresh loads being constantly brought in ox-waggons from the fields. Toiling away for their very lives in the broiling sunshine, the poor little wretches kept a constant eye on a formidable cow-hide whip, wielded by a negro who stood by, ready to crack it across their bare backs if they attempted to idle or eat the sugar-cane.

Inside the building we were shown the whole process of sugar making, from the raw cane to the boxes of sugar ready packed for export. The owner of the plantation was very proud of his machinery bought in England, in France, and in America. That used in crushing, boiling, refining, etc., was the best the world has yet produced, or human ingenuity invented, to supply the place of human labour.

At some of the machines negresses worked, at others Chinese and Africans. In some parts of the building the heat was so intense that negroes and Chinese, though stark naked with the exception of a cloth round the loins, were pouring with sweat. As many stood in the vats in which the boiling sugar had cooled and hardened, breaking up the mass with picks and treading out the lumps with their bare feet, while the perspiration poured off them, the fact became evident that more foreign matter enters into the composition of sugar than is generally known. Certain quantities of pure lime are mixed with the cane juice to destroy the acid in all kinds of sugar, while in the manufacture of the coarser qualities molasses are largely used.

From the mill we proceeded to the negro barracks, as their quarters are termed, consisting of brick buildings one story high, enclosing a large square, entered through double iron gates. As we passed in, two ferocious-looking Cuban blood-hounds, chained one on either side of the gate, sniffed suspiciously near our legs, but, being trained to run down or attack negroes only, did not molest us.

On the ground-floor, opening on to the court-yard, were the negroes' rooms, secured by heavily barred and padlocked doors. Opening one of these we found ourselves in one of the most horrible dens imaginable. Walls black with dirt, uneven clay floors about fourteen feet square, no means of admitting daylight or air except by the door, a wooden table, bench and bedstead the sole furniture. On the latter hung the remnants of a filthy blanket, while the worst filth covered the floor, furniture and walls, which also were alive with vermin. In each of these pestiferous dungeons, a whole family lived in a condition more foul and degraded than any beasts of the field. We looked into several and found them all alike, while from an open drain a few feet from the doors a most sickening stench proceeded.

Mounting a wooden staircase, at the foot of which was chained another bloodhound, we passed through a trap-door on the upper floor, and found ourselves in wide gallery running round the court. On this gallery opened large and tolerably well ventilated rooms, used as nurseries, sick-wards, lying-in rooms, saddle's rooms and stores. Dozens of naked children of every age, from the fly-devoured baby in its cradle to the black-eyed, round-bellied urchin of three or four years old, swarmed along the gallery. Their number and various shades of colour, from jet black to nearly white proved that the negro women were certainly not barren, and that the white man did not disdain to make a concubine as well as a slave of the African. A few old women too sick to work in the fields, or others not yet recovered from child-birth, looked after the children, who seemed happy enough, tumbling over each other, and playing with some bloodhound puppies, little thinking of their own unhappy lot, or the use to which these same puppies would shortly be put.

Outside the lying-in rooms some half-a-dozen young negresses were seated, evidently about to add to the population, engaged sewing cotton garments for themselves, not for the expected infants, covering of any sort being considered superfluous for coloured children of either sex on a Cuban plantation. In the punishment cells we saw only one culprit, a young negro with his feet in the stocks, the rest of the offenders being employed at this busy time of year working in chains in the fields. In the kitchen we found a filthy old negress preparing a scanty meal for the slaves, of sweet potatoes, nothing else apparently being cooked for their dinners.

Maturin Murray Ballou
Due South; or, Cuba Past and Present
(Boston: Houghton Mifflin and Company, 1885), 236–38

The first sugar plantation established in Cuba, was in 1595, nearly three hundred years since. These plantations are the least attractive in external appearance, but the most profitable pecuniarily, of all agricultural investments in the tropics, though at present writing there is a depression in prices of sugar which has brought about a serious complication of affairs. The markets of the world have become glutted with the article, owing to the enormous over-production in Europe from the beet. The planta-tions devoted to the raising of the sugar-cane in Cuba spread out their extensive fields, covered with the corn-like stalks, without any relief to the eye, though here and there the graceful feathery branches of the palm are seen. The fields are divided off into squares of three or four acres each, between which a roadway is left for ox-teams to pass for gathering purposes. On some of the largest estates tramways have been laid, reaching from the several sections of the plantation to the doors of the grinding-mill. A mule, by this means, is enabled to draw as large a load as a pair of oxen on plain ground, and with much more ease and promptness.

About the houses of the owner and the overseer, graceful fruit trees, such as bananas and cocoanuts, with some flowering and fragrant plants, are grouped, forming inviting shade and producing a picturesque effect. Not far away, the low cabins of the blacks are half hidden by plantain and mango trees, surrounded by cultivated patches devoted to yams, sweet potatoes, and the like. Some of the small gardens planted by these dusky Africans showed judgement and taste in their management. Chickens and pigs, which were the private property of the negroes, were cooped up just behind the cabins. Many of these plantations employ from four to five hundred blacks, and in some instances the number will reach seven hundred on extensive estates, though the tendency of the new and improved machinery is to constantly reduce the number of hands required, and to increase the degree of intelligence necessary in those employed. Added to these employees there must also be many head of cattle—oxen, horses, and mules. The annual running expenditure of one of these large estates will reach two hundred thousand dollars, more or less, for which outlay there is realized, under favorable circumstances, a million five hundred thousand pounds of sugar, worth, in good seasons, five cents per pound at the nearest shipping point.

There are a few of the small estates which still employ ox-power for grinding the cane, but American steam-engines have almost entirely taken the place of animal power; indeed, as we have shown, it will no longer pay to produce sugar by the primitive processes. This creates a constant demand for engineers and machinists, for whom the Cubans depend upon this country. We were told that there were not less than two hundred Bostonians at the present time thus engaged on Cuban estates. A Spaniard or Creole would as soon attempt to fly like a bird as to learn how to run a steam-engine or regulate a line of shafting. It requires more intelligence and mechanical skill, as a rule, than the most faithful slaves possess. A careful calculation shows that in return for the services of this small band of employees taken from our shores, this country takes eighty per cent. of all the sugar produced upon the island! Twelve per cent. is consumed by peninsular Spain, thus leaving but eight per cent. of this product for distribution elsewhere.

During the grinding season which begins about the first of December and ends in April, a large, well-managed sugar plantation in Cuba is a scene of the utmost activity and most unremitting labor. Time is doubly precious during the harvesting period, for when the cane is ripe there should be no delay in expressing the juice. If left too long in the field it becomes crystallized, deteriorating both in its quality and in the amount of juice which is obtained. The oxen employed often die before the season is at an end, from overwork beneath a torrid sun. The slaves are allowed but four or five hours sleep out of twenty-four, and being worked by watches during the night, the mill does not lie idle for an hour after it is started until the grinding season is closed. If the slaves are thus driven during this period, throughout the rest of the year their task is comparatively light, and they may sleep ten hours out of the twenty-four, if they choose. According to the Spanish slave code,—always more or less of a dead letter,—the blacks can be kept at work in Cuba only from sunrise to sunset, with an interval of two hours for repose and food in the middle of the day. But this is not regarded in the sugar harvest season, which period, after all, the slaves do not seem so much to dread, for then they are granted more privileges and are better fed, given more variety of food and many other little luxuries which they are known to prize.

William Drysdale
In Sunny Lands
(New York: Harper and Brothers, 1885), 56–58

A visit to a sugar plantation is one of the best parts of coming to Cuba, and no Northern visitor should come here without seeing one. The difficulties in the way of it, once you are here, are not so great as they seem, for the Cuban sugar planters are the most hospitable people in the world, and an introduction to some one of them is not hard to obtain. There came down to the steamer one evening a party of ladies and gentlemen from a plantation about twenty miles out of Cienfuegos. They were Americans, friends of the captain and all the officers, and came to make a visit and to invite the captain and other officers to go out and spend a day with them. The captain and purser were unable to leave the ship, but before the evening was over it was arranged that Steward Petersen and I should take the early train out next morning, spend the day on the plantation, and return to the ship in the evening. As the party were in on horseback, they were to make an early start in the morning and reach the plantation in time to send a volante over to the station for us. There seemed to be no flaws in a neat little excursion like that: an early morning ride by rail twenty miles into the interior of the island, then a volante ride, a day on the plantation, and home again by dark. The only drawback was that we had to be up at four in the morning to get a bite of breakfast and be in time to catch the five-o'clock train. But early morning is always a pleasant part of the day in Cuba, and this was hardly an objection. The plantation to which we were kindly invited was the one known as the "Hormiguero," owned by Messrs. E. & L. Ponvert, at Palmira, about twenty miles from Cienfuegos—an estate comprising three or four thousand acres, and supplied with all the latest improvements in sugar-making machinery. So we looked forward to a first-rate time and we had it. . . .

This "Ingenio Hormiguero" (Ingenio being the Spanish term for sugar estate) is a little principality in itself. With its three thousand acres, nearly, of sugar-cane, its rich lands, its great mill filled with the most expensive new sugar machinery, its more than comfortable dwelling-house, and its large number of smaller dwellings for the workmen, it is one of the finest sugar estates in Cuba. The Messrs. Ponvert are, I believe, both natives of America, of French decent, and they have given their attention to this plantation for many years. Here they live throughout the "grinding season," from December to April, every year, sometimes spending the remainder of the year in New York or Paris, and sometimes staying there through the entire year. Both the gentlemen having families, there is plenty of company in the large house, and they do not suffer from the lonesomeness of the situation—for a sugar plantation is necessarily isolated, and its owners are compelled to rely upon their own resources for amusement. The house, like all Cuban country-houses, is one story high, with a broad, steep, tiled roof, and with the cool front veranda so shaded with green vines that the house can scarcely be seen. Such a dark, cool, and airy sitting-room as the veranda thus becomes invaluable in a hot place like the south side of

Cuba; even before nine o'clock we began to feel that we were
down in latitude 18. With its cool brick floor and its rows of
comfortable rocking and easy chairs, it is just such a place as one
would want to find in the middle of a hot day to doze away an
afternoon in. And that is about all that any one cares to do in
Cuba, for the heat in the middle of the day makes it not only
uncomfortable but unsafe to be long exposed to the sun. The
veranda, in all these southern countries, is the best part of the
house. It is the parlor, the library, the general living-room. Without one, and a good one, a house in a tropical climate would
scarcely be habitable. We were taken at once into an airy bedroom
to get rid of the portions of railroad earth we had brought with us,
and then, seated in the shade of the vines on the veranda, had a
chance to take a first look at a big sugar-mill. The mill stands
immediately opposite the house, two or three hundred feet away,
and as it is open throughout, without walls to obstruct the view,
the owners can sit on the veranda and watch every motion of
machinery. If anything goes wrong they can be on the spot
instantly and help set it right. As the machinery is nearly noiseless,
and there are none of the objectionable sounds or smells inseparable from most mills, this is an admirable arrangement. Indeed,
they carry it even further than this, and the ladies make a sort of a
sitting and sewing room of one end of a raised platform which
supports the evaporators, and keep there a table and a collection
of rocking-chairs to be used when wanted. From this elevated
position they can watch every piece of cane that goes between the
rollers, see the entire interior of the mill, and at the same time
keep an eye upon every person who goes in or out of the house. It
is a rare place for a lady who takes an interest in the sugar
business, and all the ladies at Hormiguero do, and can tell to a
nicety just what proportion of juice the cane is yielding, whether
the engine is running steadily, and whether the last new team of
mules is likely to turn out well.

Breakfast-time in Cuba is about eleven o'clock, and Mr.
Petersen and I were quite ready to sit down in the cool dining-
room and send some reinforcements after the few bites we had
taken before starting. After breakfast Mr. Ponvert took us over to
the mill, and explained the whole process of sugar making. The
entire plantation is laid out in lots of three or four acres each, with
many miles of streets or roads between them, and eight or ten

miles of railroad track running from one end of the place to the other, on which the cane is brought to the mill in cars. There are so many of these lots that a map is kept, on which the condition of each lot is indicated by a different color. If the cane on one lot has just been cut the fact is indicated by one color; if it is ready to be cut, by another color. The cane is brought to the mill and stored in great heaps in a convenient place near the rollers that crush the juice out of it. There are three large, heavy, iron rollers, and after the cane goes between them it is squeezed dry. It is carried up to the rollers automatically on a moving platform like that on which the horses walk in a threshing-machine, and comes out crushed and sapless. The juice is carried off in pipes to the boilers, and is boiled down and run through evaporators and other contrivances till all the liquid part of it becomes molasses and all the solid part sugar. The cane now yields a much larger percentage of juice than it did a few years ago, under the improved machinery for extracting it; but this machinery costs money. It comes from New York, most of it, and the engines, boilers, evaporators, and all the other machines necessary for setting up a complete modern sugar-mill, cannot be purchased for less than $200,000. About that amount has been put in this mill at Hormiguero within the last year, and still there are additions to be made. There is a locomotive to be purchased, for instance, to take the place of oxen in drawing cane to the mill, and electric lights are to be put in next season for working by at night, for in the grinding season the mill runs night and day, Sundays and holidays, without any cessation. But through the other eight months of the year all this machinery stands idle and earns nothing for its owners. The cane, after the juice has been extracted from it, is spread out in a drying yard to dry, which it does under this hot sun in a very short time, and eventually it finds its way into the furnaces, where it makes steam for the grinding of fresh piles. The outlook in the sugar business is not so bright as planters would like to see it. Prices are so low, and transportation charges in Cuba and export duties so high, it barely pays the cost of production. And hundreds of thousands of gallons of molasses are being thrown away or poured over the land for fertilizing, for it costs more to send a hogshead of molasses to New York this year than it is worth when it gets there. The production of these large sugar-mills is enormous. No plantation is considered a large one unless it turns out from 5000 to 15,000 hogsheads of sugar in a season. I forget the exact number of hogsheads made annually at Hormiguero, but think it is from 8000 to 10,000.

Some of the large sugar estates are still worked by slaves, but at Hormiguero there is none but free labor. Mr. Ponvert is beginning a new system—of letting out small tracts of land to farmers, furnishing them with a dwelling-house and barn, oxen, and everything necessary, and stipulating that the land shall be worked according to the directions of his overseer and the cane brought to his mill. The farmer eventually pays for his stock and implements out of the proceeds of his sales of cane, a little each year, and the productiveness of the land is thus much increased. This system, so far, has been found to work well, and nobody, I think, would be willing to go back to the slavery days, free labor having been found to be much more profitable in the end. Like many another business, sugar making is rapidly going into the hands of a few wealthy firms. Although the modern sugar machinery is terribly expensive, it does its work so much more completely and economically that the small planter, with his old-fashioned boiling kettles and crude machinery, has no chance and cannot compete successfully. Still, there are quite a number of these large concerns. Here, in this district around Cienfuegos, one can stand almost anywhere and see the steam that has been grinding rise from a dozen chimneys.

There are plenty of amusements on a sugar estate to kill time when business does not press. Everybody on the place is fond of horses—men, women, and children—and all are capital riders. Each one has his own pet horse and takes delight in scampering over the country. The boys have their amateur photographic apparatus, with which they take pictures of everything in the heavens above and the earth beneath. There is a daily mail from Cienfuegos, bringing letters and papers from New York by way both of Havana and of Nassau. The gentlemen, at least, find no difficulty in amusing themselves, for about such a place there is always plenty to be done that nobody can attend to but one of "the bosses."

After a thoroughly enjoyable day, made doubly pleasant by the hearty hospitality and great kindness of our hosts, we started off in time to catch the four-o'clock train for Cienfuegos, and were taken down to the station in grand style once more in the volante; but this time with a guard of honor composed of half a dozen horsemen, all the young gentlemen on the place, who amused themselves at the station while we waited for the train with jumping their horses over all the high fences and hedges they could find. Mr. Petersen being something of a horseman himself, could not decline an invitation to mount one of the horses and join in the sport, and as he went flying over fences and walls I confidently expected to have nothing but his mangled remains to take back to the ship. But he rode like an old soldier, and we were in Cienfuegos safe and sound before five o'clock.

III

Slaves and Slavery

Alexander von Humboldt
The Island of Cuba
Translated by J. S. Thrasher
(New York: Derby and Jackson, 1801, 1856), 211–15, 227–29

In no part of the world, where slavery exists, is manumission so frequent as in the island of Cuba; for Spanish legislation, directly the reverse of French and English, favors in an extraordinary degree the attainment of freedom, placing no obstacle in its way, not making it in any manner onerous. The right which every slave has of seeking a new master, or purchasing his liberty, if he can pay the amount of his cost; the religious sentiment that induces many persons in good circumstances to concede by will freedom to a certain number of negroes; the custom of retaining a number of both sexes for domestic service, and the affections that necessarily arise from this familiar intercourse with the whites; and the facilities allowed to slave-workmen to labor for their own account, by paying a certain stipulated sum to their masters, are the principal causes why so many blacks acquire their freedom in the towns.

The customary rate of hire is ten cents on each $100 of the value of the slave for every working-day. There are about two hundred and ninety working-days in the year, Sundays and church holidays being considered days of rest. In addition to the above-mentioned facilities for attaining freedom, the slave has the privilege of paying his master small sums of money on account, and thus becoming a coowner of himself. Thus, if his value be $600, by paying his master $25 he becomes the owner of one twenty-fourth of himself; when he has paid $50 he owns one-twelfth, and so on; and in hiring his time, he pays to his master rent only on the remaining due. The law obliges the master to accept these partial payments; and should the owner over-value the slave at the time of commencing them, the negro can appeal to the syndic, who is annually appointed to protect the slaves. A slave who has partially manumitted himself is styled *coartado*. Many redeem themselves excepting the sum of $50 or $100; and on this pay a rent to the master for the rest of their lives, no matter how much wealth they may acquire. A careful study of individual reasons, among the blacks in Cuba, for adopting this course, might perhaps develop some unobserved peculiarities of the negro mind. It may sometimes arise from ties of affection, sometimes from interest, and it may be found to result, in some cases, from an intuitive desire, or an idiosyncrasy on the part of the negro to have some immediate and tangible superior, to whose opinion he can look with respect, and from whom he can claim protection in calamity.

The position of the free negroes in Cuba is much better than it is elsewhere, even among those nations which have for ages flattered themselves as being most advanced in civilization. We find there no such barbarous laws as have been invoked, even in our own days, by which free negroes are prohibited from receiving donations from the whites, and can be deprived of their liberty, and sold for the benefit of the State, should they be convicted of affording an asylum to escaped slaves.

Until the closing years of the eighteenth century, the number of slaves on the sugar plantations in Cuba was extremely small, and what most surprises us is, that a prejudice founded on "religious scruples," opposed the introduction there of females (they costing in Havana one-third less than males), thus forcing the slaves to celibacy, under the pretext that vicious habits were thus avoided. . . . Although the census of 1775, which is undoubtedly very imperfect, gave 15,562 female and 29,336 male slaves, we must bear in mind that this census embraced the whole island, while the sugar plantations, even at the present time (1825), do not contain the entire slave population.

From the year 1795, the Consulado of Havana have seriously entertained projects for increasing the slave population, independent of the fluctuations of the slave-trade. Don Francisco de

Arango [y Parreño, 1765–1837; creole planter and educator], whose labors have always been pure and judicious, proposed the imposition of a tax upon those plantations which did not contain one-third females among their slaves. He also proposed the imposition of a duty of six dollars upon each male negro imported from Africa. Although these measures were not adopted, for the colonial juntas always refused to adopt coercive measures, yet, from that time, there has arisen a desire to increase the number of marriages, and to take better care of the children of the slaves; and a royal order (22 April 1804) recommends this policy to "the sense of right, and the humanity of the colonists."

The census of 1817 gave . . . 60,322 female, and 106,521 male slaves. In 1771, the proportion of female to male slaves was 1 to 1.9; so that, in forty years, it had altered very slightly, it being, in 1817, 1 to 1.7. The small amount of this change must be attributed to the large number of African negroes imported subsequently to 1791, and to the fact that the importation of females has been large, only during the years between 1817 and 1820: the slaves retained as servants in the cities are only a small fraction of the total number. . . .

The mortality of the negroes varies greatly in Cuba, according to the kind of labor, the humanity of the masters or overseers, and the number of women employed in taking care of the sick. I have heard discussed with the greatest coolness, the question whether it was better for the proprietor not to overwork his slaves, and consequently have to replace them with less frequency, or whether he should get all he could out of them in a few years, and thus have to purchase newly imported Africans more frequently. But these are the reasonings of avarice when one man holds another in servitude.

It would be unjust to deny that the mortality of the blacks has diminished greatly in Cuba, within the last fifteen years.

Many proprietors have studied how they might best improve the rules of their plantations. The mean mortality of the newly imported negroes is still from ten to twelve per cent., and from observations made on several well conducted sugar plantations, it may fall to even six or eight per cent. This loss among the newly imported negroes varies much according to the time of their arrival; the most favorable season for them is from October until January, those being the most healthy months, and most abundant in provisions on the plantations. In the hot months, the mortality *during the sale* is sometimes four per cent., as was the case in 1802.

An increase in the number of female slaves, so useful in the care of their husbands and their sick companions; their relief from labor during pregnancy; greater attention to their children; the establishment of the slaves by families in separate cabins; an abundance of food; and increase in the number of days rest; and the introduction of a system of moderate labor for their own account, are the most powerful and the only means to prevent the diminution in numbers of the blacks. Some persons who are well informed as to the old system on the plantations, believe that in the present state of things, the number of slaves would diminish five per cent. annually if the contraband traffic should entirely cease.

Robert Francis Jameson
Letters from the Havana, during the Year 1820
(London: John Miller, 1821), 36, 40–45

During the first ten subsequent years (viz. from 1789 to 1799) 41,500 negroes were imported into this island, or rather more than 4000 annually. During the next four years, 34,500 were imported, or about 8,600 annually. From that time to the year of the abolition treaty (1817), being a period of 13 years, above 150,000 negroes were introduced, or more than 10,000 annually. In the years 1817, 1818, and 1819, there was a great increase of importation nearly 60,000 having been brought to the island during that period.

Thus in the last thirty years more than 200,000 negroes have been brought from Africa to this island, and it is no vague supposition to presume, that 50,000 more have perished in the transit. . . .

The slaves of Cuba must be considered either as *field labourers* or *domestics*, because in this more than any other island, the condition of these respective classes varies. Those employed in household duties will, of course, be expected to possess advantages, and to have been selected for qualities, not enjoyed by the others, and frequently, either from the good nature or negligence of their masters, live in a state of ease and comparative happiness. Pride and luxury have accumulated numbers round themselves; some, in the Havana, have no less than sixty household slaves, encumbering the ease they are meant to supply, and forming a grandeur which is more confusing than dazzling. There are, indeed, some wealthy proprietors, whom I gladly except, that are surrounded by these hordes, less for state than from a wish not to alienate those born under their roof, and bearing their name.

These domestics, born in hereditary service, are commonly the associates of their young masters during their juvenile years and, not uncommonly, the pets of their mistresses. They are seen sprawling and sporting at the feet of their owners with the young whites of the family, and are accustomed to the free range of the house with their associate lordlings, thus acquiring habits of familiarity not easily got rid of when the nature of their service is changed. This occurs when their white fellows become masters and require their companions to be menials. They are, then, either suffered to serve with a kind of familiar air, which to a casual observer looks very like insolence, or otherwise, are repulsed and commanded harshly, a treatment which they feel keenly, and are sure to testify. But, in whatever way they are treated by their masters, the love of liberty soon renders them restless. They see numbers of their colour enjoy freedom, and the laws sanction their attempt at attaining the same immunity.

Every slave, under the Spanish colonial law, who tenders his master the sum he was bought at, is entitled to enfranchisement, *nor can his master refuse it.* It is equally permitted him to purchase a *portion of his freedom*, by instalments as his ability allows, being then said to be *coartado* or *cut*, and such are, in consequence, entitled to a license to work where and with whom they please, paying to their master a *real* per day for every hundred dollars remaining of their value beyond the instalment they have paid. Many who are not *coartado* are allowed by their owners to labour where they please under similar conditions, by which means an industrious slave may in few years procure sufficient to ransom himself. The excellence of such a regulation it is easy to appreciate. The permission to purchase freedom by portions is both a wise and merciful policy. It satisfies the master with a high interest, during the period the slave is working out his freedom, and it imbues the latter with habits of cheerful industry while he is, as it were, knocking off his chain link by link. . . .

The laws I have detailed apply to both classes of slaves, though circumstances make their benefits less available to the *field* than the *domestic* negroes. In one respect they are all equal—in the state of utter ignorance they are kept in. Nowhere is the axiom better understood, that, *knowledge is power*.

The *field* negroes are either *bozales*, or slaves sent thither, and retained there, who are either too dull to be used as artificers and domestics, or whose faults in these latter capacities are punished by this species of banishment. To be sent *"al monte"* is the severest punishment a domestic negro can be threatened with. This is sufficient to show the distinction between their conditions.

The parts of the island where the *ingenio's*, or sugar plantations, and the *cafetales*, or coffee estates, lie, are remote from the Havana and towns where the proprietors reside. They are consequently left to the management of *overseers*, men, in all the islands, usually of indifferent characters and desperate fortunes, or if they are not are, at least, in that rank of life where prejudice is less likely to be checked by education, or feeling, to have attained any degree of refinement. The slaves committed to their charge depend entirely on temper, and are too remote from the society of their more favored fellows to learn the rights the laws have given them. From their locality they are also debarred from the advantages of extra labour, or a charge of service; they are penned up amidst the mountains, and the only remedy for suffering is, either patience or revolt. Not a year passes without instances of the latter. Last winter a body of 700 took to the hills, and it was two months before the military sent against them could compel them to surrender. It is vain to talk of men being well treated when they risk their lives to ameliorate their condition.

Abiel Abbot
Letters Written in the Interior of Cuba
(Boston: Bowles and Dearborn, 1829), 39–41

It is a matter of serious inquiry with me, how slaves are treated by the different nations, who compose the population of this island, and in the different species of culture sugar and coffee. There is a marked difference in the methods in [South] Carolina and Cuba, of employing their slaves; in Carolina, all work on land is done in tasks, and the task is the same on all plantations, and for all hands, male and female;—one hundred and five feet square, which is duly staked out for every negro, is his task for the day, which performed, his master has no claim upon him for further service for that day. The vigorous and active perform the task by three or four o'clock, sometimes by one or two, the strong are seen to help out the weak, the husband the wife, the parent the child, and good feeling is promoted among the gang. In Cuba, they have no measured task on coffee or sugar estates. With the exception of part of Saturday, and a part of Sunday, the whole time of the slave is his master's. They rise at daybreak, and commence their toil; and with short intervals to take their food, they labor till the light is gone, and renew it on some plantations, by the light of the moon or stars, or a blazing fire. As they move to the field in Indian file, the driver brings up the rear with a word and a harmless snap of his whip, to quicken their pace; and in the field they work near together, and occasionally the driver rouses the gang to a quicker movement by an inspiring call, like a carter speaking to his oxen. . . .

It astonishes one to see with what rapidity they pass over a field of weeds and bushes with their machete, an instrument like a butcher's cleaver, leaving neither root nor branch behind. This, as I should esteem it, *uncouth* instrument, is wielded with a rapidity and effect, which imply sleight of hand, and strength of wrist, even in females of fourteen or sixteen. Some planters give them the common hoe of our country, in weeding ground not stony; and esteem it a more efficient instrument, and it is certainly a more humane one, as the machete requires the laborer to bend his body low, to work with effect, which must be fatiguing and exhausting under a tropical sun.

It is certain that they work more hours than the farmers in the north of our own country, and I verily believe in each hour accomplish as much and more. There is no conversation among them, no lounging or leaning on the hoe, no slouch in their gait, and every stroke seems to tell. I should not think the opinion extravagant, that the slaves in Cuba accomplish one third more labor than the tasked slaves of Carolina.

So far as I have been able to observe, they have wholesome, and even delicious food, and as much as they desire. It is not generally measured to them, as in Carolina, nor left to their own cooking. They come to the cook-room with their gourd and take as much as they choose of the delicious plantain; they have rations of fish, indeed, of jerk beef, and of hearts and skirts, to make a variety. A pretty good sized codfish is cut into three parts, and one of them given to a laborer for the day. A pound of jerk beef also, is a ration. . . .

It is generally agreed that the labor on sugar estates is most exhausting to the negroes, and it is confidently said, that on many estates there is a loss of from 10 to 15 per cent of their laborers each year. This, however, does not take place on well conducted estates. The severity of the toil on sugar plantations seems acknowledged by the circumstance, that some estates purchase males only, and where both sexes are employed there is often little or no increase of population. As difficulties are thrown more and more in a way of importation of slaves from Africa, a greater attention is paid to pregnant females, to preserve the stock of the plantation. I trust there is with many, I know there is with some, a commiseration of female slaves in that delicate situation. They are exempt from labor for a month before and after the birth, to nurse themselves and the child, and have hours of the day for months after for the same purpose, during which others are at work.

Henry Tudor
Narrative of a Tour in North America, Comprising Mexico, the Mines of Real del Monte, the United States, and the British Colonies with an Excursion to the Island of Cuba
(2 vols.) (London: James Duncan, 1834), II:131–33

On again reaching Matanzas, I ascertained that a slave-ship had just entered the port from the African coast, with 250 slaves on board. She had been chased by the British schooner Skip-Jack for some hours before making the harbour, and I regret much to say, for the cause of humanity, that she had escaped it during the darkness of night. On proceeding to the quarter where these wretched beings were confined, I found them all huddled together in a large room, in which they were exposed to sale like a drove of pigs, in a state of complete nudity, with the exception of a bandage tied round their loins. They were disposed in lots of graduated ages, and were seated on the floor in groups of eight and ten, feeding out of a parcel of buckets, or rather devouring a miserable mess of the coarsest plantain, with a meagre sprinkling of bones and rice, exhibiting a colour as black as ink. It was, in truth, a species of pottage that I should have refused giving to my swine. Three of these miserable outcasts were extremely ill, from the effects of close confinement during a long voyage; particularly one of them, who appeared in a dying state, utterly unable to stand up, and who lay prostrate and groaning on the ground as naked nearly as he was born. The unhappy creature was literally nothing but skin and bone—a complete *anatomie vivante*, or I should rather say, *mourante*. Not a single person showed him the slightest sympathy, or gave him either clothes, food, or medicine; as if his merciless owners apprehended that the money expended on him would be entirely lost in consequence of his death, which there was too much reason to fear was fast approaching. . . . You will scarcely believe, that notwithstanding his deplorable condition, and that of his two countrymen, they were immediately put up to *auction*, in order to wring from the stony-hearted speculators on human flesh standing around, as many dollars as might be bidden for them on the desperate chance of their surviving. During the biddings the prostrate negro was attempted to be raised on his feet, to shew that he was not *actually dead*, and therefore not without hope to a possible purchaser. But famine and disease had eaten into his soul, and he sunk down in utter exhaustion. The gamblers for human blood, however, unutterably strange to say, offered money for his thus wasted body, and for those of his two sick countrymen; and they were finally knocked down for some score or two of dollars. On inquiring the following morning, I was informed that this forlorn victim of the white man's inhumanity had *expired* during the night, and thus escaped for ever from his cruel persecutors.

Joseph John Gurney
A Winter in the West Indies
(London: John Murray, 1841), 209–11

In the afternoon, after an early dinner at the Consul's, we sallied forth on an excursion of rather a delicate nature; it was to visit the barracoons—receptacles where the newly imported Africans are stowed, and offered for sale. Our two young friends went in one direction; M. Day and myself, under the guidance of a young Guernseyman, in another. He and I visited three out of six of these establishments, all of them being within two miles of the city. They have been built, and are conducted, on private speculation, and although the whole business is utterly illegal, their proprietors set at defiance all notions of shame, or of concealment from the eye of Government. We were not very successful in our attempt. The first barracoon at which we called was empty, and after walking over it, we had only to acknowledge that it was commodious and airy—for these places, for filthy lucre's sake, are intended to be curative of the effects of the middle passage. At the second, the keeper, who was the friend of our young guide, gave us an equally easy admission. We found in it about forty invalid Africans who had just been imported. They looked emaciated and melancholy. A child lying on a dresser, wrapped in a blanket, was in the article of death. The whole scene, with the exception of an idle laughter, was one of mute sorrow and suffering—heart-rending to ourselves. This barracoon was built to contain one thousand negroes. Just at sundown we arrived at a third of similar size. It is close by the garden of Tacon, which is a place of constant public resort. It was evidently full of negroes, whose voices we distinctly heard. We walked unbidden into the court yard, and saw the keeper turn the key of the last lock, after having shut them up for the night. Our guide timorously approached the scowling master, and begged admission for us into the dormitories. He gruffly replied, "No son negros aqui"—*there are not negroes here.* We were therefore obliged to retire, not being much disposed to be ourselves incarcerated in this den of iniquity. On the grass outside of the gate, however, there were sitting, dressed in coarse shirts marked with the letter D, about forty young men—a lot which had just been selected and purchased. The buyer was standing over them as if they had been oxen. Good cause had he for an attentive survey of their persons, for he had probably given 400 or 500 dollars per head, for them—from 16,000 to 20,000 dollars for the lot. Work them as he may, we could not conceive that this nefarious investment in human flesh and blood, could answer his purpose—especially as so large a proportion of these miserable beings dies in the seasoning. Our young friends found their way to a fourth barracoon, where they saw several hundred newly imported children. They were in lean condition, and many of them with marks on their skins, of bruises or blows, probably received from rubbing against the panels of the vessel, in which they had been unmercifully crammed, like herrings in a barrel. We returned to our quarters at night, well satisfied with having seen these horrors, and with the information which a most interesting day had afforded us, but heart-sickened and afflicted.

John George F. Wurdemann
Notes on Cuba
(Boston: James Munroe and Company, 1844), 257–62

With so many different dispositions to curb or direct, it will readily be seen that the treatment of the slaves must vary much. They are, indeed, governed more by the fear of punishment than are the slaves in our Southern States. . . . The chief object in Cuba seems to be never to let them remain idle; and I have excited the astonishment of many a Creole, by stating the quantity of leisure our slaves enjoy after their daily tasks are over; they could not believe they would remain disciplined. Nor was their astonishment lessened when I told them that in my native State, South Carolina, some planters paid missionaries to preach to their slaves, had chapels erected on their estates, and sometimes exhorted them in the absence of clergymen.

The laws in Cuba regulating slavery are, however, very liberal to the slave. Thus by them every owner is bound to instruct his slaves in the principles of the Catholic religion, after the labor of the day has been finished, to the end that they may be baptized and partake of the sacrament. On Sundays and feast-days they are not to be employed longer than two hours, for the necessary labor of the estate, the feeding the animals, etc., except when the gathering of the crop admits of no delay. They are required to have daily six or eight plantains, or an equivalent in potatoes, yams, yucas, or other edible roots, eight ounces of meat or fish, and four ounces of rice or flour. The quantity of clothes is also prescribed, and the treatment of women who are *enciente* or nursing, with respect to the amount of their labor, diet, and lodgings.

Except during the harvest of the canes on sugar estates when they may be employed sixteen hours daily, they are not to be worked longer than nine or ten hours; and on Sundays and other holidays they must be allowed to attend to their own gardens and private occupations. Those only between sixteen and sixty years can be employed in tasks, nor shall any who are disabled by injuries or old age be liberated, without granting them sufficient funds for a permanent subsistence.

Illicit intercourse shall be prohibited by their owners, and matrimonial alliances encouraged; nor shall the slaves of different masters be forbid to intermarry. When this takes place, and neither master will sell his respective slave for a reasonable price, that they might live together under one roof, both slaves united in marriage shall be sold to a third person. Owners who maltreat their slaves shall be compelled by a magistrate to sell them, and if a slave desires to buy his freedom, he shall obtain it for the actual valuation decided by arbitration. . . .

Liberty and fifty dollars shall be bestowed on any slave who shall have given information respecting a conspiracy of his fellow-slaves or of free persons: the purchase of his freedom and the reward to be paid out of the public funds from fines inflicted on slave-owners. No owner is allowed to give more than twenty-five lashes to a slave, and for offenses calling for a severer punishment, the latter must be tried before a magistrate. Criminal processes shall be instituted against those who maim or otherwise seriously injure their slaves, whom they shall then, moreover, be compelled to sell. Other penalties, in fines of twenty to two hundred dollars, shall be inflicted on the owners who disobey the laws relating to slavery.

No slave shall leave the estate of his master with arms, unless accompanied by the latter, when he may carry his machete, not when alone, without a license. At night they shall all be enclosed within the boheas, the general gate of which shall be secured by a lock; and the two guards placed to watch at night, shall inform the mayoral of any disturbance among them. After nine o'clock they must all retire to their rooms, and only on Sundays and feast-days shall they be permitted to play on their drums, or indulge in their national dances and other amusements. . . .

These laws are not all observed, but so many are, that the slave in Cuba is in some respects better off than the European peasant. With respect to the religious and moral government of them, baptism and burial in consecrated ground are alone enforced. On a few Spanish estates prayers are repeated to them before going to work in the morning, and before retiring to their dormitories; but no attention is paid to the matrimonial compact, some being polygamists, and others making mutual exchanges of their wives when tired of them. In the country the slaves do not often compel their masters to sell them to other owners more to their liking, but this not unfrequently is done in cities; and both on plantations and in towns many annually purchase their freedom against the will of their owners. . . .

During the winter, when the labor on the sugar estates is very great, many of the slaves abscond, and lead a roving life in the woods. They often make extensive depredations on the hogs and plantains of the coffee-planters, and are sometimes hunted by bloodhounds. The greatest number are captured by the slaves on the different estates, who obtain from the captain of partido four dollars for each prisoner; and they are as active in the chase, as they would be in their native forests to collect a supply for the slavers. On a single estate, where I resided, ten runaways were caught in a few months by three or four of the negroes, who at their own request were permitted to patrol about the grounds after the last curfew. Notwithstanding all these means, some contrive to lead a wandering life for several years; and the mountains about the Pan of Matanzas, and several of the savannas, have ever been favorite hiding-places for them. Armed with spears, made of the hard woods of the island, and the machetes they had stolen from their masters, they are often very formidable to those who with bloodhounds make it a business to ferret them out of their retreats.

William Henry Hurlbert
Gan-Eden; or, Picture of Cuba
(Boston: John P. Jewett and Company, 1854), 189–95

It was my fortune to see in Cuba perhaps the mildest form of agricultural slavery. Among the slave-holders of my acquaintance are numbered some of my most valued friends, men of candor and of character, with whom one could speak as unreservedly on the subject of slavery, as with high-minded officers

on the subject of war. Under their auspices I saw the system in its
most favorable aspects. Moreover, the Spanish slave laws rather
resemble those of the East than those of America. There is a
master too, above the masters in Cuba, and though the supreme
authority is exerted less to benefit the slaves than to oppress the
slave-holders, still there are circumstances of great superiority in
the condition of the Cuban over that of the American slave. The
American slave has no hope but that of which man cannot deprive
him, the hope of immortality. His earthly destiny is taken completely out of his own hands. He has no majority, and like a child
or a beast, must look to receive from another his good or evil
fortune, without an effort on his part. The Cuban slave is protected
by the law in the enjoyment of a certain amount of property, and
may apply his earnings to the purchase of his own liberty. An
authoritative arbitration may settle his value, on his own appeal,
and so soon as he shall accumulate fifty dollars, his master is
obliged to accept that sum as an installment of the slave's price
which buys for him a proportionate command of his time, and in
the event of his sale to another owner before he has accomplished
his liberty, shall be carried to his credit. I have seen slaves who
were free for five or six days out of seven, and would soon
emancipate themselves entirely....

The mildness of the climate is in favor of the Cuban negro.
And on the great estates, the slave quarters, the *baracones*, are
usually as neat and well arranged as on the best, the *exceptional*
plantations of the South. The *baracon* is generally divided into
separate domiciles which are about as large as an average Welsh
cottage, and are rarely so dirty as the homes of the paradise of
consonants. To the *baracon* a hospital is always attached, often
under the charge of some African Sangrado, skilled in leeching
and bleeding and in the compounding of "snake-butter," and
other astonishing specifics, but always superintended by a physician who visits the estate once or twice a week, or even oftener,
according to its size. The older women, exempted from harder
labor, (for Cuba does not traffic much, like New Orleans, in
second hand muscles), take care of the children in a great nursery. The children are not often numerous, for the growth of the
slave population in Cuba is sadly checked by the influence of the
slave-trade, which keeps up an alarming preponderance of the
male sex.

The greatest severity of toil is endured by the slaves, who in small bands of three or four men, denied even such savage semblance of family life as the great estates afford, are worked upon the small tobacco-farms, by owners whose poverty of means, and love of luxury make them utterly inhuman. Under the moonlight, as under the sunlight, these hapless wretches, with little rest and no comfort, must plant and tend and gather the pleasant poisonous weed. From that so famous "tobacco of the Vuelta Abajo," a cunning alchemist might draw secrets more fatal than its hidden nicotine!

Even on the best of the great estates, from November to May, the negroes are required to work sixteen and sometimes nineteen hours a day. They work, like sailors, by watches, making the "night joint laborer with the day," and startling the stranger from his midnight sleep, with prolonged wailing cadences of their barbaric chants. In this excessive toil both sexes bear an equal part. It may, perhaps, be doubted whether this particularly aggravates the case. The hoe in the fields may possibly be less deadly to body and to soul, than the needle in the garret.

The number of slaves in Cuba probably rather exceeds than falls short of 350,000. Of this number fully one half are Bozales, *muzzled ones*, (so runs the expressive phrase,) who cannot say whence they came. These are the native Africans, most of whom have been imported in defiance of the treaties with England, and are therefore entitled to their freedom. The complicity of several Captain-Generals with the slave-trade is a matter of notoriety in the island. . . . The energetic English consul has occasionally succeeded in bringing a number of newly landed slaves before the mixed commission, but the slave-trade still goes on profitably, and for the most part in American bottoms, sailing under the American flag. The excitement which is sometimes created in America by the news that a British cruiser has boarded an American vessel in the Cuban waters, would, doubtless, be considerably mitigated, did our patriotism reflect upon the disgraceful way on which our so-called "national honor" is constantly made to serve as a shield for the pirates of the slave-trade. The frequent advertisement in the Havana journals, of "a new, handsome, and swift American barque, entirely ready for sea," has a meaning easy to be mastered. The demand for these vessels is permanent, for after a slave-ship has discharged her fearful cargo, she is usually scuttled and sunk. The profit on victims who can be sold in Cuba at from six hundred to seventeen hundred per cent profit on their cost in Africa, amply repays the great expenses of these horrible speculations.

Robert Baird
Impressions and Experiences of the West Indies and North America in 1849
(2 vols.) (Philadelphia: Lea and Blanchard, 1850), I:222–27

Before leaving Cuba, I did my utmost to get as accurate information as possible, as to the general condition of the slave population; but the details differed so much, that it was next to impossible to lay down any statement of general application. The system is so very a despotism, and masters differ so widely, that what is true of one is untrue of another, and the shades of difference in the treatment of their slaves are just as numerous as the men. A few particulars, however, I ascertained as facts beyond dispute.

In the first place, the domestic slaves, those employed in the performance of menial offices in the families of their owners, are in general very well treated. Nor are they indiscriminately selected from the general body. The office is as it were hereditary; the children, if there are any, being brought up to the performance of domestic work as the parents die. It is plain that ties will thus be formed between the master and mistress, and their families, and their domestic servants, which will go far to soften the hardships of slavery, and to secure the comparative good treatment of slaves. So it is in Cuba. The best-informed parties in Havana assured me, and my own observation led me to the same conclusion, that, on the whole, the household slaves were a favoured race compared with their fellows in the field, and that instances in which *domestics* were ill treated were the exceptions, and not the rule.

Among the slaves, and particularly among the domestic slaves, it occasionally happens that a slave works out his or her freedom, under the operation of a law known as giving rise to what is called the *Coartado* system. By this system a slave can purchase his freedom if so inclined. If he has been purchased by his master, the price so paid is held also as the price which he must pay for his liberation; while, if he has been born in slavery to his master, he is entitled by law to have a price put upon himself by valuation, at which price he has the right to redeem himself from bondage. After this valuation, on paying one-sixth of the price, the slave becomes master of his own time, becomes free, as it were, for one day in the week; another sixth, two days, and so on; so that the capacity for acquiring freedom, as well as the desire so to do—like Virgil's impersonation of fame—*vires acquirit eundo.* . . .

The field-labourers are however, as a body, in a very different situation. As a general rule, their labour is very severe, and their treatment very harsh—during the process of sugar-making, especially so. When once the grinding or pressing the cane—the first step in sugar-making—is begun, it proceeds day and night, with the exception of Sundays and other holidays, (and ofttimes without even these exceptions,) till the whole is completed. The slaves work in gangs, and for six hours or so at a time—being kept closely at their work by the fear of the lash, and by its frequent application. In some estates there are no women—in others there are very few; and the men are, during the hours devoted to sleep, penned up in barracoons like so many cattle. No doubt the treatment varies on different estates. On some it is much more humane than on others, but as a general rule it is the very reverse of humane; and I could not, although I diligently inquired, hear of any estate on which a number of labourers was kept up by births on the estate itself. Indeed, the idea of making the slave population supply itself is the last thing that seems to enter a Cuban's mind; and it will be so so long as, by violating the contract made with, and paid for by England in 1817, and by encouraging the disgusting slave trade, he can buy *much* cheaper than he can breed. To *breed* slaves is bad enough, but it is an evil unquestionably *second* to the stealing and selling of them; and thus it is, it should be remembered, that to end slavery we must begin at the beginning: we must first put an end to the slave traffic. That is unquestionably the natural way.

Indeed, as to the condition and treatment of agricultural slaves in the island of Cuba, these two well-ascertained facts speak volumes, and render further inquiry almost unnecessary. In the first place, the Negro population is far, very far from supporting itself. The number of victims annually robbed from Africa and

taken as slaves to Cuba, Porto Rico, and Brazil, are estimated at
seventy-eight thousand. Of these the Spanish colonies get one-
half. But whatever number may be landed at Porto Rico in the
first instance, few are allowed to remain there, for the reason
already pointed out when writing of the labouring population of
that productive island. It is therefore within the truth to estimate
the numbers annually taken to Cuba at thirty thousand; and that
this amount of importation is required to make good the ravages
by death, is proved by the fact, that whenever, through the
vigilance of British cruisers or otherwise, there has been a failure
in the number imported, the price has immediately and rapidly
risen. . . .

   In the second place, it is now but too well known that the
average life of a slave, after he reaches Cuba, does not exceed
seven or eight years. This acknowledged fact requires no comment. It contains in itself at once the evidence and the explanation
of the inhuman treatment which these unfortunates receive at the
hands of their oppressors.

John Glanville Taylor
The United States and Cuba
(London: Richard Bentley, 1851), 226–28

   As may be supposed, a great many negro slaves annually
make their escape from their masters. These are two kinds of
runaways; those who merely leave on account of some temporary
pique, or fright, and others who really start thinking to get back
to their country. The former seldom stay away long, and generally
lurk about the house itself, and are mostly soon caught or come
back of themselves. But the others, who try to get away entirely,
have a different idea, for as they came by sea, so do they expect to
get back to Africa by land, and always make for the east.

   Now, at the very eastern end of Cuba, within the triangle
between the cities of St. Jago [Santiago de Cuba] and Baracoa,
and Point Maysi, a wild and rugged tract of country exists, and in
the centre of all, an immense mountain, called the Sierra del
Cristal, which I have often seen from the sea. Hither no adven-
turous topographer has yet directed his steps, but were the proper
measurements made, I am almost certain, the Cristal would be

found the highest eminence in Cuba. On this mountain range every one unites in declaring that the runaway negroes, stopped by its inaccessible summits, have established a large settlement. Collections of wild Indians, or negroes, so established, are called *Palenques*, and the people, "Apalancadoes." For the capture of what is called a "cimarron simple," a mere runaway, that is, any slave found wandering more than twelve miles from his master's house without a passport, a reward of four dollars is recoverable from the owner, and many poor Spaniards turn a penny by looking out for such chances. The Palenques come under a different regulation. Sometimes they form themselves in more accessible districts, and a settlement of runaways is termed a palenque when there are more than seven congregated. The business is superintended by an official, called a Contador del Consulado, and the court a Consulate.

Expeditions for the reduction of Palenques must be undertaken under the auspices of this tribunal. If the expedition be considered one of extreme danger, special rates of reward are offered. In that case, *extirpation* is probably determined on; but such cases have rarely happened. Otherwise they are governed by the following rules:—If the number, killed, wounded, and prisoners, amounts to twenty, eighteen dollars a-head are paid to the captors; if they exceed twelve, sixteen dollars; and if six, ten dollars; but nothing is paid *for* those, who either die or are so badly wounded that their masters will not have them; and they may refuse them if the expenses of the capture amount to more than the value, which might easily happen, as about one shilling sterling per diem is exacted for costs of maintenance, and one shilling and sixpence for every league they are brought back. The rewards are equally divided among the party, only one-sixth part more is awarded to the captain.

The great Palenque of the Cristal, however, remains as much a mystery as ever, and some even doubt if the Spanish Government does not leave it purposely as a kind of safety-valve for the discontented, for no expedition of importance enough to reduce it has ever been undertaken, although small parties are annually formed in Baracoa, who hover about it, and capture a great many negroes. Common report says, that the settlement is high up on an elevated plateau, only approachable by one pass, which is fortified by overhanging rocks, kept ready to hurl on the invaders, and strictly guarded by wary sentinels; and that on this plateau, whose inhabitants are said to amount to many hundreds, grain, tobacco, etc., are grown sufficient for their wants.

Fredrika Bremer
The Homes of the New World: Impressions of America
(New York: Harper and Brothers, 1853), 331–35

The plantation is much larger than the one I visited in Limonar, and a considerable portion of the slaves—two hundred in number—have lately been brought hither from Africa, and have a much wilder appearance than those I saw at Ariadne. They are worked also with much more severity, because here they are allowed only four and half hours out of the four-and-twenty for rest; that is to say for their meals and sleep, and that during six or seven months of the year! Through the remaining portion of the twelve months, the "dead season," as it is called, the slaves are allowed to sleep the whole night. It is true, nevertheless, that even now, upon this plantation, they have *one night* a week for sleep, and a few hours in the forenoon of each alternate Sunday for rest. It is extraordinary how any human beings can sustain existence under such circumstances; and yet I see here powerful negroes who have been on the plantations for twenty or thirty years. When the negroes have once become accustomed to the labor and the life of the plantation, it seems to agree with them; but during the first years, when they are brought here free and wild from Africa, it is very hard to them, and many seek to free themselves from slavery by suicide. This is frequently the case among the Luccomees, who appear to be among the noblest tribes of Africa, and it is not long since eleven Luccomees were found handing from the branches of a guasima-tree—a tree which has long, horizontal branches. They had each one bound his breakfast in a girdle around him; for the African believes that such as die here immediately arise again to new life in their native land. Many female slaves, therefore, will lay upon the corpse of the self-murdered the kerchief, or the head-gear, which she most admires, in the belief that it will thus be conveyed to those who are dear to her in the mother-country, and will bear to them a salutation from her. The corpse of a suicide-slave has been seen covered with hundreds of such tokens.

I am told here that nothing but severity will answer in the treatment of slaves; that they always must know that the whip is over them; that they are an ungrateful people; that in the disturbances of 1846 it was the kindest masters who were first massacred with their whole families, while, on the other hand, the severe masters were carried off by their slaves into the woods, there to be concealed during the disturbances. I am told that, in order for a man to be loved by his slaves, he must be feared. I do not believe it; such is not human nature; but there is a difference between fear and fear. There is one fear which does not exclude love, and one which produces hatred and revolution.

The slaves have here, in a general way, a dark and brooding appearance. They go to their work in the sugar-fields sleepy and weary. As they drive the oxen to and fro, I frequently see them sucking sugar-cane, which they are very fond of, and of which they seem allowed here to have as much as they like. This is, at all events, a refreshment. They are not fed here on rice, but principally upon a species of root called malanga, which, it is said, they like, but which seemed to me insipid. It is yellow, and something like a potato, but has a poor and somewhat bitter taste; each slave receives a portion of such root boiled for dinner, and eats it with his salt meat. They have for breakfast boiled maize, which they bruise and mix with wild tomatoes, the fruit of the plantain, or vegetables; for they are allowed a little land on the plantation where they may sow and reap for themselves, and besides this, each family has a pig, which they kill yearly and sell.

[Today] is the Sabbath, and forenoon; but the sugar-mill is still grinding, and the whip-lash sounds commanding labor. The slaves will continue to work the whole day as if it were a week-day. Next Sunday, they say, is the one on which the slaves will rest for some hours, and dance if they are inclined; but—they look so worn out!

There are in Cuba plantations where the slaves work twenty-one out of the four-and-twenty hours; plantations where there are only men who are driven like oxen to work, but with less mercy than oxen. The planter calculates that he is a gainer by so driving his slaves, that they may die within seven years, within which time he again supplies his plantation with fresh slaves, which are brought hither from Africa, and which he can purchase for two hundred dollars a head. The continuance of the slave-trade in Cuba keeps down the price of slaves. I have heard of "gangs" of male slaves, six hundred in each gang, who are treated as prisoners, and at night locked up in a jail; but this is on the plantations in the southern part of the island. . . .

Yet even here I have derived some little comfort with regard to the condition of the slaves on this plantation, at least from the visit which I have paid to their bohea [*bohio*]. This is a large, square, but low fortress-like wall, in which the slaves live as at Ariadne plantation, and in which they are secured by bolts and bars during meal-times, and I have always felt it a refreshment to witness their vigorous life and their cheerfulness; nevertheless, I have seen countenances here steeped in such gloom, that not all the tropical sunshine would illumine, so hopeless, so bitter, so speechless were they—it was dreadful! The countenance of one young woman, in particular, I shall never forget!

The little ones are not here familiar and merry as they are on the plantations in America; they do not stretch out their little hands for a friendly salutation; they look at the white man with suspicious glances—they are shy; but the very little Bambinos, which are quite naked, fat, and plump, as shiny as black-brown silk, dance upon their mother's knees, generally with a blue or red string of beads around the loins, and another round the neck; they are the very prettiest little things one ever saw; and the mothers, with their strings of beads round their necks, their showy kerchiefs fastened, turban-wise, around the head, look very well too, especially when, with delighted glances, and shining, pearly teeth, they are laughing and dancing with their fat little ones. Such a young mother, with her child beneath a banana-tree, is a picture worthy a pencil of a good painter.

I saw in those dark little rooms—very like those at Ariadne plantation—more than one slave occupied during the short time allowed him for rest in weaving little baskets and hats of palm-leaves, and one of them had constructed a fine head-dress of showy patches of cock's feathers!

In other respects the slaves live in the bohea very much like cattle. Men and women live together and part again according to fancy or whim. If a couple, after having lived together for some time, grow weary of each other, the one will give the other some cause of displeasure, and then they separate. In case of any noisy quarrel, the mayoral is at hand with his whip to establish peace.

Maturin Murray Ballou
History of Cuba; or, Notes of a Traveller in the Tropics
(Boston: Phillip Samson and Company, 1854), 180–82

Cuba has been called the hot-bed of slavery; and it is in a certain sense true. The largest plantations own from three to five hundred negroes, which establishments require immense investments of capital successfully to manage. A slave, when first landed, is worth, if sound, from four to five hundred dollars, and more as he becomes acclimated and instructed, their dull natures requiring a vast deal of watchful training before they can be brought to any positive usefulness, in doing which the overseers have found kindness goes a vast deal farther than roughness. Trifling rewards, repaying the first efforts at breaking in of the newly imported negro, establishes a good understanding at once, and thus they soon grow very tractable, though they do not for a long time understand a single word of Spanish that is addressed to them.

The negroes are from various African tribes, and their characteristics are visibly marked, so that their nationality is at once discernible, even to a casual observer. Thus the Congos are small in stature, but agile and good laborers; and Fantee are a larger race, revengeful, and apt to prove uneasy; those from the Gold Coast are still more powerful, and command higher prices, and when well treated make excellent domestic servants. The Ebros are less black than the others, being almost mulatto. There is a tribe known as the Ashantees, very rare in Cuba, as they are powerful at home, and consequently are rarely conquered in battle, or taken prisoners by the shore tribes in Africa, who sell them to the slave factories on the coast. They are prized, like those from the Gold Coast, for their strength. Another tribe, known as the Carrobalees, are highly esteemed by the planters, but yet they are avoided when first imported, from the fact that they have a belief and hope, very powerful among them, that after death they will return to their native land, and therefore, actuated by a love of home, these poor exiles are prone to suicide. This superstition is also believed in some other tribes; and when a death thus occurs, the planter, as an example to the rest, and to prevent a like occurrence among them, burns the body, and scatters the ashes to the wind!

The tattooed faces, bodies and limbs, of the larger portion of the slaves, especially those found inland upon the plantations, indicate their African birth; those born upon the island seldom mark themselves thus, and being more intelligent than their parents, from mingling with civilization, are chosen generally for city labor, becoming postilions, house-servants, draymen, laborers upon the wharves, and the like, presenting physical developments that a white man cannot but envy on beholding, and showing that for some philosophical reason the race thus transplanted improves physically, at least. They are remarkably healthy; indeed, all classes of slaves are so, except when an epidemic breaks out among them, and then it rages more fearfully far than with the whites. Thus the cholera and small-pox always sweep them off by hundreds when these diseases get fairly introduced among them.

Richard Henry Dana, Jr.
To Cuba and Back: A Vacation Voyage
(Boston: Ticknor and Fields, 1859), 243–55

It is difficult to come to a satisfactory conclusion as to the number of slaves in Cuba. The census of 1857 puts it at 375,000; but neither this census nor that of 1853 is to be relied upon, on this point. The Cubans are taxed for their slaves, and the government finds it difficult, as I have said, to get correct returns. No person of intelligence in Cuba, however desirous to put the number at the lowest, has stated it to me at less than 500,000. Many set it at 700,000. I am inclined to think that 600,000 is the nearest to the truth. . . .

To ascertain the condition of slaves in Cuba, two things are to be considered: first, the laws, and secondly, the execution of the laws. The written laws, there is no great difficulty in ascertaining. As to their execution, there is room for opinion.

At this point, one general remark should be made, which I deem to be of considerable importance. The laws relating to slavery do not emanate from the slave-holding mind; nor are they interpreted or executed by the slave-holding class. The slave benefits by the division of power and property between the two rival and even hostile races of whites, the Creoles and the Spaniards. Spain is not slave-holding, at home; and so long as the laws are made in Spain, and the civil offices are held by Spaniards only, the slave has at least the advantage of a conflict of interest and principles, between the two classes that are concerned in his bondage.

The fact that one negro in every four is free, indicates that the laws favor emancipation. They do both favor emancipation, and favor the free blacks after emancipation. The stranger visiting Havana will see a regiment of one thousand free black volunteers, parading with the troops of the line and the white volunteers, and keeping guard in the Obra Pia. When it is remembered that the bearing arms and performing military duty as volunteers is esteemed an honor and privilege, and is not allowed to the whites of Creole birth, except to a few who are favored by the government, the significance of this fact may be appreciated. The Cuban slaveholders are more impatient under this favoring of the free blacks than under almost any other act of the government. They see in it an attempt, on the part of the authorities, to secure the sympathy and cooperation of the free blacks, in case of a revolutionary movement—to set race against race, and to make the free blacks familiar with military duty, while the whites are growing up in ignorance of it. . . .

The laws also directly favor emancipation. Every slave has a right to go to a magistrate and have himself valued, and on paying the valuation, to receive his free papers. The valuation is made by three assessors, of whom the master nominates one and the magistrate the other two. The slave is not obliged to pay the entire valuation at once; but may pay it in installments, of not less than fifty dollars each. These payments are not made as mere advances of money, on the security of the master's receipt, but are part purchases. Each payment makes the slave an owner of such a portion of himself, *pro parte indivisa*, or as the common law would say, in tenancy-in-common, with his master. If the valuation is one thousand dollars, and he pays one hundred dollars, he is owned, one-tenth by himself and nine-tenths by his master. . . .

There is another provision, which, at first sight, may not appear very important, but which is, I am inclined to think, the best practical protection the slave has against ill-treatment by his master: that is, the right to a compulsory sale. A slave may, on the same process of valuation compel his master to transfer him to any person who will pay money. For this purpose, he need establish no cause of complaint. It is enough if he desires to be transferred, and some one is willing to buy him. This operates as a check upon the master, and an inducement to him to remove special causes of dissatisfaction; and it enables the better class of slave-holders in a neighborhood, if cases of ill-usage are known, to relieve the slave, without contention or pecuniary loss.

In making the valuation, whether for emancipation or compulsory transfer, the slave is to be estimated at his value as a common laborer, according to his strength, age, and health. If he knows an art or trade, however much that may add to his value, only one hundred dollars can be added to the estimate for this trade or art. Thus the skill, industry and character of the slave, do not furnish an obstacle to his emancipation or transfer. On the contrary, all that his trade or art adds to his value, above one hundred dollars, is, in fact, a capital for his benefit. . . .

As to the enforcement of these laws, I have little or no personal knowledge to offer; but some things, I think, I may treat as reasonably sure, from my own observation, and from the concurrent testimony of books, and of persons of all classes with whom I have conversed. . . .

The laws respecting valuation, the purchase of freedom at once or by instalments, and the compulsory transfer, I know to be in active operation in the towns, and on plantations affording easy access to towns or magistrates. I heard frequent complaints from slave-holders and those who sympathized with them, as to the operation of these provisions. A lady in Havana had a slave who was an excellent cook; and she had been offered $1700 for him, and refused it. He applied for valuation for the purpose of transfer, and was valued at $1000 as a laborer, which, with the $100 for his trade, made a loss to the owner of $600, and, as no slave can be subsequently sold for a larger sum than his valuation, this provision gave the slave a capital of $600. Another instance was of a planter near Matanzas, who had a slave taught as a carpenter; but after learning his trade, the slave got himself transferred to a master in the city, for the opportunity of working out his freedom, on holidays and in extra hours. So general is the enforcement to these provisions that it is said to have resulted in a refusal of many masters to teach their slaves any art or trade, and in the hiring of the labor of artisans of all sorts, and the confining of the slaves to mere manual labor. I heard of complaints of the conduct of individuals who were charged with attempting to influence the credulous and too ready slaves to agree to be transferred to them, either to gratify some ill-will against the owner, or for some supposed selfish interest. From the frequency of this tone of complaint and anecdote, as well as from positive assertions on good authority, I believe these provisions to have considerable efficacy.

As to the practical advantage the slaves can get from these provisions in remote places; and as to the amount of protection they get anywhere from the special provisions respecting punishment, food, clothing, and treatment generally, almost everything lies in the region of opinion. There is no end to statement and anecdote on each side. If one cannot get a full and lengthened personal experience, not only as the guest of the slave-holder, but as the companion of the local magistrates, of the lower officers on the plantation, of slave-dealers and slave-hunters, and of the emancipated slaves, I advise him to shut his ears to mere anecdotes and general statements, and to trust to reasonable deductions from established facts. The established facts are, that one race, having all power in its hands, holds an inferior race in slavery; that this bondage exists in cities, in populous neighborhoods, and in remote districts; that the owners are human beings, of tropical races, and the slaves are human beings just emerging from barbarism, and that no small part of this power is exercised by a low-lived and low-minded class of intermediate agents.

Julia Ward Howe
A Trip to Cuba
(Boston: Ticknor and Fields, 1860), 216–23

The black and white races are, by all accounts, more mingled in Cuba, than in any part of our own country. People who have long been resident there assure us that some of the wealthiest and most important families are of mixed blood. Animadvert upon this as you will, it is nevertheless certain that it weaves close bonds of affinity between them, and ties of Nature which, though ignored, cannot be unfelt. I have not seen in Cuba anything that corresponds to our ideal separation of the two sets of human beings, living in distinctness one from the other, hating and wronging each other with the fierceness of enemies in the death-grapple. . . .

The slave children wear oftenest no clothing until five or six years old. They look well-fed and healthy, only the prevalence of umbilical Hernia shows a neglect of proper bandaging at birth,—the same trouble from the same cause is very observable in the south of Italy. The increase of the slaves is, of course, an important test of their treatment,—it is small throughout the Island, and amounts to little save on the best plantations. There is now a slow improvement in this respect. The repression of the slave-trade has caused such a rise in the price of negroes, that it is become better economy to preserve and transmit their lives than to work them off in eight or ten years, leaving no posterity to supply their place. Vile as these motives seem, they are too near akin to the general springs of human action for us to condemn them. Is it otherwise with operatives in England, or with laborers in Ireland? Emigration lessens their numbers, and raises their value,— it becomes important to society that they shall be fed and sustained. . . .

We have heard of horrible places in the interior of the Island, where the crack of the whip pauses only during four hours in the twenty-four, where, so to speak, the sugar smells of the blood of the slaves. We have heard of plantations whereon there are no women, where the wretched laborers have not the privileges of beasts, but are only human machines, worked and watched. There, not even the mutilated semblance of family ties and domestic surroundings alleviates the sore strain upon life and limb. . . .

The slave laws of Cuba are far more humane than our own. It is only to be doubted whether the magistrates in general are trustworthy in carrying them out. Still, it is the policy of the government to favor the Negroes, and allow them definite exist-ence as a third class, which would be likely to range with the government in case of civil war. It is affirmed and believed by the Cubans that the colonial President has in his hands orders to loose the slaves throughout the Island, at the first symptoms of rebellion, that they may turn all their old rancors against their late masters. The humane clauses of which we speak are the following:

In the first place, every slave is allowed by law to purchase his own freedom, when he has amassed a sum sufficient for the purchase. He can moreover compel his master to receive a small sum in part payment, and then, hiring himself out, can pay the residue from his wages. The law intervenes also, if desired, to fix the price of the slave, which it will reduce to the minimum value. Every slave has the right to purchase his child before birth for the sum of thirty dollars, a fortnight after, for fifty, and so on, the value of course rising rapidly with the age of the child. Again, a slave who complains of ill-treatment on the part of his master may demand to be sold to another, and a limited space of time is allowed, during which he can exert himself to find a purchaser. These statutes do not seem to contemplate the perpetuity of slavery as do our own institutions.

Rachel Wilson Moore
The Journal of Rachel Moore Kept during a Tour to the West Indies and South America in 1863–1864
(Philadelphia: T. Ellwood Zeil, 1867), 25–29

Having travelled through all the Southern States when slavery existed, we never saw it in so horrible a form as on the island of Cuba. We did not visit the calaboose, at Havana. We daily saw passing our boarding-house a large number of slaves, heavily loaded with irons, and chained together, going into different parts of the city, to labor on public works; such as repairing pavements, cleaning out sewers, or anything else of the most menial character. As all are chained together, one could make no move unless all moved, which must have given them in their irons the most excruciating pain. We saw them down in deep sewers, amid mud and filth, not only performing labor, daily, in those wretched ditches, but taking their meals (if they might be so called), surrounded with this stench. . . .

As we were riding out one evening, on the Paseo, in the finest part of the city, in company with our friends, G. Bernado and wife, of Philadelphia, we passed a gang of slaves, apparently in great wretchedness, with a driver behind them with an uplifted whip. They were probably being driven out to a plantation. We saw them every day while on the island, always under great oppression, and were informed by a gentleman from one of our Eastern States, that he had recently returned from a visit to a slave-ship, which had just come in with eleven hundred slaves on board, valued at eleven hundred thousand dollars. He was invited by a friend of his, residing in Havana, to go with him to witness the enormity of the slave-trade.

I will give the relation, as nearly as I can, in his own words. "They went," he says, "in the darkness of the night, to a certain point on the island, where slave-ships generally unload their cargoes"—it being an isolated spot. "We there saw a large number of planters on the shore waiting for the arrival of the anticipated slave-ship. We waited there for several hours, in the darkness of the night, until at last she made her appearance. On reaching her moorings, the cargo was hurried out of the ship, with all the rapidity possible, and placed upon the shore, many of them, poor miserable creatures, not being able to stand. I had heard of the horrors of the slave-trade, but the sight of these poor creatures, torn from their native land, in their filth and degradation, beggars all description—few of them having the appearance of human beings. After the ship was cleared of its inmates, the gentlemen who had invited me to go with him, insisted on my going on board the ship, which I did, and never can I forget the horrid spectacle that met my vision. The ship, from stem to stern, was a mass of filth and noxious vapor; it looked as if all the excrements accumulated on the passage, were there deposited, during a voyage of ninety days. I queried to know how it was possible, eleven hundred could be stowed into that ship? His answer was, 'I will show you,' pointing to that part between decks, where seats were formed like stairs, and in every part where they could be placed, in the same way. I said, 'They cannot all be seated here,' when he replied, 'They could not, except as they are made to fit each between the limbs of the other, having just room to crawl from their seats to a certain spot, nigh at hand, too horrible to reflect upon.' Never could I have contemplated so revolting a sight.

"We hastened away from the ship as rapidly as possible, fearing to remain many minutes in so noisome a place. We returned to the shore, and there found an auction going on. The many planters, who had been waiting for the arrival of the ship, were now making purchases of such as suited them best.

"In the course of an hour or two, all were gone, not a vestige being left of the blackened crime and shameful exhibition we had been witnesses to. The ship was then towed out into the sea and scuttled; which is the custom with the owners of slave-ships after discharging their cargoes, so that no trace shall be seen that such a ship has brought a cargo of slaves to the island. I queried with a gentlemen how it could be allowed, as it was contrary to the laws of Spain, as well as all other civilized countries. He said the people there got along easily with that; as money will do anything. So many doubloons handed the Captain-General, and all will be right; which has since been confirmed by a Cuban in my own house."

Antonio C. N. Gallenga
The Pearl of the Antilles
(London: Chapman and Hall, 1873), 119–26

The shrewd and matter-of-fact, though often perverse, English dealer in ready-made clothes whose authority I have repeatedly quoted, whenever he is questioned on the subject of the emancipation of the Cuban slaves invariably answers, that it is already "an accomplished fact," and that every negro in the island has been for several years "virtually free." By long living and flourishing among Spaniards, my trusting friend has caught their trick of using and accepting words for deeds, and looking upon mere promise as actual performance. The liberation of the slaves has been, it is true, determined on paper; and the Moret Law is usually pointed out as a proof that the Spanish Government, so far as the matter lay within their power, have in this respect acquitted themselves of their task, and paid the debt their country owed to modern civilization. . . . The law of 1870, which took its name from the then Minister for the Colonies, Senor Moret y Prendergast, late Minister for Spain at the Court of St. James, enacted in the first place, that every slave who had attained his 60th year in September, 1868, should from that very moment be declared free; and moreover it proclaimed the *vientre libero*, or, in other words, at once emancipated all the unborn offspring of slaves. It bound the proprietors to rear and bring up all children born on or after the date of the "glorious September Revolution," to keep them at their own expense up to their eighteenth year, and only to exact from them, in return for their maintenance, such work as they might be fit for up to that period of their lives; after which they should be allowed to do with themselves as they pleased. . . .

The clause which manumitted the unborn, had it ever been observed without any redeeming provision, would have laid an enormous and an unjust burden on the slave-owners, without really benefiting the future freed-men; as, during eighteen years of their lives, the new-born children would grow up in a thoroughly slavish condition, and would be compelled to work by the same discipline as had compelled their fathers before them. The law did not designate upon whom the task of fitting the new generation for a free life, in other words, of educating them, should devolve; and all that the negro of the future could learn was that the day would come in which he should only work when he liked. The only advantage that might be expected from a gradual emancipation was thus lost; and, at the end of eighteen years, the whole mass of the slaves would be found in as hopeless a state of ignorance and brutality as it now is. There would always be the same question to be dealt with: "How to dismiss the 300,000 or 350,000 slaves from the sugar estates, and to turn them loose and wild upon the unsettled districts of the Island, without reproducing the worst calamities of San Domingo, Jamaica, and the Southern States of the American Union." To redeem and reclaim the slaves is a task as difficult to accomplish before as after their emancipation. . . .

The scheme upon which the slave-owners have hit in order to tide over the catastrophe, which they admit to be inevitable, is, as I before stated, the immediate association of free with slave labour, and the gradual substitution of the one for the other. They propose, first, that the slaves should be contracted, indented, or apprenticed to their present masters for a certain number of years and upon a certain amount of wages; secondly, that a subscription should be opened to bring in a number of free labourers corresponding to the number of the present slaves, for it is expected that "no amount of remuneration can make two free labourers do more than the work that is now obtained from one slave." But in the opinion of Don Juan Poey, who has given the utmost attention to these subjects, there is something appalling in the sacrifices to which the land and slave-owners will have to submit if they are at the same time to allow wages to the slave who is now working for his bare sustenance, and to bear the expense involved by the importation of free labourers and by their wages. These sacrifices are so heavy that the greatest number of those who are to bear them must, if we may rely on Señor Poey's authority, succumb to them. There are, he says, in round numbers, 1500 sugar estates in Cuba, of these about 1200 yield to their owners in "dry sugar;" that is, without taking molasses, etc., into account, only 4 percent on their capital. The remaining 300 give a return of 6 to 8 1/2 percent on the capital; though the proprietors of one-half of these are so deeply indebted and mortgaged that they can scarcely be said to cultivate their estates for their own account. There remain therefore, only 150 estates whose revenue could enable their owners to bear the new burdens, and these alone would be expected to survive the contemplated reforms. It is needless to say that the income is larger in those estates upon which greater care and intelligence, and above all things, greater capital is bestowed. . . . So artificial and precarious is this wonderful prosperity of Cuba that it can only be kept up for a time on the present terms; that is, by working the slaves to the full extent of their power. The moment this high-pressure is removed a general collapse will necessarily ensue. The causes of the distress of a great number of Cuban proprietors, besides their own improvidence and want of skill, must be sought in the heavy and ill-assessed taxes imposed by the rapacity of the Spanish Government, and by the charges of the four years' Civil War which have been exclusively borne by the Colony.

Maturin Murray Ballou
Due South; or, Cuba Past and Present
(Boston: Houghton Mifflin and Company, 1885), 60–62, 278–81

There are comparatively few slaves to be found on the plantations or elsewhere in the vicinity of Cienfuegos: in fact, slavery is rapidly disappearing from the island. "Slave labor is more costly than any other, all things considered," said a sugar planter to us. "I do not own one to-day, but I have owned and worked six hundred at a time," he added. "We pay no tax on the laborers we hire, but on slaves we pay a heavy head-tax annually." An edict has been promulgated by the home government, which went into force last year, and which frees one slave in every four annually, so that on January 1, 1888, all will have become free. In the meantime the commercial value of slaves has so decreased in view of their near emancipation that they are not appraised on an average at over fifty or sixty dollars each. The law has for a period of many years provided that any slave who pays to his master his appraised value shall at once receive his free papers. Many purchase their liberty under this law, and then hire themselves to the same master or to some other, as they may choose,—at low wages, to be sure, but including food and shelter. Slaves have always been entitled by law in Cuba to hold individual property independent of their masters, and there are few smart ones who have not accumulated more or less pecuniary means during their servitude. They have had no expenses to meet in the way of supporting themselves. That has devolved upon their owners, so that whatever money they have realized by the several ways open to them has been clear profit. Many slaves have anticipated the period of their legal release from servitude, and more will do so during the present year. We also heard of planters who, realizing the inevitable, have manumitted the few slaves whom they still held in bondage, and hiring them at merely nominal wages, believed they saved money by the operation.

It will be seen, therefore, that slavery as an institution here is virtually at an end. Low wages will prevail, and this is necessary to enable the planters to compete with the beet sugar producers of Europe. In truth, it is a question how long they will be able to do so at any rate of wages. The modern machinery being so generally adopted by the sugar-cane planters, while remarkably successful, both as to the quality and the quantity of the juice it expresses from the cane, not only is expensive in first cost, but it requires more intelligent laborers than were found serviceable with the old process. To supply the places of the constantly diminishing slaves, emigrants, as they were called, have heretofore been introduced from the Canary Islands; men willing to contract for a brief period of years, say eight or ten, as laborers, and at moderate wages. These people have proved to be good plantation hands, though not so well able to bear the great heat of the sun as were the negroes. . . .

The slaves who still remain upon the plantations appear in all outward circumstances to be thoughtless and comparatively content; their light and cheerful nature seems to lift them above the influence of brutal treatment when it is encountered. That they have been called upon to suffer much by being over-tasked and cruelly punished in the past, there is no doubt whatever, but it may be safely stated that their condition has been greatly improved of late. The owners are obliged by law to instruct the slaves in the Catholic faith, but this has never been heeded to any extent by the planters, though all the children are baptized in infancy. The law relative to the treatment of the negroes also prescribes a certain quantity and quality of food to be regularly furnished to them, but the masters are generally liberal in this respect, and exceed the requirements of the law, as their merce-nary interest is obviously in that direction. The masters know by experience that slaves will not work well unless well fed. With no education or culture whatever, their intelligence remains at the lowest ebb. "With plenty of food and sleep," said an owner to us, "they are as easily managed as any other domestic animals."

Until latterly the slaves have been carefully watched at night, but nearly all these precautions against their escaping from ser-vitude seem to have been dropped. They are no longer locked up in corral, their special night quarters. Of course they are kept within certain bounds, but the rigorous surveillance under which they have always lived is no longer in force. The two sexes are nominally separated, but as there is no strict recognition of the marital relation, the free intercommunication between them really exists, the state of morality may be imagined. It has always been customary for mothers to receive certain consideration and partial relief from hard labor during a reasonable period prior to and subsequent to their confinement, with encouraging gifts from the masters, which has caused them generally to covet the condition of maternity. Still the proportion of female slaves on the plantations has always been so small, compared with that of the other sex, that not nearly so many children are born as would be supposed. Female slaves have generally been sent to town service, even when born on the plantations.

It has always been clearly understood that the births on the part of the negroes in Cuba have not nearly kept pace with the number of deaths among them, even under apparently favorable circumstances. One has not far to look for the reason of this. Promiscuous intercourse is undoubtedly the predisposing cause, which is always an outgrowth of a largely unequal division of the sexes. On the plantations the male negroes outnumber the females ten to one. In the cities the males are as five to one. When the slave trade was carried on between Africa and the island, the plan was to bring over males only, but it was hardly practicable to adhere strictly to the rule, so women were not declined when a cargo was being made up and nearly completed. Thus a disparity was inaugurated which has continued to the present day, with only a slight equalizing tendency.

The present plan of freeing the slaves recommends itself to all persons who fully understand the position, and if it be honestly carried out will soon obliterate the crime of enforced labor upon the island. A sudden freeing of blacks, that is, all at once, would have been attended with much risk to all parties, although justice and humanity demand their liberation.

Every reasonable Cuban has long realized that the freedom of the blacks was but a question of time, and that it must soon be brought about, but how this could be accomplished without rendering them liable to the terrible consequences which befell St. Domingo was a serious problem. The commercial wreck of Jamaica had less terror for them as an example, since of late their own condition could in that respect hardly be worse. Therefore, the manumitting of one slave in every four annually, so organized that all shall be free on January 1, 1888, is considered with great favor by the people generally, except the most radical of old Spaniards. All are thus prepared for the change, which is so gradually brought about as to cause no great shock. It is not unreasonable to believe that the instantaneous freeing of all slaves would have led to mutual destruction of whites and blacks all over the island.

IV

Crime and Punishment

James Edward C. B. Alexander
Transatlantic Sketches
(2 vols.) (London: Richard Bentley, 1833), I:350–59

Turn we now to penetrate and explore the gloomy saloons of the most horrid receptacle of crime in the civilized world, the Carcal [*cárcel*], or prison of "the cultivated city of Havannah," as the Spaniards delight to call it. I visited this dreadful place, and though it is almost impossible to obtain circumstantial details regarding it, owing to the extreme jealousy of the Spaniards, and their unwillingness to expose the great want of order, and entire absence of decency which prevail within its detested walls, yet I am enabled from personal observation and hearsay to lay before my readers a sketch of the Carcal as it now exists.

The entrance to it is on the southern side of the governor's house, and the gratings of the back cells open into the very patio, or court-yard of the palace. The gaol itself contains a long paved court, in looking into which through a grated door, where was a strong guard of soldiers, I saw some of the most cut-throat looking characters I ever beheld. They were of all classes and colours, black, yellow, and white, and many had gambled away all their clothes, save a thin pair of drawers. From the murderer to the petty thief, all were allowed to mingle indiscriminately. Not the least classification was attempted. At night the prisoners are disposed of under the piazzas which surround the court, and sleep on plank couches, retiring to rest at nine o'clock. Up stairs is a large sala, or strong room, (having no connexion with the yard,) also for male prisoners of all kinds. On the left-hand side of the entrance on the first floor, I observed a separate apartment for women, and opposite to it is the "Sala de distincion," or state-room for chance customers, such as drunkards, and other disorderly persons, arrested after improper hours in the streets, and who can afford to pay for superior accommodation. Mutinous sailors, run-away negroes, and others, whose offenses are light as well as their pockets, are thrust into the court-yard with the *canaille*, and have to fight out accommodation for themselves. I was told by some American sailors, who had been incarcerated by their captain for asking higher wages, that they witnessed such scenes of vice and depravity every night, that they were obliged to keep regular watch on one another.

All the prisoners are allowed to exercise, within the prison, any trade or handicraft they may have followed, barring that one which procured them a lodging in the Government-house, although they sometimes find opportunity to practice even that also. The produce of their honest industry, such as plaiting straw-hats, huckstering fruit, etc., is applied partly to defray the expenses of the prison establishment; and the residue is given up to their entire disposal. Even the assassins enjoy this privilege until sentence of death is pronounced upon them, when they are removed to separate cells up stairs.

Murders are often committed in the Carcal in the following manner: Three men gamble in the daytime, and one of them wins the money of the other two. The losers then conspire together to murder and rob the winner; at night they watch where he lies down to sleep in one of the saloons, and each goes to the lamps at the ends of the sala; they extinguish them simultaneously, draw their knives, and make a rush at the place where their victim lies; they stab him in the dark, and sometimes one or two others on each side of him to make sure of him; then strip the body or bodies of their money, and thrust them down the sink.

The prison is a rich Golconda for the Havannah lawyers. Persons accused on the slightest grounds of any offence or crime are incarcerated without examination, being afterwards permitted to exonerate themselves through the agency of these pests of the island society, who never fail to extort the utmost fee from their unfortunate clients. Persons of the better classes and state prisoners are generally confined in one or other of the forts, and some of them are allowed the liberty of their limits. When the common gaol is overstocked, as often happens, the surplus is transferred to the cells of Fort Cabanas.

In a city, the population of which is so mixed, the habits of the lower classes so demoralised, among whom gambling and its concomitant, drunkenness, is so prevalent,—in a city where there is no police, and where, by paying the priests handsomely, absolution maybe obtained for the most atrocious crimes, no wonder that robberies and assassinations are of almost daily occurrence. Sometime ago no fewer than seven white people were murdered in different parts of the city in one day. I remember when on one occasion I visited Hydrabad, a den of miscreants in the East Indies, in the guise of a Mussulman, (for none in European costume could enter its walls with safety,) three were murdered there that day in the streets; but that was nothing to Havannah.

In this latter city people are robbed in open day in the following manner: Two villains come on each side of a pedestrian, displaying long knives under their arms; while a third deliberately takes out his watch, purse, gold shirt buttons, etc. and whispers that if the least noise is made, the knife will do its office; and though the plundered individual may afterwards recognise the robbers, he is afraid to give evidence against them, and must just put up with his loss. . . .

When the least scuffle takes place in the streets, all the doors and windows are hastily closed in the neighbourhood; the inmates of the houses are so much afraid of being called upon to give evidence in case of a murder. I walked about at all hours, and fortunately escaped molestation; but I was fully prepared for a skirmish, with an iron-cane, a very handy weapon, something between a poker and a crow-bar. On looking at it, no one could suspect its weight until they felt it. I recommend this to travellers instead of the piked sticks of Dr. Kitchener, for it strengthens the chest and arms, and disables an antagonist without killing him.

The bodies of the murdered are exposed for a day in the street, behind the gaol, in order that their relatives may claim them. One forenoon, I happened to be passing the government-house with my friend Mr. Jackson, and observed a small crowd collected; we looked over the shoulders of the people, and saw a ghastly sight. In an open bier, with legs and handles to it, lay the corpse of a white man, about forty years of age, rather good-looking, and wearing a grim smile on his countenance. A dreadful gash was in his throat, his hands were also cut in the death-struggle, and his trousers and shirt were torn, and literally steeped in gore. This was a Gallician shopkeeper, who had been murdered in his own store, two or three hours before. He was a sober and industrious man, had arrived in Havannah a few years before, and had become possessed of twenty houses, and eighty thousand dollars in cash. His negro wench informed two of her black paramours where the money was kept. The miscreants went in the morning, on pretence of purchasing rope; the Gallician stepped to a corner of the store to supply them; they sprang upon him like wolves, held his mouth, threw him down, cut his throat, and carried off two coffee-bags of gold. All this took place within a few yards of the custom-house guard, with perfect impunity to the murderers. . . .

I have described some deeds of violence, but I have not yet brought any culprit to condign punishment. I am tired of horrors, and am afraid my readers are so likewise; but I think it will be satisfactory to describe an execution, which does not happen quite so often as it ought to do at Havannah. If a criminal has money, he may put off capital punishment for years, even after sentence is passed upon him; but he who is friendless and pennyless, mounts the scaffold immediately after he has been found guilty of a capital offence. The Spaniards have a great objection to see a white person executed at Havannah, because it degrades their order in the eyes of the coloured inhabitants. They bribe the civil authorities and priests to procure respites, and even if the culprit is not entitled to the least mercy, they will go to the governor and solicit a pardon by the *impegnio*, or private petition, which it is not generally the custom to refuse. A white woman had made mince-meat of her husband, and had put the mangled body into a beef-barrel; she was found guilty, but by means of bribery and the impegnio, the punishment was delayed for two years; at last, to the great annoyance of the fair Havanneras, she was placed on the fatal *garoté*, and her hands and feet tied to the chair, a collar of iron received her neck, to which a screw and winch were attached. A priest prayed with the condemned, and on a signal the executioner stepped behind the culprit, turned the winch, the neck was dislocated in a moment, and "the bitter sherbet of death tasted."

On passing the Carcal one afternoon, I saw a cross and lanterns displayed before a black cloth opposite the door of the prison chapel; this was the signal for the execution of a criminal on the morrow. In the chapel was a tall negro, pinioned and guarded, with a priest sitting beside him; I asked what the crime was for which he was about to suffer, and was told that he had been attached to a negress, but discovering that she favoured a mulatto, he waylaid them whilst they were proceeding on horseback into the country, and murdered man, woman, and horse, in a solitary place.

I rose at five o'clock next morning to witness a Spanish execution. The condemned, dressed in a white frock, was taken from the chapel, and drawn in a hurdle for some distance, and then compelled to walk for a mile and a half to the plain without the city, which is washed on two sides by the sea; here was the gallows. The cross and lanterns preceded the coffin. He was attended by the Brothers of Charity in black robes and white capes, one of them bearing a bottle of brandy and a glass; the "Companios Urbanos," or city guard, in leather caps, green jackets, carbines, and swords, were on each side. Arrived at the fatal tree, where a multitude waited in anxious expectation of the sight, the culprit got a large dose from the bottle, and then, with a ferocious-looking negro (the executioner), mounted the double ladder, and the rope was adjusted; the executioner then whispered something in the ear of the culprit, probably to throw himself off, but he did not do so, when the executioner gave him a hitch with his elbow, and away he swung; the executioner then sprang into the air with the agility of a Clias, seized the rope, and alighted on the shoulders of the murderer, and there sat kicking his breast with his heels. When the executioner had satisfied himself, by stooping down and looking in the face of the culprit, that it was all over with him, he slid down by the legs and mingled with the crowd. Then a priest mounted the ladder, and pointing to the dead, delivered a short and impressive homily. The body was left on the gallows till mid-day, and then taken down for the purpose of being decapitated, and the head to be placed on a pole at the spot where the foul deed had been done.

John George F. Wurdemann
Notes on Cuba
(Boston: James Munroe and Company, 1844), 59–61, 235–39

The Prison of Havana is a noble monument, among many others, of the good effected by Tacon [Miguel Tacón, 1775–1855;

governor general, 1834–1838] during his residence on the island.
It is situated without and near the gate of La Punta, not far from
the sea; the fresh breezes play freely through it, and protect its
unfortunate inmates from those pestilential fevers arising from
crowded and ill-ventilated rooms. It is quadrangular, each side
being about 300 feet long and fifty high, and encloses a central
square planted with shrubbery, and watered by a handsome
fountain. It can contain 5000 prisoners, and had more than 1000.
The style of its architecture is simple but grand; and although
unenclosed by walls, and built with a chief care for the health of
the inmates, its strongly ironed windows and doors, and large
guard of soldiers, afford ample testimony of its security. It is said,
its erection did not add to the expenses of the city; that it was built
by the labor of the convicts, and with funds, which, before the
administration of Tacon, had been dishonestly appropriated by
the civil officers, and of which he deprived them.

As I strolled with a friend to view it, and to enjoy the sea air
from the rocks on the coast, I passed a long shed near to the
prison, under which about a hundred convicts were busily employed in breaking stone. They were under a guard of soldiers,
and seemed very attentive to their work, perhaps from the dread
of a heavy whip, which an overseer held in his hand. All did not
have the chains generally worn by them; but these may have
been confined for lesser crimes. Continuing my walk, I passed
close to the old Castillo de la Punta, the spot where the day
before, a soldier had been shot by order of a court-martial, for
burglary with threatening to take life. Two regiments were paraded
on the occasion; and the criminal, who was permitted to choose
the manner of his death, between the garrot and the balls of his
comrades, selected the latter. The bloody turf had been upturned,
but many traces of the execution still remained on the blood-
stained chips and other rubbish around the spot.

Military executions are not unfrequent; and when it is recollected that the soldiers are all from old Spain, often fresh from
scenes of murder and robbery, in which perhaps not a few of
them have participated, the strict discipline to which they are
subjected in Cuba, will be felt indispensable. It was but last winter
that a small guard with their officer, who had been sent from
Matanzas to relieve the garrison of a fort near by, on the bay,
deserted in a body, officer and men turning robbers. An unfortunate party they met were roughly handled; a small lad belonging

to it, having had his fingers wantonly cut off by one of the soldiers. Their brigand career was, however, a brief one, for they were soon all captured.

Near the spot where the soldier had been shot, was the post to which the garrot is fixed when required for use. This instrument consists of an iron semi-circle to fit the front of the neck, which is placed in it; while behind, a screw, on the principle of those used in copying letters, presses against the first vertebra, near its junction with the skull. By a sudden turn the iron crushes the bone and spinal chord, near the point where the latter joins the brain, the medulla oblongata. Death produced in this manner, and that caused by the bursting of the heart, or rather of the arch of the aorta, as in aneurism of that vessel, are the only two which are sudden, and in which consequently but a momentary pang is felt. It is preferable to hanging, which, although intended to crush the spinal chord by means of the dental process of the second vertebra, often from want of skill in the adjustment of the rope, destroys life by the lingering and painful process of suffocation. . . .

No statistics of crime have ever been officially published, but the following informal report will give data by which the aggregate may be roughly calculated. In here giving the number of criminals confined in the Havana prison in 1842, it must be premised that many are brought from a distance, and that it includes all within the jurisdiction of the capital, a population of 631,760: the greater number from the ignorant population of the country.

Accused of	Whites	Colored	Total
Murder	11	38	49
Wounding	86	152	238
Robbery	132	137	269
Forgery & passing counterfeit money	14	7	21
Carrying prohibited arms	24	122	146
Quarrels (reyertas)	68	46	114
Inebriety and riot	74	83	157
Serious injury	50	56	106
Rape and ravishment	12	4	16
Adultery	4	0	4
Uncontrollable anger (servicia)	1	0	1
Prohibited games	44	31	75
Vagrancy	33	10	43
Deserters from those condemned to hard labor	17	19	36
Deserters from the army	35	0	35

Non-observance of police laws	180	282	462
Suspected of various transgressions	192	191	383
Minor offenses	108	64	172
Sent to prisons or other jurisdictions	45	62	107

From this number must be deducted 107 sent to the prisons of the jurisdictions where the crimes were committed; also the convict deserters and the soldiers, 71. Of the 383 suspected persons, it is calculated that 288 at least will be found innocent, for persons in Cuba are often imprisoned on very slight grounds of suspicion. The 462 arrested for non-observance of police laws, cannot be classed among criminals, and added to the preceding, make the number 928 to be deducted from the total, leaving 1506 criminals.

The same year, 19 lunatics were confined in the prison until proved fit subjects for the Lunatic Asylum, making the total 2453; that for 1841, was 2551, at the end of which year 482 remained confined, and at the end of 1842, only 287, showing a decrease in crime. The following table shows the comparative number of particular crimes in the two years.

	1841	1842	Diminution
Accused of murder	74	49	25
Accused of wounding	340	238	102
Accused of robbery	372	269	103
Rape and ravishment	21	16	5
Incendiaries	5	5	0

Let us follow the author of the above table, for which I am indebted to the Noticioso y Lucero de la Habana, and see the final destiny of those incarcerated in 1842.

Liberated	1512
Confined for correction and hard labor	202
Condemned to hard labor alone	329
Deserters sent to their garrisons	69
Sent to Casa Beneficencia	21
Sent to the Lunatic Asylum	19
Sent to the Section of Industry of the Soc. Econ.	2
Died in the hospital	7
Executed	5
Remaining	287

The following curious comparative statistic of crime and education, reported in 1837 to the Patriotic Society, by the Captain-General, is not without interest. Of 888 prisoners in the Cabanas, 494, charged with grievous offenses, had not had even a primary education: to which may be added, 239 sick prisoners sent to the hospital San Juan de Dios, making the total 1127 persons accused of crime. The 4407 scholars in Havana and its suburbs, compared to the accused, give a per centage of 26, and to the 1105 convicted in the capitania-general, give 25 per cent. The same comparison between the scholars and prisoners, gave for Cuba [Santiago] 24 per cent., Baracoa 28 per cent., Jiguani 21 per cent., Bayamo 5 per cent., and for San Juan de los Remedios 20 per cent. The greater number of the prisoners in these places had not received even a primary education.

Let the reader compare the foregoing with the statistics of crime in countries, where the forms at least of religion are generally observed, and ample means of education are free to all. Let him also recollect that persons are arrested in Cuba for many acts which are often committed with impunity in the United States,— the carrying of concealed weapons, and other offenses which a depraved public opinion permits, if it does not encourage, in our country. Let him then contemplate the miserable police system of Cuba, and mingle with the people during their festivals, the heterogeneous masked crowds of the Carnival, where almost unlimited freedom is allowed; let him travel alone through districts, once the domain of the robber and the assassin, now safe as the highways of the most civilized country in Europe; let him compare the amount of crime in Cuba with its population and its preventive means, and he will discredit many of the popular aspersions on the character of the Creole.

Two chief causes contribute to the present peace of Cuba. Intoxication is very rare, the dormant passions are not aroused by it; and the laws are enforced. With all the corruption of the bench in Cuba, the murderer very seldom escapes from punishment; and so well is justice administered in certain cases, that foul excrescence on civilization, and most deliberate defier of the laws of God, the duellist, receives no mercy, and the crime is now *unknown* on the island.

Nor are the intelligent of Cuba idle lookers on the moral condition of their fellow-citizens. Unremitting efforts are made to improve it by encouraging industry in the youth. The section of

Industry and Commerce [Sociedad Economica] has made a grati-
fying report to the society, so often referred to, on the subject of
apprenticeship, for 1842. They have already snatched from vagrancy 1411 boys, and placed them in situations to learn trades
and the arts; of these, 257 were bound in 1842. It is also a chief
object with this section, to see to the interests of the apprentice,
and truly have their labors been great. During the past year they
adjusted 621 quarrels between the masters and the indented, and
their parents or trustees; and so satisfactory were their decisions
to both parties, that only five of the disputes were referred to a
magistrate. Of the whole number indented, 72 have become
masters of their trades, and are now working for themselves; 84
changed masters by mutual consent; 11 died; 159 absconded, but
153 of these were retaken and returned to their occupations. In
all, only 50 were lost, many of these having been removed by
their own parents or trustees; 14 were sent to the work-shops of
the Lanceros as a punishment; and 32 have been arrested by
different peace-officers for public offenses. Notwithstanding all
these difficulties, the section continues to be sanguine of success,
and the report of their secretary, Senor Garcia, breathes a spirit
of patriotism and benevolence highly honorable to his feelings as
a man and a Christian. The philanthropist will rejoice to learn that
the different branches of the Sociedad Economica, established
throughout the island, imitate the example of the parent society,
and that in several other cities their reports have been favorable.

Richard Henry Dana, Jr.
To Cuba and Back: A Vacation Voyage
(Boston: Ticknor and Fields, 1859), 191–95

Dr. Howe had seen the Presidio, the great prison of Havana, once; but was desirous to visit it again; so he joined me,
under the conduct of our young friend, Senor ———, to visit that
and the hospital of San Juan de Dios. The hospital we saw first. It
is supported by the government—that is to say, by Cuban revenues—for charity patients chiefly, but some, who can afford it,
pay more or less. There are about two hundred and fifty patients.
This, again, is in the charge of the Sisters of Charity. As we came
upon one of the Sisters, in a passage-way, in her white cap and

cape, and black and blue dress, Dr. Howe said, "I always take off my hat to a Sister of Charity," and we paid them all that attention, whenever we passed them. Dr. Howe examined the book of prescriptions, and said that there was less drugging than he supposed there would be. The attending physicians told us that nearly all the physicians had studied in Paris, or in Philadelphia. There were a great many medical students in attendance, and there had just been an operation in the theater. In an open yard we saw two men washing a dead body, and carelessly laying it on a table, for dissection. I am told that the medical and surgical professions are in a very satisfactory state of advancement in the island, and that a degree in medicine, and a license to practice, carry with them proofs of considerable proficiency. It is always observable that the physical and the exact sciences are the last to suffer under despotisms.

The Presidio and Grand Carcel of Havana is a large building, of yellow stone, standing near the fort of the Punta, and is one of the striking objects as you enter the harbor. It has no appearance of a jail without, but rather of a palace or court; but within, it is full of live men's bones and of all uncleanness. No man, whose notions are derived from an American or English penitentiary of the last twenty years, or fifty years, can form an idea of the great Cuban prison. It is simply horrible. There are no cells, except for solitary confinement of "incomunicados,"—who are usually political offenders. The prisoners are placed in large rooms, with stone floors and grated windows, where they are left, from twenty to fifty in each, without work, without books, without interference or intervention of any one, day and night, day and night, for the weeks, months or years of their sentences. The sights are dreadful. In this hot climate, so many beings with no provision for ventilation but the grated windows—so unclean, and most of them naked above the waist—all spend their time in walking, talking, playing, and smoking; and, at night, without bed or blanket, they lie down on the stone floor, on what clothes they may have, to sleep if they can. The whole prison, with the exception of the few cells for the "incommunicados," was a series of these great cages, in which human beings were shut up. Incarceration is the beginning, middle and end of the whole system. Reformation, improvement, benefit to soul or body, are not thought of. We inquired carefully, both of the officer who was sent to attend us, and of a capitan de partido, who was there, and were positively assured that the only distinction among the prisoners was determined by the money they paid. Those who can pay nothing, are left to the worst. Those who can pay two reals (twenty-five cents) a day, are placed in wards a little higher and better. Those who can pay six reals (seventy-five cents) a day, have better places still, called the "Salas de distincion," and some privileges of walking in the galleries. The amount of money, and not the degree of criminality, determines the character of the punishment. There seems to be no limit to the right of the prisoners to talk with any whom they can get to hear them, at whatever distance, and to converse with visitors, and to receive money from them. In fact, the whole scene was a Babel. All that was insured was that they should not escape. When I say that no work was done, I should make the qualification that a few prisoners were employed in rolling tobacco into cigars, for a contractor; but they were very few. Among the prisoners was a capitan de partido (a local magistrate), who was committed on a charge of conniving at the slave-trade. He could pay his six reals, of course; and had the privileges of a "Sala de distincion" and of the galleries. He walked about with us, cigar in mouth, and talked freely, and gave us much information respecting the prison. My last request was to see the garrotte; but it was refused me.

James Williams Steele
Cuban Sketches
(New York: G. P. Putnam's Sons, 1881), 150–52

During all my residence in Cuba, watching as vigilantly as I might the drift of events, I have never known a man who had money to suffer capitally, though they sometimes remain a long time in confinement. There has always been a terrible drag in their cases, but they finally went free. But I have seen the swift punishment of negroes, Chinamen, and the general scum. The consciences of the officials are duly awakened when they can afford to make an example of somebody. When a negro who has killed an overseer one morning is led out and shot the next, when you may go out in the street and take the census of the chain-gang and find in one division of it sixty Chinamen, eighteen negroes, and no white men, and when you know at the same time half a dozen men who have testified absolutely to the intentional and premeditated killing of people before the fiscal, and know that the subjects of this uncontradicted testimony went free, and when this kind of thing passes under your observation for years, and nobody ever denies it, and everybody considers it a matter of course, it begins to seem as though there were a peculiar fatality in color and accompanying poverty.

I have mentioned a chain-gang. It is the Spanish penitentiary, and the lineal descendant of the galleys. The prisoners are used in the making of roads, and in general public slavery. They are usually chained in couples, otherwise the prisoner usually carries his leg-chain over his shoulder, or slung to his waist, and has his ulcerated and iron-eaten ankle wrapped in rags. They go clanking along the streets, and it seems as though you were never out of hearing of the horrible tinkling. Punishment for crime is undoubtedly necessary, but a system which parades its chained, beaten, half-starved, ragged, and squalid penitents in gangs upon the streets does not seem the best system. But it is better than the galleys.

Since the beginning of the Cuban [Ten Years] war, the course of criminal justice has drifted almost entirely into the military courts. These are institutions entirely to the liking of the rulers of the island, who are soldiers. Civilians do not understand them. Their course of justice is of the "drum-head" order, so swift that there is no time for question or appeal. It is a good way to be rid of bad men. Death and the chain-gang end all. Its sessions are secret, and its members not in any way responsible to the rest of mankind. For years all offenses criminal have had their adjudication between two rows of colonels, captains, and lieutenants sitting at a table behind closed doors.

V

Church, State, and Religion

Abiel Abbot
Letters Written in the Interior of Cuba
(Boston: Bowles and Dearborn, 1829), 15–17, 69–72

The ecclesiastical state of this important and opulent island, develops itself to a stranger gradually, by facts, some of which are freely reported on Spanish authority, as well as on European and American. A very singular fact in a Catholic country, holding the celibacy of the clergy as indispensable, is, that most of the padres have families; and few of them are bashful on the subject, or think it necessary to speak of their housekeeper as a sister or cousin, or of the children that play about the house, as nephews and nieces. They even go further, and will sometimes reason on the subject, and defend habits contrary to the ecclesiastical authority, upon principles of nature and common sense. Certainly an unnatural and unscriptural imposition, which is so unblushingly evaded, should not be attempted to be enforced; but should be revoked. The fearless violation of one law of a community weakens the authority of the whole statute book.

Of some of the padres, the morals, in other respects, are quite as glaringly corrupt, as in the particular just mentioned. They are bold, eager, and contemptible gamblers. They go from the table to mass, and from mass to the table; and I do not speak on light authority, not without unquestionable examples, when I say, that some have been known to *delay* mass, to see the end of a cock fight, and to pit their own cock against the cock of any slave in the circle who has an ounce or a real to lay on his head. . . .

There are two distinct codes of laws, which govern the island, the civil and ecclesiastical. By the latter, baptism is required of blacks and whites. In regard to foreigners, however, this law is not rigidly enforced. Neglect is winked at, and passes *sub silentio*. The padres, the best of them, stand ready to give certificates of Christian character, without much examination into faith or manners, more especially if the applicant has subscribed to the building of the city or village church. Pecuniary evidence is highly satisfactory, and with many weighs heavier than *judgment, faith, and the love of God.* The padres have an interest in baptism, receiving seventy five cents fee, a part of which goes to the bishop, and the rest is their perquisite. And this is very considerable when whole plantations are baptized. There is a season of the year, I know not which, when for a few days they are entitled to but three bits, that is, half price. If, however, the prudent planter would avail himself of this economy, the padre is usually *mal*, indisposed, or engaged in another direction. Some planters, who wish to conform to the law, and yet do it prudently, have a negotiation with the padre; and he performs the service by job and at a discount.

While many of the padres fully deserve the censures lavished upon them, some are said to be amiable, and in general correct and respectable men. I hear the bishop of Havana spoken of in terms of high respect. His princely income is munificently expended in mercy, and in beautifying the city, where he resides. He is said to be a man of liberal views; too much so to suit the high toned feeling of ecclesiastics at home and in the colony. He has been once recalled; but the sentiment of the community was in his favor, and certificates from physicians that it would be dangerous to his health to remove, have preserved him to the diocese. His name is Juan Diaz de Esplando. . . .

I sallied out to witness the scene in the church, and to join in the devotion, so far as a Protestant conscientiously might, and on a consecrated spot at least to be devout in my own way. I have been analyzing my motives for going: and possibly, *curiosity*, a *desire* to form an equitable idea of Catholic worship, that I might do it no injustice in my thoughts, or my descriptions, and the love I feel for a house of God, and for anything, which can seem sincere worship of the Supreme Being, all entered into a complex motive, which carried me abroad so early, for it was yet dark, when I reached the church. The doors were not yet opened, and I surveyed the exterior, and measured as well as I could, its length and breadth. It is larger than I had judged it to be. The length of the building is about 135 feet. This measure, however, includes the appendage to the west end, which is, I suppose, the residence of the priests, as well as the vestry. . . .

Over the centre is a concave, and a semi-concave on three sides. There is nothing elegant in the material or finish of the exterior, nor of the interior, except that the altars are with gorgeous ornaments; twisted pillars, adorned with brass or gold leaf. Over a side altar, I observed a small glazed recess, the shrine of the Virgin, I believe in wax. In two recesses or niches, with splendid apparel, were two saints . . . ; one, patron saint of the city, with a mitre and a crosier, and the other, with something like a crown. It was still dark when I entered the church, and I passed a devotee near the door, the only one arrived. He was contemplating a painting of the Saviour, I think as baptized of John; and stood crossing himself, with much appearance of mental prayer. Soon after, he advanced to a picture of the Virgin, and his devotions were renewed, and near that spot, he sunk on his knees. An attendant came in, and from a lamp burning in the centre of the church, lighted two wax tapers, and set them on the front altar. Worshippers began to come in, and I recognized the faces of most whom I had seen there before, which led me to think that they were nearly the same individuals, who always attend. The old men were the same, and some of the women. Three negro boys, well dressed, came in and kneeled on their handkerchiefs; after awhile, they rose, and went near a side altar, and kneeled again, and in the most solemn part of the service, they advanced beyond all others, and kneeled on the step leading towards the front altar, where the priest was officiating. A black woman decently dressed, advanced far, and kneeled; rose and kneeled again close to a side altar, and after service, if I was not mistaken in the individual, she was full ten minutes kneeling and confessing to a priest. Several ladies came in and kneeled on rugs, spread by a servant, who kneeled behind them. Some of them had prayer books in which they read; and then, closing them, clasped their hands, looking to the altar and cross, as if in mental prayer. The countenances of several, which I had seen in church before, were those of sincere and intense devotion. I saw none that came in without crossing themselves, and most of them, after touching the holy water; the first that I mentioned, who was alone in the church when I entered, made sundry applications to the font, and then to his crown, and face and breast. The service was . . . short

and inaudible; full of genuflections, bending of the body, oscula-
tion of the altar, elevation of the host, and parting of the hands, as
the priest turned and looked at the people.

After the service was closed, the officiating priest retired into
the vestry and returned in a black gown and sat in one of the
confessionaries. The negro, just mentioned, was the first to confess, was long and earnest, resting her hand against the side of
the confessionary, holding a shawl up, as if to prevent being seen
and heard. She applied her mouth to a tin plate full of small holes
or perforations, as of a grater, on one side, and the priest his ear
of the other. When she retired, several were in waiting, kneeling
near by, and one or two of them reading in their prayer book. But
the priest beckoned an infirm old man, and he approached and
kneeled on his footstool in front. The priest rested his hand on
the penitent's shoulder, and their heads being near together, a
short confession was made, and I presume, absolution given, as
he was one of two only, who kneeled a little while after, at the side
altar, and received the wafer. As soon as he retired, an elderly
woman kneeled at the side of the confessionary, and was soon
dismissed. A young lady then kneeled, with her face turned to the
wall; but the priest for the present, neglecting his office, beckoned
to an officer in partial uniform, several times. He, however, not
understanding his intention, or perhaps, wishing to decline confession, kept his place in the floor. The priest then descended
from the confessionary and reached out his hand to him, for a
pinch of snuff, which was readily granted, and he returned to
listen to the youthful and beautiful sinner, still patiently kneeling.

James Edward C. B. Alexander
Transatlantic Sketches
(2 vols.) (London: Richard Bentley, 1833), I:338–41

Some think that the masses in the Havannah were excel-
lently performed, but I cannot say I am of that opinion; for instance, in repairing to a church in the morning, the senoras, in
their black dresses and mantillas, would come in and seat themselves on the floor on a mat, whilst their black slaves would kneel
behind them, and a few men, either old Spaniards or brown
monteros, would stand beside the pillars. A priest in flowing

robes, and preceded by two attendants bearing candles, would then advance to the altar, burn incense, and commence a chant, which was answered from the gallery in such a lively strain that one was more reminded of a concert-room than of the house of prayer. He would then hurry through the service in Latin, but so fast and so indistinctly that it was a perfect mockery, even if his auditors had understood the language, which they did not, though I believe some of the most devout of the female worshippers had a translation to assist them. During the pauses in the service I remarked smiles and conversation behind the fans, and I invariably retired from the scene, sincerely pitying those who, content with the mere ceremonials of religion, are not aware that these are altogether insignificant compared with its precepts.

The priests in the Havannah exceed four hundred in number, and appear to enjoy the good things of this life as well as their brethren elsewhere, for they generally look sleek and fat. Some of the elders, I remarked, were dignified in their appearance, but the greater number had a very sensual and unintellectual air about them. The Bishop of Havannah is a very superior personage, and expends his income of one hundred and ten thousand dollars in acts of charity, in beautifying the city, and repairing churches; his good deeds will embalm his memory, and, like the rose, he will leave a sweet savour even after his demise. But it would be well for the island, of which he is the brightest ornament, if, as the Spaniards say, he "would live a thousand years."

Some of the country priests employ their time honourably in instructing the youth of their parishes, and . . . if the priests of each parish would do the same, what reproachful examples of idleness, gambling, and cock-fighting would at once disappear, and the moral desert blossom luxuriantly; then an enlightened population would inhabit the rich valleys of Cuba, peace and prosperity would attend them, the lawless bands of ruffians who occupy the Sierras would be suppressed, and then there might be some hopes of free labour superseding that of slavery.

Many of the country padres are excessively idle and openly vicious, and a perfect disgrace to the church. I heard a liberal ecclesiastic lament over the sins of his brethren, and regret that marriage was not permitted in the church. Many of the padres have a handsome niece to keep their house in order, but it is better this than exciting the jealousy of husbands. One of these gallant priests, some time ago, had justly excited the indignation of a Spaniard by attentions in a quarter where he had no business; and as the priest alighted from his volante at a ball-room, he received a foot of steel between his ribs and perished on the spot.

Though the moral character of the bulk of the people is not high, yet they are fully aware what the clerical office ought to be, and that the hands of those who elevate the host and impart the sacred wafer should be unspotted and pure as ermine. What respect can a clergy be held in when they are too often bold and eager gamblers? From mass they go to the cock-pit, and from the cock-pit to mass, and sometimes delay the mass to see the end of a fight. They might be seen at Guanabacoa, in full canonicals, watching with intense interest a combat between a favourite cock and that of a negro slave, who had staked his money against that of the unworthy priest.

Of late years there has been a great decay of religion in Cuba. The writings of Voltaire and Rousseau have corrupted the people, made them indifferent to the Catholic religion, and given them no substitute. After the negro insurrection in St. Domingo, and the expulsion of the French from the island, they flocked to Cuba, sneered at the mental slavery of the Spaniards, as they termed it, and scoffed at religion in every shape. The young Dons became infected with the free-thinking of their visitors, and affected to despise the religion of their fathers.

John George F. Wurdemann
Notes on Cuba
(Boston: James Munroe and Company, 1844), 47–50, 164–67

The great wealth once possessed by the monks in Cuba is well known. They owned large tracts of the richest soil on the island, and their revenues from their plantations were very great. Their possessions within late years have all been confiscated, and with them their power has passed away. Most of them have left the island, their number in Havana, by the census of 1842, being reduced to one hundred and six, to which may be added one hundred and eighty-eight nuns—all that now remain of those once numerous bodies. Two of their establishments, St. Augustine and St. Domingo, have been converted into store-houses by the government for its use, and severe restrictions are imposed on all who still retain the order.

It must have required some glaring vices in these celibates, to encourage the government to seize on their long coveted wealth, and to have justified the measure in the eyes of a Catholic community. I have listened to many a scandalous tale, told by some of the older inhabitants of Havana, of the pranks these worthy sons of the church played in their days. The St. Augustine convent was so notorious for the joyous life its inmates led, that many young men of the first families entered it; not for the purpose of relinquishing the vanities of the world, but that they might enjoy them the more freely. The Belenites, especially, were celebrated for their great wealth, having a revenue of about a million dollars to be divided between twenty-two, of which their order consisted. One of my friends, who had dined with them, told me that they were excellent boon companions. The usual order of furnishing the table was, by the steward receiving from each monk a list of what he desired, so that the dishes were as various as their respective tastes; and as each daily invited his particular guests, and all sat down to a common table, the most fastidious could have his palate gratified.

Of all these numerous churchmen, who must once have swarmed in the city, but one or two may now occasionally be seen passing through the streets; his humility unaffected, and apparently his greatest care being to prevent his large shovel-shaped hat from being knocked off by the passing throng. Although their rich cane-fields and valuable coffee estates have long been advertised for sale by the government, few purchasers have as yet been found. Much of their landed property had been bequeathed to them for the express purposes of religion; and the fear that if bought by individuals, lawsuits might be instituted for its recovery by the heirs of the legators, has deterred persons from buying, for no faith is placed in the government substantiating the claims of the purchasers.

The church of San Felipe is the resort of the fashionable, and having seen service performed in the more humble edifice of Santa Clara, I took my seat the next Sunday among the worshipers of this. It was the anniversary of Santa Lucia, and the church was nearly half filled with gentlemen, among whom were a few military officers in rich uniforms. Not more than a dozen ladies were present; the rest of the females were colored, and there were only a few children. The central benches were occupied by the gentlemen alone, but the two races were not separated; and here, as in Santa Clara, the colored mostly were near the sacristy; one old woman, in a shabby attire, kneeling on the very steps, and almost touching the gown of the officiating priest.

During the performance of mass, two capuchins entered and sat down among the congregation, whispering and laughing with the gentlemen near them, but never failing to join in the crossing whenever the ceremony required it. Before its close, two colored men, attended by richly-liveried footmen, bearing silver baskets filled with engravings of Santa Lucia, passed among the worshipers, presenting to each person one, to myself among the rest; while two large bouquets of fresh flowers were given to two ladies near the altar, but why they were so distinguished I could not learn. A preacher now left the sacristy, where he had received the benediction of the priest, and entering the pulpit, addressed his auditors in an impassioned strain on the virtues of Santa Lucia. His actions were very graceful, and it was delightful to listen to his pure Castilian, which is never used here in conversation. The audience, both whites and colored, were very attentive, and all retained their places until he had finished. Nearly the whole now dispersed, and I was left with a few who lingered to offer a final prayer at the foot of a side-altar.

The embellishments of the interior of this church were in better taste, and the architecture more imposing than that of Santa Clara; but it contained no fine paintings or statues, on which the eye could delight to rest. Even the massive pillars and wide-sprung arches supporting the roof, had something rude in them, and seemed like abortive attempts at architectural beauty.

From their churches, one can always learn much of the past and present state of religious feeling in a people, and I resolved to visit one more, the Cathedral. It is situated near the mansion of the Captain-General, in the calle del Ignacio; and its towers and pillared front of discolored and worn stone, on which the hand of time had strongly impressed its age, reminded me of those Gothic monuments of bygone sacerdotal power, that arrest the attention of the traveller in almost every European town.

Its large doors were closed, but the clerk seeing me loiter about the porch, beckoned to me, and led me through the yard and sacristy into the interior. The *tout ensemble* here, was more imposing than that of any church I had seen in my own country. The ceiling and dome were ornamented by paintings in fresco, and ranged along the walls were many oil paintings, some well executed. Among these was one of St. Christophal, the patron saint of Havana, bearing on his shoulder an infant Jesus with a world in his hand. Another was a Maria Conceptionis, the patroness saint of the Cathedral, standing on the world and crushing the serpent's head with her heel. There was also one of the Virgin and her Child, offering an olive branch to several figures, who were in purgatorial flames at her feet; and in whose faces the feelings of hope, joy, and humility were severally well expressed. . . .

They can scarcely be said to pay any regard to the ceremonies of their religion, having a too poor opinion of their spiritual teachers to place any faith in their doctrines. The bible is, however, always an acceptable present to them, and, perhaps from its novelty, is greedily devoured. Tracts, that do not treat on sectarian points, are also received with readiness, and may with due caution be distributed with impunity; but if relating in the remotest degree to the institution of slavery, would subject the pseudophilanthropist to imprisonment and hard labor. A medical friend, who has taken up his residence in Cuba, chiefly from philanthropical views, was requested by a padre to operate for cataract on the eyes of one of his slaves. Desirous to improve every opportunity that was offered to distribute some tracts he had, he gave a few to the messenger who showed him the way to the padre. These, to his great annoyance, the man carried openly in his hand; but his anxiety greatly increased, when, on reaching the padre, they were submitted to his inspection, with the demand, if he could read them without injury to his spiritual welfare. The latter had no sooner seen them, than he suddenly left the room carrying the books with him; but my friend, who was as yet a stranger in Cuba, and had his brain filled with ideas of Spanish intolerance, soon had all his fears dissipated by the return of the padre, with a bundle of similar tracts in his hand, who assured the man that he could not read better books, and distributed the rest, which he had received from New York, to several other visitors. Yet this very son of the church, like nearly all his brethren in Cuba, was an opponent to the rules of celibacy, and had a large family living with him under the same roof; except in the vows of matrimony, obeying all its laws,—protecting a single woman, and maintaining her children. Nor do the island padres hesitate to defend their position, having only usurped a privilege, which some of the priesthood of Italy, Spain, and Germany have at different times petitioned the Pope to grant to them,—marriage.

In those parts of the island much traversed by strangers, and where many foreigners have settled, the padre is no longer seen at the cock-pit; but in the less frequented spots, like Puerto Principe, where the procession of the host still brings every one down on his knees, and the people are a century behind the present age, he is often found among the greatest betters on that debasing sport; an employment, it must, however, be acknowledged, not more unclerical than horse-racing and fox-hunting in England. The current anecdotes of their vices, and which are freely circulated by their own parishioners, if true, in many cases place them on a level with the lowest characters; still many are found among them, whose gentlemanly deportment, and devotion to their peculiar forms of worship, secure the love and respect of their flock, and who in other respects act the part of faithful pastors.

On the whole, there is more toleration of religious opinion here, than in many European Catholic communities; certainly far more than in those of Germany and Ireland. No one can hold property or practice any of the professions, without first acknowledging in writing that he is an Apostolical, Roman Catholic; but those who have tender consciences leave out the middle term, and it is winked at. The term *judio*, Jew, is also applied to foreigners, including Spaniards, more in jest than derision, and without any particular reference to its sectarian application: and I have not met with as much inimical feeling in the Creoles towards Protestants, as the sects of the latter manifest towards the Catholics in our northern states. The secret is, that the Cubans are not priest-ridden; they are in the same state that the French were under Charles X with a church establishment forced on them. But if tomorrow all hindrance to the preaching of other doctrines were removed in Cuba, her Roman Catholic clergy would be soon purified of many of their vices, and her churches, like those in France at the present time, be again filled with worshipers. No other nation can be pointed out, in which less of religious duties is publicly taught, and more order and obedience to the laws are observed. Were it open to all sects, Cuba would form a rich field for the missionary, but in her present condition all means to improve the morals of her people must be silent and covert.

Although at present the churches are thinly attended, there was a time when the ceremonies of their religion occupied much of the time of the Creole. In Havana alone, 525 festivals were celebrated annually in the 29 religious establishments that it possessed, besides vespers, ave Marias, masses, and sermons. In pomp and solemnity they were unrivalled by any in Europe; and that, like in Lima, more wax was consumed in candles for the churches of Havana in one month, than in other cities for the whole year, the wax being moreover of the finest quality, from Castile. The tithes collected in 1811, from the 42 parishes under the bishopric of Havana, amounted to $328,309; the income of the bishop was $38,333. From the same bishopric, $3,137,736 were collected in tithes in eight years, from 1813 to 1821.

Richard Robert Madden
The Island of Cuba
(London: C. Gilpin, 1849), 108–10

The state of religion in this island is most deplorable. Slavery, that contaminates every thing it touches, has not spared even the Church, or its ministers, in Cuba.

The clergy, in every slaveholding country that I have known, are incapable of exercising their ministry with advantage or effect. The Government would not suffer them to do so. The slaveholders would persecute and discredit them with the authorities, if they dared to do their duty as ministers of religion, preachers and teachers of justice, mercy, and purity of life. Woe betide the priest who should dare to admonish his flock to abstain from buying, or bidding for those slaves on the Lord's day! Woe betide the priest who should be so forgetful of the tender mercies of a captain-general, and so remindful of his duties to his God, as to exhort his flock to be obedient to the law of the land, that forbade the crime of the slave-trade! Woe betide the confessor, who might be so fearless of banishment, or so indifferent to the vengeance of authority, as to counsel a penitent in high office, who sold his connivance at slave-trading crimes, by the cargo, for ten dollars for every stolen man—to give the bribes he had received to the poor, and their rights to the robbed! Woe betide the priest, who thought so much of the people, and so little of an intendant's power, as to enjoin his parishioners to refrain from gambling in the lottery, or betting in the cock-pit, and thereby injuring, by his precept, the revenues of the Crown. I have asked priests, who were not lost to every sense of Christian duty, why they did not do some of these things, and the answer was—either a shrug, or a look towards heaven, or a mournful admission that they dare not do their duty; nay, one of them, a parish priest, referring to the subject of the partition of the fees for administering the sacraments that go to the State, said to me, in a tone which I cannot easily forget, and with all the solemnity of a man inwardly moved and grieved in his spirit:—"The system is so bad, that the very ministers at the altar must sell the holy things for money."

The royal hankering after Church Property, and the practice of providing for the needy nobility out of the funds set apart for the service of religion, have been indulged even in providing, still more amply in late years, out of those funds, for the titled beggars of the Spanish court. The pension for the Royal Order of Charles the Third was partly secured, by its august founder, by an assignment of 40,000 dollars on the tithe revenues of the cathedrals of the Indies; the amount levied on the part of the Havana, being 2,500 dollars—1,000 on the Mitre, and 1,500 on the Dean and Chapter.

The order of the Jesuits was extinguished in the Havana in 1767. The sale of their temporalities immediately followed. The property of this church sold for 30,000 dollars; the college for 25,900; and their other effects for 303,000 dollars—which went to Spain, to be applied towards the payment of the national debt. Altogether, church property contributes to the treasury 133,212 dollars a year—a sum equivalent to twenty per cent on the tithes and other church revenues.

Richard Burleigh Kimball
Cuba and the Cubans
(New York: Samuel Hueston, 1850), 152–57

Among the many reasons for sad reflection afforded by the present situation of the beautiful Queen of the Antilles, there is none so appalling as the low and wretched condition of religion. The seeds of infidelity which were so widely diffused through the world at the close of the last century, have been greatly checked within late years; and the Christian observer now rejoices daily more and more at the general extension of the Gospel influence. But in unhappy Cuba those fatal seeds seem to have found a more propitious nurture under the influence of depressing and deteriorating government; and nowhere therefore is presented a more dark and distressing picture of unbelief, corruption, and immorality.

Twenty-five years ago, if one happened to be an inmate of any respectable Cuban family, one would be sure to meet with religious practices and feelings which, even to a foreigner of a different creed, appeared cheering and grateful. At the hour of twilight, a church bell rung through the city would create every where a sudden and simultaneous excitement. It was the *"Angelus,"* and at its sound all persons, of all classes, would at once rise to say their evening prayers; children and servants would, at its conclusion, ask a blessing from their parents or masters; while every carriage and passenger would pause in the street, every workman would suspend his toil, and a general manifestation of religious reverence would be exhibited. In those days frequent sermons, from pious and eloquent preachers, would awaken the congregations that filled the churches to the solemn truths connected with their spiritual welfare; slaves and free blacks were instructed in the precepts of the Saviour, and the service of the temple was attended with devotion and decency.

At the present day, in all the churches of Cuba, a brief mass, scandalously hurried through, and witnessed by a very small portion of the inhabitants, is all that attests the Sabbath of the Lord. And even this poor and meagre performance of the solemn services of the church whose creed bears sway in the island, by whom and how is it attended? By few others than those who resort to it as a public place of meeting, gayety, and flirtation. The ladies ply the telegraphic fan and the same airs of coquetry and playfulness as they may have done the evening before at the theatre, or as they will probably do the same evening at the opera. The young gentlemen attend at the doors for the interchange of glances with their fair friends, and perhaps for a glimpse of the pretty ankles ascending the steps of the *volantes*, in waiting. All seem intent on showing, by their smiles and their undisguised disrespect, that they are neither believers, nor ashamed of their unbelief. In the church itself, are no expounding—no reading, even of the Gospel—no visits of the pastors—no consolations carried to the dying—none of the charitable communities that abound in other countries, both Catholic and Protestant.

Among the shopkeepers and artisans, is manifested the same utter disregard, not to say scorn, of the Christian Sabbath and the Christian faith; for with wide-open doors and windows, and on the public street, they pursue, without even the affectation of a difference, the customary employments of the week in labor or traffic.

But to explore further the moral results of the state of things thus imperfectly described, go to the aged head of a family, and behold him incapable of exercising any influence over his own offspring, who have never been taught the divine mission of Christ; to the neglected wife, who weeps over the cruel and mortifying treatment experienced from a depraved partner, and see her endeavoring to forget her griefs at public amusements, at cards, or elsewhere, ignorant of, because never taught, the only balm that can restore peace to the most embittered soul; to the injured husband, and there witness a similar hollow wretchedness of the heart, searching vainly for the relief he knows not how to search for aright; or, what is more probable, behold him plunged in the most deadly course of debauchery and vice.

Leaving the cities, go to the country, and see the poor African, condemned to a toil not less incessant than severe—doomed to remain forever sunk in the imbruted ignorance in which he was torn from his native and distant land—adoring a serpent—and encouraged to suicide, by the superstition which be believes, of the immediate return of his body to Africa after death. Few of them are baptized; scarcely any married; but they live together for the most part in the most disgusting habits of promiscuous intercourse; while none are ever instructed in the consoling and humanizing truths of the Gospel. Look farther around to the white laborer who commands the negro as overseer or *mayoral*, or who tills a piece of land, or who moves along the road with his cart or draught horses; look, too, at the countryman's family— and every where will be found the same indifference, and in general worse than indifference, the same sneering contempt of all that their ancestors revered as holy.

The gentry also—the masters of estates—the officers of government—nay, the very priests themselves—exhibit the same painful picture of an all-pervading, all-demoralizing infidelity. The country curates may, in general, and as a class, be set down as an example of all that is corrupt in immorality, all that is disgusting in low and brutal vice. Of the number there is one—Don Felix del Pino—too notorious, too illiterate, and too shameless to care for even this publication of his name, whose career presents so shocking and frightful an example of vice that I will mention a few of its characteristic traits, as a proof of what is possible in the island of Cuba at the present day. This man, who is the curate of an interior town, is in the habit of exacting $200 for an insignificant pretended attempt at the great ceremonies of a funeral. On one occasion, at a meeting of his low associates, he announced that he was preparing for a pleasure trip to the city of Havana, and in reply to their inquiries as to the pecuniary means on which he relied for that object, he simply answered, that a certain respectable old woman, whom he named, was on the eve of death, and that her funeral expenses would supply him the means. Having afterward ascertained that she was unexpectedly improving, he vowed that she *should* die, and hastened to her bedside, where, prostituting the rights of his sacred ministry, he labored to dissuade her from any hopes of recovery, and harassed her mind with such agonizing and terrible pictures, in such a tone, and with such evidently evil design, that the friends of the poor despairing sufferer felt compelled to interfere, and rescue her from his guilty hands. On another occasion he informed a couple who wished to marry, but whose family relation of consanguinity required a dispensation from Rome, that he could obtain the grant for that purpose at Havana. He therefore went to that city, and shortly afterward returned with the full license, as he pretended, to perform the marriage; to which, however, he insisted on naming the attesting witnesses, or the *godfather* and *godmother* of the ceremony. He accordingly married the parties, and received six hundred dollars as his reward. When the couple, at a later day, discovered that no such authority could be procured at Havana, and that they had been made the victims of a foul deception, they called on him and were met by a cool denial of his having had any thing to do in the matter; in support of which he exhibited his books, where he had carefully omitted to set down the case. He was, however, arrested for a time in consequence, but no more serious penalty ever ensued. His last act was one which, indeed, can hardly be credited, though its truth is beyond question. In a letter coarsely written, in the most obscene and revolting

language, to his brother in Havana, he expatiates on the violation
of a young white female, for whom he had paid to her own father,
and says that on the occasion of his first possession of her, he had
ordered the bells of his church to be rung! The signature of the
letter he acknowledged to be his; and the young girl, only thirteen
years of age, was found at his house, and the truth of the case so
fully proved by her testimony, and other corroborating evidences,
as to cause the imprisonment of the father, and the suspension of
the priest from the office so foully scandalized. Of course, it must
not be understood that there are many priests in Cuba who have
reached such a depth of corruption as is exhibited by this revolting and hideous instance; but the general degradation of the
clergy and the church, and the deep demoralization of the country where such a monster is not at once visited with signal
punishment, must be sad indeed. This wretch may, on the contrary,
be seen even now, though suspended from his parish cure, attending in his clerical robes on the public ceremonies of the
Church at Havana!

The responsibility of this dreadful state of things, in reference
to the religious and moral condition of the island of Cuba, should
not be considered as resting upon the Romish Church or creed. It
would be illiberal indeed to carry to so unjust a length those
prejudices of Protestantism which are doubtless founded in reason, and which cannot but be stimulated to a great degree at the
exhibition of Roman Catholicism in Cuba. Yet in the United
States no one can deny that it is a very different institution, both
in its spirit and its practice, from that which is presented to the
eye of the most superficial observer in Cuba. The Church proper
is not the responsible cause, but the corrupt political government
which has invaded its domain, paralyzed all its good energies,
corrupted its entire organization, and poisoned its very fountains
of spiritual purity. The central military despotism, in the hands of
the Spanish officials, clustered in and about the palace of the
captain-general, may be said to have absorbed to itself the Church,
with every other good institution possessed by the island in its
better days. Its influence has been destroyed, its revenues and
property, together with all the patronage of ecclesiatical appoint-
ments, appropriated by the government. The nominations to all
religious offices are made, directly or indirectly, *by* the creatures
of the government, and given, directly or indirectly, *to* the creatures of the government. The very members of the chapter of the

cathedral at Havana are now named at Madrid, in disregard of the canonical proposals from the board according to law. Day after day and year after year have been suffered to pass without an appointment to fill the long vacant bishopric of Havana, and thirty years have elapsed since the sacrament of confirmation, as it is termed by the Roman Catholics, has been administered in the several districts of the diocese, which should be regularly visited once a year.

John Glanville Taylor
The United States and Cuba
(London: Richard Bentley, 1851), 294–97

It is unnecessary perhaps to remind [my readers] that Cuba is, most strictly speaking, a Catholic country, though, its being a country of Catholics may be apocryphal enough; for I declare that during my whole residence, I do not know an instance of *men* going to church; and it is my firm belief that if they do, in other places where I have not been, and where perhaps good music (for one thing) may be heard, it is for other seasons rather than their attachment to the Catholic, or *any* religion. We see none of that superstitious or half idolatrous reverence for churches, padres, images, or Saints, that we read of as existing in countries like Peru, or even Mexico and Brazil, or under the Portuguese; and as for the procession of the Host, even it may pass unnoticed. I do not speak of Havana, for I have never been there. I see it is among the local printed ordinances of that city, that passengers should kneel to the "Viatico;" *that* perhaps may enforce it, but I doubt—. The only two "Padres" I knew were respected as the legal media for obtaining the celebration of the rites of matrimony and baptism; and otherwise, as right "jolly good fellows;" nothing more. As for *fasts*, it is a most remarkable matter, that in regard to the island of Cuba, the Pope, every year regularly goes through the form of granting a general indulgence on that score to all its inhabitants; giving them free leave to eat meat during the whole of Lent, and on every Friday throughout the year. As I do not imagine it would be any way more difficult to keep a fast there than in Italy, I confess I am at a loss to account for His Holiness' kindness in any other way than by supposing he "knows his neighbours' ways," and that in any case the "olla" would be cooked. In the meantime, the *Government* professes to be as strictly Roman Catholic as ever, and the Bible is rigorously inter- dicted at the Custom Houses, though if you get one ashore in your pocket, and thereafter possession of it is never noticed against you in any way. In the year 1837 or –8, I think it was, that the Spanish Government made great exertions to induce capital- ists and others to settle in Cuba, by, among other immunities, promising them ten years' exemption from ordinary taxes, and even after that, giving them more privileges than even the natives themselves. How many greedily availed themselves of this I need not say, and at the present moment perhaps the government rather regrets thus having filled the country with Americans and others, who might at any moment create the utmost confusion, and even go far to upset that very government itself. However, I was going to say, that in this manifesto of the Spanish Government, every settler is represented to be a Catholic, and in fact, "no others but Roman Catholics can be inhabitants of the island." This seems somewhat strange when one discovers it for the first time, after having lived, as was my case, more than a year, and completely settled myself, in the country, without knowing a syllable about it. The law further is, that "no one can be three months in the country without taking out a letter of domiciliation," and yet only a small majority of those I knew had done so. Those who had, had been forced to it, by threats from some connected with the law. They merely considered it a civil regulation, and that religion had nothing whatever to do with it, but that they had to conform to it, because it was the law of the land. Thus it is in a country so situated, having once taken the first step, *the rest must be gone through to match*; as for the morality of the thing, it in- volves some nice points, but having altogether done with the whole business, I do not care to discuss them; merely satisfied with warning my reader, who may perhaps be an intending settler, that such is the fact; but as I said before, no public demonstration of Catholicity is ever expected from strangers; indeed they are well known to be Protestants, in general, nor do *they* consider themselves any the less so, because the Government chooses to believe them otherwise.

Richard Henry Dana, Jr.
To Cuba and Back: A Vacation Voyage
(Boston: Ticknor and Fields, 1859), 237–43

No religion is tolerated but the Roman Catholic. Formerly the church was wealthy, authoritative and independent, and checked the civil and military power by an ecclesiastical power wielded also by the dominant nation. But the property of the church has been sequestrated and confiscated, and the government now owns all the property once ecclesiastical, including the church edifices, and appoints all the clergy, from the bishop to the humblest country curate. All are salaried officers. And so powerless is the church, that, however scandalous may be the life of a parish priest, the bishop cannot remove him. He can only institute proceedings against him before a tribunal over which the government has large control, with a certainty of long delays and entire uncertainty as to the result. The bishopric of Havana was formerly one of the wealthiest sees in Christendom. Now the salary is hardly sufficient to meet the demands which custom makes in respect of charity, hospitality and style of living. It may be said, I think with truth, that the Roman Catholic Church has now neither civil nor political power in Cuba.

That there was a long period of time during which the morals of the clergy were excessively corrupt, I think there can be no doubt. Make every allowance for theological bias, or for irreligious bias, in the writers and tourists in Cuba, still, the testimony from Roman Catholics themselves is irresistible. The details, it is not worth while to contend about. It is said that a family of children, with a recognized relation to its female head, which the rule of celibacy prevented ever becoming a marriage, was general with the country priesthood. A priest who was faithful to that relation, and kept from cockfighting and gambling, was esteemed a respectable man by the common people. Cuba became a kind of Botany Bay for the Romish clergy. There they seem to have been concealed from the eye of discipline. With this state of things, there existed, naturally enough, a vast amount of practical infidelity among the people, and especially among the men, who, it is said, scarcely recognized religious obligations at all.

No one can observe the state of Europe now, without seeing that the rapidity of communication by steam and electricity has tended to add to the efficiency of the central power of the Roman Catholic Church, and to the efficacy and extent of its discipline. Cuba has begun to feel these effects. Whether they have yet reached the interior, or the towns generally, I do not know; but the concurrent testimony of all classes satisfied me that a considerable change has been effected in Havana. The instrumentalities which that church brings to bear in such cases, are in operation: frequent preaching, and stricter discipline of confession and communion. The most marked result is in the number of men, and men of character and weight, who have become earnest in the use of these means. Much of this must be attributed, no doubt, to the Jesuits; but how long they will be permitted to remain here, and what will be the permanent effects of the movement, I cannot, of course, conjecture.

I do not enter into the old field of contest. "We care not," says one side, "which be cause and which effect;—whether the people are Papists, because they are what they are, or are as they are because they are Papists. It is enough that the two things coexist." The other side replies that no Protestant institutions have ever yet been tried for any length of time, and to any extent, with southern races, in a tropical climate; and the question—what would be their influence, and what the effect of surrounding causes upon them, lies altogether in region of conjecture, or, at best, of faith.

On the moral habits of the clergy, as of the people, at the present time, I am entirely unable to judge. I saw very little that indicated the existence of any vices whatever among the people. Five minutes of a street view of London by night, exhibits more vice, to the casual observer, than all Havana for a year. I do not mean to say that the social morals of the Cubans are good, or are bad; I only mean to say that I am not a judge of the question.

The most striking indication of the want of religious control is the disregard of the Lord's Day. All business seems to go on as usual, unless it be in the public offices. The chain-gang works in the streets, under public officers. House-building and mechanic trades go on uninterrupted; and the shops are more active than ever. The churches, to be sure, are open and well filled in the morning; and I do not refer to amusement and recreations; I speak of public, secular labor. The Church must be held to some responsibility for this. Granted that Sunday is not the Sabbath. Yet, it is a day which, by the rule of the Roman Church, the

English Church in England and America, the Greek Church and other Oriental Churches—all claiming to rest the rule on Apostolic authority, as well as by the usage of Protestants on the continent of Europe—whether Lutherans or Calvinists—is a day of rest from secular labor, and especially from enforced labor. Pressing this upon an intelligent ecclesiastic, his reply to me was that the Church could not enforce the observance—that it must be enforced by the civil authorities; and the civil authorities fall in with the selfishness and gratifications of the ruling classes. And he appealed to the change lately wrought in Paris, in these respects, as evidence of the consistency of his Church. This is an answer, so far as concerns the Church's direct authority; but it is an admission either of feeble moral power, or of neglect of duty in times past. An embarrassment in the way of more strictness as to secular labor, arises from the fact that slaves are entitled to their time on Sundays, beyond the necessary labor of providing for the day; and this time they may use in working out their freedom.

Another of the difficulties the church has to contend with, arises out of negro slavery. The Church recognizes the unity of all races, and allows marriage between them. The civil law of Cuba, under the interpretations in force here, prohibits marriage between whites and persons who have any tinge of black blood. In consequence of this rule, concubinage prevails, to a great extent, between whites and mulattoes or quadroons, often with recognition of the children. If either party to this arrangement comes under the influence of the Church's discipline, the relation must terminate. The Church would allow and advise marriage; but the law prohibits it—and if there should be a separation, there may be no provision for the children. This state of things creates no small obstacle to the influence of the Church over the domestic relations.

John Milton Mackie
From Cape Cod to Dixie and the Tropics
(New York: G. P. Putnam, 1864), 253–55

I am sorry to be obliged to represent the Cubans as not very diligent churchgoers. In the mother country, the Spaniards are much more exemplary in the performance of the duty of attending mass and vespers; often filling not only all the seats, but even the aisles of their churches. But, on the island, the sacred edifices contained, whenever I visited them, but a paltry handful of worshippers, and always presented on the marble floors abundant space for the servants to spread the broad carpets and cushions of their mistresses. Generally, the congregations consisted one half of Africans, who are not here compelled to pray in a corner, as in our Northern churches; but who, on the contrary, often occupy the very foremost places before the altars. Always well dressed, the blacks sometimes come to church in great state even. One strapping wench I remember to have seen in a chapel, making herself conspicuous, directly in front of the high altar, on a cushion which had been brought to her for that purpose by a most respectful black boy. Being dressed in a fine pineapple, a lace mantilla, and embroidered skirt, wherein she seemed to take as much delight as if it had been bought off the altar, she sat there apparently enjoying the unction of extreme comfort and self-satisfaction. Her fan, which was opened and shut at the end of each ave and pater with all the air of a fashionable belle, was about as gay as any Senora's at opera or *paseo*. There appeared to be only one little mistake about her—her fashionable hoop had been put on backside foremost.

It was in the freshness of the early morning, and before the rays of the sun had become potent enough to require the protection of an umbrella, when I went, for the first time, to the cathedral. At that hour, the quiet of the place was not much disturbed by worshippers; and it was pleasant to stroll through the different parts of this collection of venerable edifices, hearing the music of the chant in the remotest courts, and the echoes of the organ repeated along all the corridors. In some of these inner court-yards tall trees were growing, and water was trickling from ancient fountains; while here and there were to be seen a few plants and flowers. In the course of my walk through the buildings, I observed some priests praying, some receiving confessions, some promenading and chatting, and others eating and smoking. . . .

The churches, it may be added, opened here every morning and evening to all persons who may be disposed to come in from the purpose of offering up their prayers, and much more accessible than in our Protestant States, where the sacred doors remain closed six days out of seven, and where, even then, the congregation is shut up in pews, located according to the color of the skin, and the monetary value of the worshippers.

Samuel Hazard
Cuba with Pen and Pencil
(Hartford: Hartford Publishing Company, 1871), 117–19

If the old adage be true, that "the nearer the church the farther from God," then I fear much the Habaneros have no hope of future salvation; for to almost every square in the old city, within the walls, there seems to be a church of some kind, to many of which are attached religious societies or organizations.

The priesthood and the church have probably a greater share in the life of the Cubans, particularly with the female portion, than anything else that goes to make up the sum of their simple daily life; and as one strolls along the street, he is met at almost every turn by some priest of some particular order, either in shovel or three-cornered hats, or, perhaps, like a stout old Franciscan,— whose vows prevent him from having anything *comfortable* in this world,—forced by the heat of the sun to forget his resolution of baring his head to the elements, and sporting an enormous palm-leaf, that answers the purposes of both hat and umbrella. I was considerably interested, after a while, in studying out the peculiarities of the wearers of the different hats, and I finally came to the conclusion that the shovel hats were a badge of good living,— for nearly all their wearers were stout, jovial, hearty looking priests,—while the three-cornered ones had a young, thin, unfed, Oliver-Twist-like look about them (though these hats all have their particular meanings, according to the order to which they belong).

The superior authority of the secular portion of the Cuban church is the Captain-General, as Vice Royal Patron, and as his deputy in the Arch-bishopric of Cuba, the Commanding General of the eastern department. There are attached to the church a number of dignitaries of different grades, all drawing salaries in proportion to their rank; while the government of the church is divided into four vicarages and forty-one parishes, the grand Cathedral being situated in the town of Santiago de Cuba. Besides the churches actual, there are a number of convents, monasteries, etc., belonging to the different orders of St. Domingo, San Francisco, Jesuits, San Augustine, etc., etc.

The Cuban church, in comparison with that of other countries is said to be poor, especially in the Arch-bishopric, the temples needing the magnificence and those church ornaments that the traveler on the continent of Europe admires so much. Notwithstanding, in some of the principal towns there are a few imposing structures, interesting from their great antiquity and ancient style of architecture, while upon special occasions the services carried on are tolerably rich and imposing.

There is a regular tariff of prices to be charged for all such ceremonies as in a more Christian land are thought to belong to the duties connected with the church. A baptism, for instance, for one dollar upwards; a burial five dollars; and marriages, masses, and prayers for purgatoried souls in proportion,—the poor being attended to without charge.

Richard J. Levis
Diary of a Spring Holiday in Cuba
(Philadelphia: Porter and Coates, 1872), 78–80

In the street in front and at the door of the cathedral were rows of music-stands, and a military band came up, and played some beautiful operatic selections, and I sat on the steps, enjoying at least this part of the religious ceremonies. After this was over the band entered the church, and I sat observing with curious interest the varied styles, ranks, castes, and colors of people as they arrived. The ladies came with bare heads, or were covered with veils, and many were followed by servants who carried chairs for them to sit on, and also handsome rugs to kneel on.

The day is Palm Sunday, and some unusual performances, including an abundant display and distribution of palm branches are in order; but besides the religious display the day has not the air of a Sabbath, for business goes on as usual, and some laborers are engaged in repairing the street, even in front of the church.

Within the church the congregation were generally standing or kneeling, and I walked around looking at the paintings and the stained glass of the windows. People were mingled miscellaneously in their worship, and I was impressed with the extremes of complexion—very dark white people and very light negroes—and came to the conclusion that color alone will not go very far in the distinctions of races on this island. . . .

There was much ceremonious performance in the church, which was led off by a fat priest, who perspired profusely under his exertions and the burden of his robes. One of the devotees offered me a piece of palm leaf, which I accepted without any increase of devotional feeling, and I strolled off, ruminating on the antithesis of religion as a faith and religion as a life practice—on creeds versus conduct.

Antonio C. N. Gallenga
The Pearl of the Antilles
(London: Chapman and Hall, 1873), 155–56

Even the State religion, such as it is, has no hold whatever on the masses. In towns like Manzanillo, Cienfuegos, Sagua, or Villaclara, numbering from 12,000 to 15,000 inhabitants, there is only one church with three priests. Those who are acquainted with the rites of the Roman Catholic Church well know that three priests could not, even by superhuman efforts, administer the sacraments to one hundredth part of their flocks. In an Italian town of the same size and population, there would be a bishop, one or more chapters of fat canons, a seminary, at least 300 priests, and half-a-dozen monastic communities of both sexes. Whether too few or too many priests should be considered the greater evil I would not take upon myself to decide; and certainly the Cubans do not complain of their scanty allowance of religious instructors. At Santiago there is an archbishop who is "Primate of all the Indies," a whole hierarchy, and an incessant ringing of bells; yet one hears nothing but evil reports of the priests, who, like the lay functionaries, are mostly Spaniards bent on making money, and enjoying life, and anxious to go back to the Mother Country with the spoils of the Colony. A planter near Cienfuegos, the other day, visited with some misgivings as to his duties, wished to have the small fry of his negroes baptized. It was time, he thought, that the poor Africans should cease to be brought up like dumb cattle, and it was well that they should be made Christians before they aspired to be free men. The priest who performed the ceremony claimed the fee of one gold ounce ($17, or 3.8s) for each of the christened children; and enforced payment; but the result was to deter other slave-owners from bringing their *cria*, or negro nursery, to the font; so that the little Africans will grow up as unmitigated heathens as their fathers have been before them. It is easy to say that so venal and debased a religion is no better than no religion at all; but no religion in Cuba is tantamount to no instruction and no morality.

Alexander Gilmore Cattell
To Cuba and Back in 22 Days
(Philadelphia: Press of the Times, 1874), 33–35

Although not expecting that in Havana there would be the strictest observance of the Sabbath, we were somewhat surprised to find the day so generally disregarded; apparently there was no suspension of business amongst the cafes and retail stores, and a greater portion of the wholesale establishments were not closed.

In the afternoon crowds flocked to the "Bull-fight," and at evening the Circus, Opera at "Theatre Tacon," and other amusements attracted large audiences: while services held throughout the day at the Cathedral and other Catholic Churches, were but slimly attended.

As advised, we attended "High Mass" at eight o'clock. On entering the Cathedral we found scarcely fifty worshipers, those mostly women and children, and at no time during the service did the number present exceed one hundred. Highly interesting to us was the pompous entrance of the wealthy, aristocratic families, preceded by their slave, bearing a costly rug, which, being spread on the marble floor, all would kneel upon it, the slave first arranging the ladies' trains.

We observed that rich and poor, black and white, knelt side by side, and well might other denominations emulate the noble example of the Catholic Church in thus exemplifying that "God is no respecter of persons."

Behind the altar rail were about a dozen priests, all of whom took part in the service. In the absence of a choir they chanted the responses with the accompaniment of a fine organ located in the gallery.

Just previous to the ceremony of "Elevating the host," a priest passed through the congregation motioning all to kneel, and touched upon the shoulder with his staff those who did not immediately comply.

Soon followed a sermon in Spanish, delivered with great rapidity and violent gesticulation, the speaker utterly failing, however, to command the attention of this audience. A brief ceremonial concluded what had impressed us as an exceedingly cold and lifeless service, so unlike Catholic worship in the United States. Later we visited Havana's most fashionable church, "La Merced." The exterior of this edifice is far from imposing, but the interior having recently undergone a thorough transformation, presented a bright and cheerful appearance in contrast with the other churches of the city; as at the Cathedral, a large majority of those present were ladies, some of them most elegantly dressed, all combining to form an interesting and attractive scene. Having understood that permission of the government had been granted a Baptist clergyman, residing at "Hotel San Carlos," to hold service in its parlor on Sundays, we proceeded there only to find that it had long since been discontinued, and we were confronted with the fact that on the Island of Cuba there was not a single place of Protestant worship.

Back again at our hotel we met some who with us were desirous of acknowledging the mercy and goodness of God, and assembling, as did the disciples of old, in an upper chamber, we realized the fulfillment of that precious promise. "Where two or three are met together in My name, there I will be in the midst of them."

While our recollections of the Sunday are not wholly unpleasant, we cannot forget how flagrantly the day was violated, and though seemingly a contradiction, we assert that there is no Sabbath in Havana. Thankful are we that our laws in this particular are so different; and may every attempt to destroy the sanctity of the Sabbath in the United States be most earnestly resisted.

James Williams Steele
Cuban Sketches
(New York: G. P. Putnam's Sons, 1881), 174–81

It is the old Church, the Church "Romana, Apostolica, Catholica," *the* Church as she is and was meant to be in southern Europe that holds sway in Cuba. The man who begs leave to exercise his wicked reason, and has the temerity to doubt a dogma, who fails to see the truth of a statement or the foundation for a pretense, cannot be otherwise than in some sense opposed to her. She has her will in most things, and takes no pains to conceal the fact that she considers a heretic already doomed, and that she will not believe him under oath. She pervades the land, and in a sense she owns it. She has an essential place in the police system, and is an ingredient and necessary part of everything.

I grieve to state, however, that notwithstanding all this, the Church in Cuba seems to be poor. Pecuniarily she has fallen upon these later and evil times in which dying sinners are not permitted by heirs peacefully to endow and die, even if they would. Her buildings, while many of them are venerable, are none of them palaces, and some of them are greatly in need of plaster and paint. Her vestments are cheap, her jewels are tawdry, the lace is cotton, the gold is brass.

The church edifice of the Cuban town, of the dilapidated character already alluded to, is a peculiar building within, though doubtless much like all others in Spanish America. Its most peculiar characteristic is a want of any thing that can truly be called magnificence, with a vast and futile attempt at something like it. There are, of course, no seats. The worshipers are not to be accommodated with the irreverent appliances of ease, but are expected, once for all, to bend their legs and keep them bent. This gives rise to a curious scene of every-day occurrence. Only women go to church as worshipers. The males usually attend for the purpose of seeing them worship. Each pious dame brings a little carpet, or rather a small-sized negro brings it for her. She kneels, but in the course of a few minutes sits. An ill-bred person would say, squats. Tired with the course of the ceremonial, she at length reclines. In the middle of the service the floor is strewn with a choice assortment of ladies' dress-goods with the ladies inside of them. At certain places in the ceremonial, it is necessary for everybody to place themselves again in a kneeling posture, and there is a general struggle to attain this end. To see two or three hundred women scrambling at once from a reclining to a kneeling position, has a tendency for the moment to destroy the solemn feeling one should have under the circumstances.

The ultramontane theology is fully illustrated by the decorations of the walls, especially the pictures. Some of these last are little less than horrible, both as a objects of worship and as works of art. . . .

Here and there through the building there are boxes with glass sides, and a candle burning within, transparently painted with skulls and cross-bones, and other mortuary emblems. I do not know what these death's-head lanterns are for, and frankly confess my ignorance of what they are called. But people crawl from one to the other on their knees, and pray to them, as they do to every other object in the building. There is a life-size image of the Man of Calvary, stretched upon his cross, dreadfully realistic in its representation of a dead man who has suffered torture. The knees are bloody and abraded, the wound in the side runs blood, and each scar made by nail and thorn and scourge is there. It is horrible. There is young Saint Sebastian, looking very smiling, with his body stuck full of arrows like a pin-cushion. There are a large number of Virgins, assorted sizes and moods, sad, glad, or merely complacent, for the wonderful woman has the faculty of being four or five hundred women at once, suiting herself to all climes and races. There are a dozen or so of the regular dried saint in glass cases, all bald, all clad in red and purple gowns, all having the general look of having been made in the same factory, after the same general model, and all producing the vague impression that if they are in heaven and look like that, one does not wish to go there.

At intervals stand the confessionals. These are wooden boxes, with a comfortable seat inside for the priest, and sides of perforated tin. At almost any hour, you may see some sin-stricken soul kneeling on the floor with her lips to the tin partition, pouring her iniquities into the ear of a red-faced priest. And here we arrive at the secret of the whole business, and obtain the key to the power of Roman Catholicism. The shames, crimes, and unhappiness that come to the ear of the Church, the causes for assassinations, jealousies, hatreds, suspicions; the secret springs and motives of life and society; the nameless things that mothers, husbands, and brothers do not know: all these things Mother Church knows. It was a shrewd invention of the fathers. By it she indeed holds the keys, and is infallible, if infallibility means not guessing, but knowing.

There is only one occasion, however, upon which the average male Cuban or Spaniard goes to confession. That is, when he is on the eve of matrimony. If he declines to do so, then the Church declines to marry him, and as there is no such thing as a civil marriage he has no remedy. Thus, once in the life of almost every man, the long-delayed penance is sure to fall, the long-retained fee sure to be paid. Then, in many cases, the hardened sinner goes away, and tells the boys what the priest asked him, what he answered, and how he did not do any penance whatever. It is sadly true that it is the feminine soul, and not the masculine, that respects the sacraments. The great majority of men cherish an ill-concealed dislike to the faith of the fathers, though refusing to countenance any other. He is disposed to have a private opinion of the infallibility of the Church, the purity of the priesthood, the divine authority of dogma, and the pecuniary disinterestedness of the whole sacred college. He believes a little competition is necessary to enliven ecclesiastical routine and reduce the fees.

I have said that the Church in Cuba seemed not to have attained great wealth. I have never yet attended services where the establishment was rich enough to afford an organ. In the little towns of Mexico the band and instruments of the last night's *baile* are good enough for choir-service the following morning. It is not greatly different here. The unsanctified cottage "organ" so called, the *quincum-quancum* of country churches, the musical sister of the sublime accordion, is the ordinary devotional instrument. But there is nothing strange in the celebration of mass without a single worshiper. It is all the same. The church is always open, and something is always going on. An old cock-fighting *roué* may be off at one side repeating an assorted selection of prayers to atone for misspent Sundays and ounces, and a gay mulatto, burdened with more amours than she can carry, which is saying a great deal, kneels at the confession cupboard. Idle boys play here and there, and grown-up vagabonds loaf around, apparently engaged in counting the candles. Occasionally there is an old woman of the humbler class, going from picture to image, and taking all as they come, saying a prayer to each, and giving her moral nature a regular cleaning up. If it is not piety it is penance, the salutary dispensation of the man in the cupboard.

There are seasons of the year when religious matters are more lively than at other times, and the languid zeal of the flock is stirred up. There are, or should be, half a dozen bells in every church steeple, of all sizes, kinds, and tones. These they ring at such times,—begin early and ring pretty much all day, and ring them all at once. The tune is slam—bang,—bang, bang, bang, and *da capo*; slam—bang,—bang, bang, bang. They are all slam-banging, big and little, of all sizes and keys, with all grades of harmony and dissonance. Nobody wishes to live within a mile of the church.

Feast-days, *"fiestas,"* are a special and characteristic institution. They are a remarkable feature of religious life to the man from active and go-ahead regions like the United States. There are twenty or more of them in the course of the year, and Holy Week is a continuous seven of them at once. They could not be endured in any active northern country, and Mother Church seems to leave them out of the calendar in her dealings with the irreverent and money-getting Yankee. Everybody stops work. All the laboring classes are religious then. You must wait for your shoes, your coat, and your washing until a working-day comes again. All this time Sunday counts for nothing. There is, indeed, a little more activity and frolic than on other days. Even during the sadness of Lent, Sunday is counted out, and everybody may dance, sing, eat meat, trade horses, and fight cocks with a clear conscience. There is no Sunday in the year, and Good Friday is the nearest approach to one. The Cuban lady sews and darns on Sunday with especial industry, if ever she does.

With the numerous feast-days comes the procession. There is a mania for processions, and no end to them in point of numbers and kind. I do not know what they are good for. They are not pretty, or solemn, or of pecuniary benefit, or aids to holiness, and remain in my mind unclassified, save that I am disposed to include them under the general heading of mummery. There is a long one in May, for the especial honor of the Virgin, in which the ladies take part. Such is the theory. But the "ladies" are usually a shade darker than is fashionable. There are other processions in which only gentlemen—the military especially—march. Then you may see the Virgin, escorted by soldiers and a band, pass by, while the Dons come after, clad in their best clothes, each carrying a candle, and each doing his best to keep the wax from falling on his best coat.

On Good Friday the religious season and the processions reach their culmination together, and thereafter decline. From ten o'clock on Thursday until the same hour on Saturday, is a period of solemn and ostentatious mourning. Carriages and horsemen are suppressed by law. The streets are nearly deserted and the shops are closed, except that you can enter by the back door, and everybody who has any idea of doing the correct thing is attired in solemn black. All the day of Friday, you are distressed by a peculiar hammering sound, a noise as of continuous knocking. The devout are engaged in pounding upon boards and boxes with sticks, as an expression of grief. All the neighborhood is at it, and they keep you awake until midnight with the performance. But the church bells are not rung, which may be regarded as some compensation. About eight o'clock in the evening the grand display begins, and I can easily see how, to these people, it is a most impressive scene.

VI

Health, Education, and Charity

Abiel Abbot
Letters Written in the Interior of Cuba
(Boston: Bowles and Dearborn, 1829), 122–25

We passed a few rods, to the insane hospital, which has been just completed on an extensive and beautiful scale, but is not yet occupied by its unfortunate tenants. It has a handsome front building, through which you pass into a spacious court, the four sides of which are divided into distinct rooms or large cells, for the separate accommodation of the lunatics.

From the insane hospital we repaired to another benevolent institution in the neighborhood, the Lazaretto for lepers, a class of persons scarcely less pitiable than those who have been deprived of reason; often much more sensible of their misery, oppressed with a disease usually incurable, infectious also, and therefore requiring exclusion from the ordinary consolations of society. This benevolent institution was originally upon a large scale, and capable of accommodating many inmates, which seems to show that the disease is prevalent in this country. The institution is now evidently in considerable neglect. The gate was open, and negroes were idling around it, some or all of whom may have belonged within. It is a large open court or square, inclosed with a row of huts, some of them in bad repair. In the centre is a large building, which possibly may be the common kitchen and store-room. Some parts of the square were inhabited, and the rest were shut up. A considerable number of lepers, however, were to be seen,

179

some exceedingly disfigured in their faces, but the larger number affected in their extremities, their feet and hands. Some had
no fingers above the middle joint. An air of woe was upon the face
of all;—a sort of desperation seemed to characterize the look and
movement of a few. From one or two of the apartments came the
sounds of the guitar and voice, implying the experience of better
days, and an endeavor to recall in their seclusion the tones of
gladness and joy. When new benevolent institutions are attracting
peculiar attention, it will sometimes happen that those of larger
standing fall into comparative decay and neglect. But the com-
passionate of this city will but need a short walk within the walls
of this lazaretto, to awaken an active sympathy.

     Our next visit presented a delightful contrast to our walks in
places devoted to the dead, the lunatic, and the leprous. It was in
the magnificent institution called Casa de Beneficiencia, or the
house of mercy. It is appropriated to the subsistence and education
of orphans and friendless children. In the first instance, females
only were admitted; but with a noble accession to its funds, boys
also now share the benefit. It was commenced by the Governor,
Las Casas [Luis de las Casas, 1745–1807; governor general of
Cuba, 1790–1795], in 1795.

     A noble accession to its funds has been made by ——, in the
gift of lands in the partido of ——, estimated at $200,000. The
appearance of the buildings is very fine, extending several hundred
feet on the main street, and as many on another street, the whole
enclosing a spacious court, with a living brook, probably diverted
from the city canal, ranging through the premises, and diffusing
health and cleanliness among the numerous children and youths
of the establishment. We entered through the chapel, a neat
building, and more than sufficient for the accommodation of the
house of mercy. We ranged through the lofty and spacious halls
on the lower and upper story, under the conduct of the respectable
gentleman, who presides over the institution; and visited the
apartments of those who were slightly ill with a cold, and of those
who were more seriously ill. It was a holiday, or the hour was that
of amusement, and we saw the children and young ladies in small
groups, or sitting at their large windows, grated in the fashion of
Spanish houses, all neatly dressed, and some tastefully. Some
were amusing themselves with reading, and some with work, and
the little girls were innocently sporting from hall to hall.

Having passed over the apartments appropriated to the females, their school-rooms, their eating-rooms, their immense
hall in which their cots are arranged for the night, after the
manner of the Moravians, but decently removed to a private room
for the day, we entered on a distinct suite of rooms for the
accommodation of the boys, in most respects similar to the other.

A useful education is given in this institution to two hundred
females, and forty boys, and to all except ten, at the expense of
the institution. The ornamental kinds of needlework are taught,
as well as the more useful, and even music. In the boys' apartment
we found a Lancasterian plan adopted; the walls were hung with
the usual tablets, and the benches with slates. It is remarkable
that females once entered into this establishment remain as long
as they please, or till they are married; if married from the house,
they are portioned as daughters of the family, each bride receiving a dowry of $500. Several of the young ladies we saw in friendly
conversation with young gentlemen, their brothers possibly, and
possibly friends entertaining for them still tenderer sentiments.

James Edward C. B. Alexander
Transatlantic Sketches
(2 vols.) (London: Richard Bentley, 1833), I:341–43

One evening I walked out with Mr. Jackson to visit some
of the public institutions which have lately sprung up, much to
the credit of the Havanneros. The first we reached, outside the
walls, and near the sea, was the Casa de Beneficencia, or House
of Mercy, for the education of orphans and friendless children of
both sexes. The buildings are very extensive, and enclosed a
court through which a stream of pure water runs. The apartments
are large, and well aired; and it was extremely interesting to see
the girls, in particular, sitting at the grated windows reading, or
engaged with their needlework. The boys are taught after the
Lancasterian plan. Every attention is paid to health and cleanliness
in this noble institution, which rears three hundred of both sexes,
and afterwards establishes them in the world. If the females are
married from the Casa de Beneficencia, they receive a dower of
five hundred dollars; and the boys have a sum advanced to them
with which to begin business.

We next turned to the institution of St. Lazarus, or the lazaretto for lepers. The gate was open, and instead of the infected being shut up, I saw several of them sitting by the road side wearing an air of hopeless dejection. They were principally negroes whom I saw, many of them frightfully disfigured, and beginning to lose their lips; others were affected in their extremities. . . .

Round the court were apartments occupied by white lepers, men and women: they looked extremely dejected, for their disease is incurable; though some live forty years before they finally sink into the grave, a mass of corruption too horrible to describe. It was with painful interest that the sounds of guitar, accompanied with a feeble voice, were heard from the cell of one of the inmates, who tried to beguile his sorrows with the soothing notes of melancholy music.

The next public building we came to was the Insane Hospital (Casa de Locos) enclosed with a lofty wall, and with a handsome entrance, over which was painted a fool's cap and bells. We passed into a spacious court, and saw some noble figures of men, with the wandering eye of lunacy, lounging about. We then passed an inner gate, and found ourselves in a beautiful garden full of shrubs and flowering plants: here and there were secluded walks and arbours for the inoffensive insane.

David Turnbull
Travels in the West: Cuba, with Notices of Porto Rico and the Slave Trade
(London: Longman, Orme, Brown, Greens, and Longman, 1840), 127–28, 208–15

The state of education in the primary schools of the island of Cuba forms one of the three important objects to which the attention of the Patriotic Society of the Havana is directed. But although a corporate body, armed with considerable powers, I regret to say that, in this department of its duties, the society is not very cordially or efficiently supported. Of primary schools there are, in the whole island, for white boys, 129; and for white girls, 79; for coloured boys, 6; and for coloured girls, 8. Of course, no slave is admitted into any school in the island. The whole number of white boys who attend these schools is 6025; of white girls, 2417; of coloured boys, 460; and of coloured girls, 180. In the entire province of Puerto Principe, there is not a single school for free coloured children of either sex; and it is almost needless to say that in the white schools they are not admissible. Of those who pay for their own education there are 3255 white boys, 1557 white girls, 371 coloured boys, and 142 coloured girls. Of those taught gratuitously by the masters, there are 672 white boys, 363 white girls, 71 coloured boys, and 28 coloured girls. Of those who have the expense of their education defrayed by patriotic societies, there are 340 white boys, and 200 white girls. Of those educated by public subscription, or by local taxation, there are 1758 white boys, 297 white girls, 18 coloured boys, and 10 colored girls.

It is assumed that there are in the island 99,599 free children, between the ages of five and fifteen; and the free population of the island, according to the last census, having amounted to 417,545, it follows that the number of free children is proportionally to the number at school as 9.97 are to 1, and that the total free population, as compared with the numbers of the children at school, is as 45.98 are to 1.

In the province of Havana, the free children are to the educated children as 7.34 are to 1, and the free population to the children at school as 34.04 are to 1.

Between these extremes, in the province of Santiago, the number of free children fit for school is to the number of children at school as 13.11 are to 1, and the free population of the province to the number of educated children as 51.71 are to 1. The number of white children in that province, between five and fifteen years of age, is 65,658, and of coloured children 24,859, making together 90,517. . . .

In the *Real Casa de Beneficencia* there are five distinct branches: 1st, a school for girls; 2d, a school for boys; 3d, a female lunatic asylum; 4th, a male lunatic asylum; and, 5th, a hospital for the reception of aged and infirm persons of both sexes. There is also connected with this establishment, although deriving its funds from distinct sources, an hospital of incurables, called the *Real Casa Hospital de San Lazaro.*

At the time of my visit, there were in the girls' school 101 scholars, including twelve day scholars; in the boys', sixty-three, including two day scholars; in the female lunatic asylum, eighty-three, including five out-pensioners; in the male asylum, 102, including ten out-pensioners; and in the hospital or poor-house twenty-five. In the management of the establishment there were twelve persons employed; the slaves attached to it were seven; there had been sent there three other slaves as a punishment; and the local government had granted the charity the services of fifty of the unfortunate *emancipados*, the hire obtained for whose services was to be regarded as the Captain-General's contribution; so that the whole number of persons supported by the institution, or in any way dependent on it, amounted in all to 445.

Girls are not admitted into the institution after ten years of age; and being entirely supported there they are completely separated from their parents and their families until the time of their final removal from the establishment has arrived. They are taught the various branches of needlework and dressmaking, and receive such other instruction as may sufficiently qualify them for becoming domestic servants, house maids, cooks, or washerwomen. They are not suffered by the regulations to remain in the house after the age of twenty-one; but before that time it is the duty of the Junta or committee of management to endeavour to procure employment for them either in a private family or in some house of business. Should the circumstances of the parents have improved during the stay of their daughter at the institution, they are not suffered to take her away until they have paid for her previous board and education at the rate of fifteen dollars a month; but if the girl herself has acquired property by inheritance, or is able to improve her condition by marriage or otherwise independent of her parents, she is suffered to leave the house without any payment; and in the event of her marriage to the satisfaction of the Junta, a little dowry is provided for her, amounting to $500, from a fund created by prizes in the lottery, the produce of tickets presented to the institution. Six such marriages had taken place, and six dowries bestowed from this fund, in the course of a single year.

The boys are taught the usual branches of education of primary schools, such as reading, writing, and arithmetic; and at the periodical examinations those who distinguish themselves by the greatest proficiency are rewarded by admission into select classes, where several of the higher branches of a good education are taught. The greater number of them are instructed in some business suited to their humble station in life, such as that of a tailor or a shoemaker. The masters in these departments, besides receiving a moderate salary, are allowed, as a further stimulus to their exertions, the benefit of any profit they may be able to make from the labour of their scholars.

In the course of my visit to this institution I had the opportunity of convincing myself that the boys, as well as the girls, were sufficiently supplied with good wholesome food; that their clothing was well suited to the climate; that the dormitories were airy and comfortable; the galleries for exercise well shaded and the play-grounds spacious, well enclosed, and sufficiently protected. Yet in spite of all these advantages I observed with regret that in both branches of the institution, the young people in general were of a pale and sickly frame of body, and, in regard to health and activity, appeared to be decidedly below the average of young persons of their age and station in other parts of the city. This fact I am persuaded cannot fairly be ascribed to any want of care or tenderness on the part of the managers of the institution, but must at once be referred to an inherent fault in the system prevailing in all climates and under all circumstances where young people are congregated in large numbers, completely separated from their families, and deprived for a long period of the numberless and nameless attentions which are only to be found under the parental roof.

In the two lunatic asylums dependent on this great charity, I observed also with pain and regret, that while the physical wants of the patients were adequately attended to, and while every care was bestowed on the preservation or restoration of their bodily health, no provision whatever was made for that moral culture and reclamation so well understood and so successfully practised in the great public institutions for the recovery of the insane in many parts of Europe and in the United States of America. In my visit to the lunatic branches of the charity I had the advantage of being accompanied by my friend Dr. Madden, who has studied this branch of his profession with so much enlightened and practical zeal, that I trust he may one day or other be induced to give the world the benefit of his experience and researches. We were informed by the medical attendant, and had previously learned, indeed, from the periodical reports, that the number of insane persons, for whom the benefit of the institution was claimed, had for many years been constantly on the increase. Among the eighty-three female patients not a single cure had been effected during the previous year. With the men they had been more successful or more fortunate,—at least credit was claimed for sixteen recoveries out of the total number of 102; but if the cures were numerous so also were the deaths, amounting to fifteen within the year.

In the poor-house department of the institution the number of inmates is inconsiderable when compared with the gross population of the city and the mendicancy prevailing there, to a degree which has certainly no parallel in any other place in the West Indies. But a life of vagabond freedom would certainly be preferred, in such a climate, to the irksome regulations of a workhouse, even if the inhabitants were less wealthy and less charitably disposed than they undoubtedly are. When this branch of the institution was first formed, the public beggars of the city and the suburban districts were arrested and sent by force to the *Casa de Beneficencia*. But the funds at the disposal of the junta having proved insufficient for the adequate support of the other branches, which were considered as of more vital importance to the public welfare, the poor-house department had for some years been reserved for the use of voluntary applicants.

Although not so productive as could be wished, the sources of the income of this charity are as various as can well be imagined. They consist of private donations; public subscriptions; government grants; rents of houses belonging to the institution; the hire of slaves and property of the establishment, of negroes sent there for punishment, and of the so called *emancipados* assigned to it for this purpose by the Captain-General; a special tax on the flour imported at the Havana and Matanzas; a tax on the public billiard tables of the capital; a poll tax; the produce of certain planks belonging to the institution, used in facilitating the landing of passengers at the wharf from the ships in the harbour; the payments received for needlework and dressmaking in the female department, and for the singing of the pupils as choristers in the responses for the dead; and, finally, the board received for such of the inmates as can afford to pay for their maintenance, in whole or in part. The private donations present also an amusing variety. The gift of tickets in the lottery is of frequent occurrence; and every imaginable article is to be found on the list of donations in kind. When sufficient employment is not to be found for the negroes belonging to the establishment, they are sent out into the market places and elsewhere to beg for donation of food; and in the last report I observe it stated that a visitor, who declined the communication of his name, had distributed some thousands of cigars among the lunatics of both sexes. The total pecuniary receipts amount in general from this great variety of sources, to $55,000, or $60,000 a year; and the funds at every balance are so completely exhausted, that a debt remains constantly due to the treasurer, and also to the Custom-house, for the advances which have been made from time to time to meet the exigencies of the establishment, varying from $6,000 to $8,000.

The hospital for incurables, called the Real Casa Hospital de San Lazaro, is chiefly occupied by leprous patients. The situation chosen for this branch of the establishment has all the appearance from its openness to a free circulation of air, and its gentle elevation, of being highly favourable to the improvement of the general health of the unfortunate inmates; and the arrangement of the buildings, consisting of small cottages, erected round an extensive area, and all looking inward from distinct terraces gives as cheerful an aspect to the scene as is at all compatible with the hopeless nature of the disease, and the necessity of protecting one class of patients from the risk of contact with others whose cases may happen to be of less virulent nature. At the period of my visit, there were seven patients in the infirmary of the institution, two of whom were white and five persons of colour. In the cottages around the square there were sixty-three patients, of whom eighteen were white and forty-five persons of colour. I was told, also, that there were ten patients who received out-of-door relief, two in the city and eight in the country. There were, also, five attendants, three slaves, and two *emancipados*, making altogether eighty individuals more or less dependent on the institution.

John George F. Wurdemann
Notes on Cuba
(Boston: James Munroe and Company, 1844), 32–34, 57–59, 220–25, 228–35

Near to the Campos Santos is the Lunatic Asylum, and I had so often heard of the filthy state of Spanish jails, etc., that I thought it was well placed so near to the cemetery I had just visited. However, determined to attempt an entrance, I informed the keeper that I was an American physician, and wished to see the interior arrangements of the establishment. He politely invited me to enter, and putting on his coat, accompanied me through the different apartments.

The building was of one story, about twenty-five feet high, with a dead wall on the outside, and separated into three different sections, each opening into a central square, and communicating with each other by large doors, while lofty porticos formed around each square cool promenades. The sleeping-rooms were very airy and clean, and it was apparent from the number of beds in several, that many were not subjected to solitary confinement at night. There were, however, in smaller rooms sets of stocks, in which, as a punishment, four or five of the more furious were confined, some by one, others by both legs. They appeared sensible of the cause of their punishment and were quiet. One, however, had just torn in pieces a strong shirt which the servant brought to the keeper, who expostulated, rather than reprimanded him for having destroyed it. There was much kindness in his bearing towards the inmates, and from his benevolent countenance, I believe it was not put on for the moment, while under the eye of a stranger.

There was one, confined in a comfortable room, busily employed in writing petitions to a friend. He asked me if I were an Englishman, and gave me one to read. It was written in pure Castilian, and no one would have thought, that the brain which had composed it, and which could so sensibly comment on the acts of the insane around him, was itself deranged. It contained, however, one glaring mark of folly; a request that his friend, on the score of his former intimacy and regard, should loan him a small sum of money. I begged him for the copy, but he brought me another, which he said was just as good, for which I paid him his charge, one real, amid the winks and smiles of the other insane inmates who had crowded around the window, and who seemed much amused at the delusion under which he labored, themselves well assured that their own brains performed their functions faithfully.

The third ward was appropriated to the colored insane, and here I found no material difference in the accommodations for Africa's sons from those for the whites. The yard was filled with clothes that had been washed, and were drying in the sun; the keeper informing me that the work was done by the inmates every two days; thus affording them an occupation, while it tended to preserve cleanliness. Next to this was a kitchen guarded by a bolted door, through a crack of which one hungry fellow was anxiously peeping at the preparing meal, but sneaked away when we approached, quite ashamed at having been thus surprised. There was a large pot of very white boiled rice, and another full of vegetables and meats, the favorite *olla podrida* of the creole, though probably not as savory as that on private tables. Still everything appeared to be clean, and the two cooks were very enthusiastic in showing me the contents of the pots, one of them at the end asking me for a fee, for which the keeper reproved him. Around the paved yard was an open drain, through which rushed a rapid stream of water, quickly removing the refuse from the whole establishment, into the open sea; while a bathing establishment, supplied by the same stream, offered that most necessary luxury to the inmates. Throughout the whole, an air of great cleanliness and comfort reigned; and as I looked upon the poor negroes and saw how well they had been cared for, and recollected the scenes of misery I had seen unrelieved at the door of the wealthy in Europe, I could not refrain from execrating the blind efforts of those who would restore the improvident slave to a freedom, for which his whole history has proved him to be unfit. . . .

Returning homeward I passed through the calle Aguiar, in which the large convent San Juan de Dios is situated, now used solely for a hospital. Its gates were open, and asking permission of the porter to enter, informing him that I was a physician and a stranger, it was granted with that grace of manners that the lowest creole knows so well to give to all his actions. It was a huge building, with high unornamented walls without, offering nothing attractive to the eye: and within, of irregular construction, with a double gallery open to the central square court.

At the end of the passage leading from the gate, a small body of soldiers were lounging on benches before their quarters, and a number of convalescents promenading under the high arches supporting the second gallery. From it a wide door led into a spacious ward on the first floor, which was very cleanly, and was furnished with iron bedsteads with plank bottoms, some covered by blankets only, others by beds. Crossed at its extremity by a still larger room, the two were capable of accommodating more than two hundred patients. Their lofty ceilings, and large windows opening high up, through the walls, rendered them cool, and afforded means of the freest ventilation. A great degree of neatness pervaded the whole place; perhaps not as much as is seen in the Paris hospitals, but certainly more than I had witnessed in those of Italy, even of Rome itself.

Many of the beds were occupied; and an air of contentment was observable in the faces of the invalids, that told they were well treated. Indeed, the bread on their tables did not appear inferior to that used in my boarding-house; and the appearance of their bed-clothes, and everything around them, showed plainly that the hand of care had been there. Ascending a narrow flight of stone steps, I entered the ward appropriated to the reception of free colored patients, and noticed with much pleasure that their accommodations were not a whit less comfortable than those for the whites. Here also the inmates seemed contented, and answered cheerfully my questions respecting their cases. Adjoining this was another ward for whites, containing about twenty patients.

As I looked at the poor invalid in his clean bed, surrounded with more comforts than his home, if he had one, could afford; and saw the convalescent, whose pale features were lighted up by the first faint signs of returning health, promenading the galleries and feasting his sight with the bright sunshine, and the green shrubs that grew in the square beneath—I could not but reflect on the different uses once made of this vast building, when perhaps it served chiefly to screen from public gaze scenes of revelry and dissipation. Nor could I refrain from rejoicing over that charity, that extended its care as well to the colored as to the white man. Whatever may be said of Spanish cruelty to slaves, the accounts of which are often greatly exaggerated, they offer in their institutions for the relief of the sick free negro, an example which might well be followed by many of our Southern States. Nor is it alone when sick that he is protected. Those who prate so much about the "cruel task-master of the South," cannot point out an instance, even on this island, where the free negro has been given up to mob violence, and his humble dwelling sacked under the eyes of the public authorities. . . .

No report on the state of education in the whole island has been made to the Sociedad Economica since that of 1836 was submitted by its able committee, Don Pedro Maria Romay, and Don Domingo del Monte. According to that paper, the island contained 41,416 boys, from 5 to 15 years of age, and 32,660 girls from 12 to 14. Havana maintained 85 white and 6 colored male schools, in which 4453 white and 307 colored boys were educated; and 55 white and 1 colored female schools, with 1840 white and 34 colored girls.

The next division of the island, [Santiago de Cuba], had 32 white and 19 colored male schools, and educated 1069 white boys; and 19 white and 5 colored females schools, with 347 white, and 145 colored girls. Puerto-Principe, the third division, had 12 white male schools, with 512 white boys; and 7 female schools, with 239 girls, not classified. The whole amounting to 210 schools, with 8460 white scholars; and 31 schools, with 486 colored scholars. Of these, 3678 received a gratuitous education; 1243 from the reachers themselves, and 2435 from funds provided by the Sociedad Economica and by subscriptions, etc.

Discouraging as this report is, that of 1842 is still more so. The committee state that the public funds for the gratuitous education of scholars, which not long before amounted to more than $32,000, has been reduced to $8,000, sufficient to support only 457 boys, and 342 girls, in 37 schools. The cost of instructing them in the articles of religion, reading, writing, arithmetic and grammar was, for each, one dollar monthly. In the large cities, the dearth of schools is not very remarkable, but extensive tracts of the richest part of the country are scarcely provided with even primary schools. Among other, Nueva Filipina may be mentioned, which, although with a population of more than thirty thousand, and containing the richest vegas of tobacco, unrivalled in commerce, has but one school of about 40 boys, recently established by its lieutenant-governor in Pinar del Rio.

The extreme poverty of the laboring class of whites in the country is one cause of this neglect of education; the children often have not clothes decent enough for school, and some have none at all; and the distance to the school in a country sparsely populated with the poor where the soil is barren, and almost exclusively occupied by the rich planter where it is fertile, is another prominent obstacle. But another cause felt by every Cuban, but which no one dares publicly own, is the depressing effect on the energies of the population by the enormous exactions of the mother country, and the extreme jealousy with which she views every attempt to enlighten the creole. Yet there are not wanting patriotic men, both in public and private life, who struggle ever against obstacles, which no one living under a free government can conceive. And with what feelings of approbation must not the efforts of the teachers be regarded. Although frequently in indigent circumstances themselves, by the report of 1836, they taught gratuitously one-half as many as all the societies and the government paid for, and in many cases adopted the scholars, to rescue them from ignorance.

I have already made mention of some of the charitable institutions of Havana, but the one most honorable to the feelings of the Creole is a kind of orphan-house, named the Real Casa de Beneficencia. It was founded, or rather translated to the present site, in 1794, amid an imposing ceremony, a record of which may be found in an old oil-painting suspended in its hall of administration. Under the guidance of its presiding director I was conducted through all its departments, beginning at the one for the reception of insane females, for the institution does not confine its care to destitute children. Their dwellings consisted of a number of rooms, in front of which a wide piazza extended its inviting shade, and a spacious yard offered the means of exercise. About sixty-five were here confined, of whom not more than a dozen were whites, the rest being of every shade from black to brown. Nearly all were walking about the yard or through the dormitories, and talking to the idle wind. There could not be a happier set of lunatics; all their wants were supplied, and they were subjected to no medical treatment when in ordinary health, and had no fear of shower-baths, bleeding and cups.

I could not learn the correct number cured by this rude treatment; but several were annually thus relieved of their infirmity, probably, chiefly from the absence of its exciting cause. A few were insane on religious subjects; of these, one, a pretty young woman, received us very courteously, and with such a constant simper, that it was hard to keep our own countenance. Another, a beautiful girl with a pensive look, answered rationally all our questions relative to her physical health; but the settled gloom dwelling on her face told of a "worm that dieth not." I must not omit to notice a stout, old negro woman, who was bustling about everywhere, and who, on being introduced to me, was at once quieted by my inquiries in English of her home. She replied hurriedly, "I am from Charleston, I belonged to Mass John Wragg, he sold me to Sam Ferguson, and then little John Miller, who kept a boarding-house, bought me." I tried to learn how she had eventually come here, but she flew off to subjects that induced me to quickly part company with her.

We next proceeded to the boys' department, passing through their dormitories, long, high, well ventilated halls, cleanly swept, in one corner of which the cots used at night were placed away. The eating room contained a spacious table, covered with clean crockery, and knives and forks for more that a hundred, with long benches placed by it ready to receive the eager throng. In the schoolroom we found 150 boys from seven to twelve years, engaged with their books, silently conning their lessons. At a signal from the teacher they all rose when we entered, resuming their seats only when directed to do so by the gentleman who accompanied me. One class was engaged in parsing a sentence written with chalk on a black-board, giving first the definition of each word; they seemed to be well prepared, and proceeded without any promptings from the teacher. With the exception of the usual pallor observed in children congregated in large numbers, there was no appearance of ill health among them.

Their infirmary, which we next visited, contained only six patients, none of which were very sick, and the nurse told me that twelve was the largest number that had been there at any one time. I could not refrain from patting the head of one retiring, modest little fellow, who was convalescent, and asking his name. With flushed cheek, proud of the notice I had taken in him, he told me it was Antonio Valdez; in itself a history of his origin. Valdez, the name of one of the oldest families of Spain, being conferred on all nameless, illegitimate children brought to the foundling hospital.

Our entrance into the school-room of the girls created quite a sensation among the scholars; one drew a loose kerchief around her bare shoulders, another arranged a stray lock of hair, and all changed their easy posture for one erect and prim, while the buzz of a general whispering pervaded the large apartment. My conductor was an elderly gentleman with a most benevolent expression in his face, and he had a kind word to say to each class; often asking who was at the head, when the downcast looks of the one would tell before her smiling classmates could point her out. They numbered about 150; very few of them were more than 13 years old, those above that age generally accepting situations as seamstresses, etc., in private families. It was pleasant to look on so many tender minds snatched from poverty and all its temptations, and to reflect that their very destitution had been turned into a blessing.

The institution was at first intended only for girls, and by its rules three years' residence within its walls entitles each on her marriage to a dowry of five hundred dollars. I asked my conductor how they got sweethearts; but he pointed to the grated windows, opening on the streets, and said many a sly token had found its way through those iron lattice frames, adding, no girl in love ever failed to let the loved one perceive her passion;—he had never travelled out of Cuba. Most, however, become engaged after they enter the service of a family, which may be one inducement to leave the institution early, for they can remain there until 21 years of age.

In the female infirmary seven were seen on clean beds, apparently with every comfort about them. One had her cot removed to the extremity of the long room, and separated from the rest by a screen. She told us she was much better, and was getting stronger, but the nurse significantly pointed to the bloody sputa; and her attenuated frame, her burning palm, and hectic flush, told too plainly that consumption's blighting touch was fast loosening the "silver chord," and that ere long would "the golden bowl be broken." This disease, when it originates in Cuba, runs its course so rapidly, that the Creole might well be pardoned for his belief in its contagiousness. So strong is this belief, that in private families, the clothes and bedding of the deceased, and even the plates, spoons, etc. used by him while sick, are destroyed. The physician now entered, to whom I was introduced by a professional friend accompanying me. Leaving the hopeless case around which we had met, he brought to me a delicate looking girl, whom, he told me, he had cured of the same affliction, showing me the numerous marks on her chest of the cups he had applied. She was but twelve years old, and possessed those characteristic features of Spanish beauty, the full dark eye and the long silken lashes; there was, moreover, so much of native dignity in the expression of her countenance, that although she was but a child, my voice insensible assumed a tone of respect, as I asked her the history of her case. With regret I saw that I could not coincide with the favorable opinion of her physician, and foresaw that the unerring shaft would, ere long, lay prostrate her exhausted frame.

The children, who are all whites, are received after the age of six years from the foundling hospital and other sources. The boys are kept until 15 years old, and are then indented as apprentices. In 1842 a proposition was made by Monsieur Antonio Cournand, a student of the high normal school of Paris, and tutor in this institution, to educate the more intelligent boys for schoolmasters, to supply the schools on the island. It was gladly agreed to by the trustees of the school, but the early death of the proposer has, for the present, unhappily frustrated the completion of the design.

In addition to the departments already described, the institution embraces also one for white female paupers, another for the free colored, and one for indigent men. The lunatic asylum, mentioned in the first pages of this work, is also a part of it. It contains besides a place for the confinement of slaves arrested for crimes, from which it receives a considerable income, in the charges exacted from their owners for their lodging and board.

The capital of the Casa de Beneficencia amounted in 1832 to $262,505, and by the report for the year 1812, read by its secretary before the Patriotic Society, its income for that year was $86,407, and its expenses $86,262. Of this sum $3,300 were for six dowries, and an additional one bestowed during that year. In the girls' department 22 had been admitted, 20 had been placed at service in private families, 2 had married, and 2 had died. In that of the boys 33 had entered, 30 had returned to their friends, or had been indented, and one had died; 156 were left, and of the girls 151. In the Lunatic Asylum 54 had entered, 28 had left, and 11 had died, leaving 130; while in the female insane department, 19 had entered, 12 had left, and 7 had died, leaving 63. Of the paupers 32 had entered, 26 had left, and 7 had died, leaving 39. The whole establishment gives shelter to 604 individuals, including 49 negroes of both sexes, and 16 slaves belonging to it. Well might the Habaneros be proud of this monument of their charity, unexcelled as it is by any similar institution in other countries, in the liberality of its regulations, and the care it bestows on its inmates. . . .

The military hospital, which has lately been established in what was formerly the Royal Factory of tobacco, is one of the finest in the world, both in regard to size and the neatness of its arrangements. The immense building is quadrangular, enclosing several separate squares, and presenting without the appearance of a large fortress; so massive and high are its walls, and so well secured all its inlets. . . .

Having been presented to the Superintendent, by the porter, as a foreign physician desirous to visit the hospital, I was placed under the guidance of an attendant, with directions to him to show me every part of the building. I will not carry my reader with me through all its numerous lofty wards, each appropriated to the reception of a separate class of diseases; nor by the prisons for the refractory, and the comfortable apartments for the insane; the bathing-rooms, where a large number of warm and cold, and shower-baths, could be given at the same time; the apothecary's hall; the cleanly kept kitchen, and the separate room with furnaces to prepare chocolate and coffee; the dispensary with its motley collection of candles, tin-pans, cups, etc., and clothes-room with shelves laden with piles of white linen and flannels. I will not lead him through them all, lest he be as fatigued by the description as I was in traversing them. Indeed, although my guide kept me at a quick step the whole time, my visit occupied more than an hour. I cannot, however, refrain from noticing the ward for afflictions of the eyes. It was about two hundred feet long, forty wide, and twenty high; and the light was admitted only through panes of green and blue glass, transmitting hues peculiarly grateful to the sight. The rooms for sick officers were better fitted up than those for the common soldier, but I saw only one lodger of a higher grade than a lieutenant, and his balcony commanded such a view of the harbor and country, that I really envied him the possession of his quarters.

The large central square was laid out in multiplied walks, with a cool fountain in the middle, and beds crowded with flowers of every variety; forming a beautiful garden, on which the extensive, cool corridors for the convalescents looked down. Attached, also, to the hospital, and within the same building, was the Anatomical School of the medical college, with a fine museum, containing specimens of anatomy in wax, *papier mache*, and a few of the dried preparations of the human body, with others in alcohol. Adjoining the museum was a small amphitheatre for the students, and below a marble table for the subject of demonstration, while the walls around were appropriately hung with anatomical plates, presenting a complete picture of the human system.

The whole building covered a large space of ground, and whoever will visit it, and witness the scrupulous cleanliness and order that pervades every part of it,—its well ventilated and comfortable wards, its spacious and cool corridors, and the attention that everywhere seems paid to the welfare of the sick inmates,—will feel his estimation of the Spanish character greatly enhanced. The physicians and officers of the different wards received me with the greatest courtesy, and my wishes were everywhere anticipated by their desire to show me everything. It contained in January 1842, 480 patients, and received that year 5622. Of these 5540 left it cured, and 204 died, leaving 358 in its wards in January 1843. . . .

The comparative mortality of Havana may in a measure be learned from the statistics of its hospitals. San Juan de Dios in 1842 lost 507 of 2299 who entered; San Francisco de Paula, for women, 181 of 479; San Lazaro 18 of 106; the foundling hospital, Real Casa de Maternidad, 32 of 169; the military hospital, just described, 204 of 6102; in all 942 of 9155,—about 9.7 of the patients entered. . . .

Of the four hospitals established by these religious orders, San Juan de Dios is the most ancient, having been founded by three brothers, hospitaliers from Cadiz, in 1603. During the 17th century, according to its tables, it had one hundred beds, and 800 sick persons were annually cured in it; but as the commerce and population of the city increased, it is probable that the number was greatly augmented; the order consisted of thirty brothers.

The hospital San Francisco de Paula, dedicated to the reception of women, is the next most ancient, having been founded in 1665 by Don Nicolas Estebes Borges, a native of Havana, and dean of the church of Cuba. In 1730 it was destroyed by a hurricane, and one rebuilt in 1745.

The Convalencia de Nostra Senora de Belen, owed its foundation to Senor Evelino, and was built to shelter those who had been cured in other hospitals, and protect them from the vicissitudes of the weather and improper diet during their convalescence. It maintained also a free school of 500 boys, 300 of whom were taught writing and two hundred reading, and all were instructed in the articles of the holy faith. Many of these scholars were so poor that the institution had to furnish them with paper, pens, and catechisms; and it is particularly noted that the teachers made no distinction between the poor and rich scholars, the mean and the noble. Yet at a later day, the scrupulous historian, Valdes [Antonio José Valdes, b. 1780, Cuban creole historian], denounced this very order for maintaining, for only three days each, a number of convalescents not averaging above a hundred; while it possessed fully two million dollars in real estate, and a great sum in capital, and consisted of only 22 brothers, who had taken the vow of charity and poverty! It was founded about the year 1695, and is now suppressed.

The list of charitable institutions would not be complete without that excellent one named by the Creole, in common parlance, *la Cuna*, the cradle. It was founded by the illustrious Valdes in 1711, at an expense of $16,000, and maintains both the nurses and the foundlings. In 1842 it received 64 children, in addition to the 105 remaining from the last year; of these, 32 died, 23 were sent out to gratuitous nursing, and 2 to the Casa Beneficencia, leaving 112 inmates: its income was $35,859, and its expenses, $31,682. The name of its founder is conferred on all infants left without one under its protection, thus perpetuating a living monument to his noble charity. There are eighteen other public hospitals on the island, located in its chief towns.

Richard Henry Dana, Jr.
To Cuba and Back: A Vacation Voyage
(Boston: Ticknor and Fields, 1859), 183–88

The Casa de Beneficencia is a large institution, for orphan and destitute children, for infirm old persons, and for the insane. It is admirably situated, bordering on the open sea, with fresh air and very good attention to ventilation in the rooms. It is a government institution, but is placed under charge of the Sisters of Charity, one of whom accompanied us about the building. Though called a government institution, it must not be supposed that it is a charity from the crown. On the contrary, it is supported by a specific appropriation of certain of the taxes and revenues of the island. In the building is a church not yet finished, large enough for all the inmates, and a quiet little private chapel for the Sisters' devotions, where a burning lamp indicated the presence of the Sacrament on the small altar. I am sorry to have forgotten the number of children. It was large, and included both sexes, with a separate department for each. In a third department are the insane. They are kindly treated and not confined, except when violent; but the Sister told us they had no medical treatment unless in case of sickness. . . . The last department is for aged and indigent women.

One of the little orphans clung to the Sister who accompanied us, holding her hand, and nestling in her coarse but clean blue gown; and when we took our leave and I put a small coin into her little soft hand, her eyes brightened up into a pretty smile.

The number of Sisters is not full. As none have joined the order from Cuba, (I am told literally none,) they are all from abroad, chiefly from France and Spain; and having acclimation to go through, with exposure to yellow fever and cholera, many of those that come here die in the first or second summer. And yet they still come, in simple, religious fidelity, under the shadow of death.

The Casa de Beneficencia must be pronounced by all, even by those accustomed to the system and order of the best charitable institutions in the world, a credit to the island of Cuba. The charity is large and liberal, and the order and neatness of its administration are beyond praise.

From the Beneficencia we drove to the Military Hospital. This is a huge establishment, designed to accommodate all the sick of the army. The walls are high, the floors are of brick and scrupulously clean, as are all things under the charge of the Sisters of Charity; and the ventilation is tolerable. The building suffered from the explosion of the magazine last year, and some quarters have not yet been restored for occupation. The number of sick soldiers now in hospital actually exceeds one thousand! Most of them are young, some mere lads, victims of the conscription of Old Spain, which takes them from their rustic homes in Andalusia and Catalonia and the Pyrenees, to expose them to the tropical heats of Cuba, and to the other dangers of its climate. Most had fevers. We saw a few cases of vomito. Notwithstanding all that is said about the healthfulness of a winter in Cuba, the experienced Sister Servant (which, I believe, is the title of the Superior of the body of Sisters of Charity) told us that a few sporadic cases of yellow fever occur in Havana, in all seasons of the year; but that we need not fear to go through the wards. One patient was covered with the blotches of recent smallpox. It was affecting to see the wistful eyes of those poor, fevered soldier-boys, gazing on the serene, kind countenances of the nuns, and thinking of their mothers and sisters in the dear home in Old

Spain, and feeling, no doubt, that this womanly, religious care was the nearest and best substitute.

The present number of Sisters, charged with the entire care of this great hospital, except the duty of cooks and the mere manual and mechanic labor necessarily done by men, is not above twenty-five. The Sister Servant told us that the proper complement was forty. The last summer, eleven of these devoted women died of yellow fever. Every summer, when yellow fever or cholera prevails, some of them die. They know it. Yet the vacancies are filled up; and their serene and ever happy countenances give the stranger no indication that they have bound themselves to the bedside of contagious and loathsome diseases every year, and to scenes of sickness and death every day.

As we walked through the passage-ways, we came upon the little private chapel of the Sisters. Here was a scene I can never forget. It was an hour assigned for prayer. All who could leave the sick wards—not more than twelve or fourteen—were kneeling in that perfectly still, secluded, darkened room, in a double row, all facing to the altar, on which burned one taper, showing the presence of the Sacrament, and all in silent prayer. That double row of silent, kneeling women, unconscious of the presence of any one, in their snow-white, close caps and long capes, and coarse, clean, blue gowns—heroines, if the world ever had heroines, their angels beholding the face of their Father in heaven, as they knelt on earth!

It was affecting and yet almost amusing—it would have been amusing anywhere else,—that these simple creatures, not knowing the ways of the world, and desirous to have soft music fill their room, as they knelt at silent prayer, and not having (for their duties preclude it) any skill in the practice of music, had a large music-box wound and placed on a stand, in the rear, giving out its liquid tones, just loud enough to pervade the air, without forcing attention. The effect was beautiful; and yet the tunes were not all, nor chiefly, religious. They were such as any music-box would give. But what do these poor creatures know of what the world marches to, or dances to, or makes love by? To them it was all music, and pure and holy.

James Williams Steele
Cuban Sketches
(New York: G. P. Putnam's Sons, 1881), 139–42

Schools in Cuba possess a striking feature to begin with,—striking, at least, as compared with our own system of public education. The sexes are always separated. Very small boys and girls are studiously kept apart. The children of a family must attend two schools unless they are all of one sex. It is the system which may be considered inseparable from the race, and nobody has, as yet, been bold enough to intimate that there is any useless trouble or expense about it. The Spanish mind is firmly fixed in the idea that when the male and female of the human species are thrown together, there is sure to be mischief of some kind concocted. It is probably true.

The schools are all managed by the Church; this of course. It is to obtain this management that a constant struggle is going on in the United States. It is one of the fixed ideas of the hierarchy. Take away a direct influence of the priesthood from the youthful mind, and the grand opportunity is lost. Mix the church—the general religious doctrines—daily with all that is taught upon other and very different themes, and the mind of the pupil unconsciously imbibes the idea that it is *all* true alike, and belongs together. Geography,—Maria; mathematics,—the quarterly confession; natural history,—the *credo* and ritual; history,—the lives of the saints; and so on through the course. This is the education of the Cuban boy, when he gets any, for there is no system of public schools, and probably will never be any.

There are generally several pedagogic priests about every boys' school. The education of the girl is conducted under the direction of some order or sisterhood of maiden ladies, who are distinguished by the wearing of rosaries and serge gowns. None of the questions regarding the education of youth which have been extensively agitated in nearly every other country, are matters of thought or discussion in either Spain or Cuba. The question is settled. Things are as they should be. Education is a boon for the benefit of the sons and daughters of those who can pay for it. That it is a means of preventing crime is not believed, and the idea is scouted as an absurdity. The girls principally learn needlework and embroidery, and it is notorious that the bright and pretty Cuban miss often ends by not even knowing that.

I have already had something to say of the Cuban young man. I have not observed any pale students. The oratorical and essay-writing future statesman is unknown. The ambitious youth here desires clothes, tight boots, an extraordinary hat, a cane, a big watch-chain and a package of cigarettes. Of course statesmen are growing up on all hands, and it is sincerely to be hoped that when they come round to it, they will distinguish themselves in the better management of their island. . . .

Noticing casually the system of education in Cuba, I have wondered what, besides mischief, might have been the themes of study in the ancient and famed universities of Salamanca and Cordova. Pursuing the theme, it has sometimes seemed to me that Church and State had undoubtedly combined to force a flimsy and inadequate system upon Cuba, the main purposes of which should be political and religious. If such is the case the plan is a manifest failure; they have never made of a Cuban schoolboy a Spaniard, or a very religious man.

VII
Rural Life

Abiel Abbot
Letters Written in the Interior of Cuba
(Boston: Bowles and Dearborn, 1829), 140–45

The largest coffee estate on the island of which I have heard consists of a million of trees; the next in size, it is said, but the information can hardly be supposed to be very exact, is the Angenora, (or Argenora,) consisting of 750,000 trees, and 450 slaves. As this vast estate is conducted on principles somewhat original, some might take upon them to say, eccentric, and yet with excellent success; and as many of the expensive arrangements have a striking character of humanity, while also they result in excellent discipline, several of my friends acquainted with the proprietor, attended me to see it. Fortunately, the planter, who is also a merchant, was on the estate, and as communicative as the inquisitive could desire. A concise, yet detailed account, may furnish hints to the enterprising and humane.

For his *batey*, or extensive square of buildings, he selected a rude spot of hill and valley, surcharged with rocks. This is approached by a broad and superb avenue, adorned in the usual manner, except that at the foot of the hill, on an elevated pedestal stands his sylvan deity, the Goddess of Silence, furnishing the name and emblem of the bachelor's estate. It is a fine marble statue in Roman costume, indicating by sign what she suffers not to pass her lips.

His principal building occupies the crown of the hill, and is 309 feet long, and 69 broad; of the latter, thirty two feet are piazza, and on the north side of the building it is glazed, that the health and comfort of himself and negroes may in a moment be consulted by letting down or suspending the side of the piazza. A cold norther was blowing, and the negroes very comfortably picking coffee behind the glass.

In the first apartment of this extensive building is a mill to grind the corn of the plantation, going by ox power, the oxen below and the stones above. The corn is rapidly shelled by a simple machine turned by a crank. The next apartments are store rooms for coffee in the cherry, competent to hold 20,000 barrels. In the centre of this building is a peeling mill, terminating in a cupola. Near by was a beautiful mill of stone, ready to be put down, hard as granite, white as chalk, nicely jointed and bevilled by his black masons, which he expects will never need alterations or repair.

It is a maxim with the proprietor that negroes should have money, and should spend it. To encourage the latter part of this plan, he furnishes a shop in an apartment of the building next to the mill, with everything they may wish to buy that is proper for them; cloth cheap and showy; garments gay and warm; crockery; beads; crosses; guano, or the American palm, that they may form neat hats for themselves; little cooking pots, etc. He puts everything at low prices; and no pedler is permitted to show his wares on the estate.

The next apartment is a carpenters' room; in which were tools and benches, some articles of household furniture; planecases neatly made, and soaking in oil; acana wood, hard to saw, and easy and smooth to plane, dark as cherry tree, a quantity of which was getting out for bars and sashes for the splendid hospital which he is building for the estate.

The next apartment is the clothes room, fitted up with cases of 300 drawers, numbered, and the name of a negro and his wife on each drawer, and their apparel made to their size, and laid away in it against the first of January, when two suits are given at once. To prevent fraud their clothes are marked with indelible ink; their tools also are marked.

To prevent any abuse from the reception of two suits of clothes at once, there is a parade day every week, when each negro is obliged to appear with one suit on, and one in his hand, accompanied with his blanket. If anything is missing the whole are assessed to replace the lost article, as he thinks no roguery takes place among them but it is generally known.

The next apartment is an elegant hall, floored with wood, an unusual thing in this country, glazed and painted, that it may be safe and warm in any change of weather. In one of the windows was an Aeolian harp of great power and sweetness, resounding at the touch of the norther.

The next apartment is a breakfast room and library; through which we passed into a spacious bedchamber. The last three apartments are hung round with pictures, many of them in fine taste.

The piazza at the eastern end of the building serves for a dining hall. In this is a fine piece of statuary, representing a water deity, with a cask on his knee and bung out, filling a marble vase with water for washing hands before and after dinner.

Connected with the eastern end of this building is a lying-in hospital and inclosure for the young creoles [in this context, children of slaves born in bondage], an interesting and populous spot. You first enter the yard, inclosed by a plastered wall, the top of which is set with broken glass. This yard has a plastered floor like a coffee-dryer, that the creoles may not be able to find dirt to eat, which they are prone to do, and which brings on swelling of the bowels, and destroys many of them. This yard, is shaded by trees set in boxes, and leads to the lying-in hospital. Here we saw a double row of cradles well filled, and a young creature only fifteen years old sitting between two of them to take care of her twins. In the whole inclosure were ninety five creoles under ten years of age; and the most discontented little thing among them became instantly quiet, when perched in naked ebony on his master's arm. Children are sometimes destroyed through the jealousy of the husbands, and also through the neglect or abuse of unnatural mothers. One woman was pointed out to me suspected of having made it easy for four of her children to die; they died. At the birth of the fifth the master warned her that if the child did not live, she should smart for it; he lives, and is one of the finest of the creoles. From the very unusual success in raising creoles on this estate, these hints deserve the consideration of planters. As a premium for rearing children, the mother of six living children is freed from labor for life, and has her maintenance on the estate.

North from the principal building, on the batey already described, beyond a valley of two or three hundred yards, and on a rising ground, is erecting a splendid infirmary for the estate. The length of the building is 126 feet, and the breadth 30. The basement story is finished, and the principal story is almost completed. The building is intended for those who are morally infirm, as well as physically. At each end of the infirmary, therefore, in the basement story, is an apartment called the stocks, the one for male criminals, and the other for female. They are spacious arched rooms, and well ventilated with spiracles.

The stocks are formed by two thick planks, with holes large enough to admit the small of the leg, cut half in the upper plank and half in the lower, and made fast together at the ends. Attached to this contrivance for securing the legs, which extends across the apartment, is a bed and bedding, and pillows, that offenders may lie without needless pain, and think over their cases.

In the basement also is another large and spacious room, occupied as a store-room, but which, in case of insurrection, is intended as a place of confinement. Smaller rooms in the basement are prepared to receive persons with contagious diseases, as leprosy, etc. There are two arched ways leading from the infirmary to the yards in the rear, one for each sex. The yard is inclosed with a high wall, and a partition separates the sexes; and each half is a kitchen and convenient offices, and a cistern into which water is poured from without, that there may be no communication between the sick and the well.

The principal story of the infirmary displays taste and humanity. We ascended into it from the front by a flight of twenty spacious stone steps. It is divided into six rooms. Two of these rooms are floored with boards, and glazed, that every delicacy of treatment may be observed towards the very sick.

The building is to terminate with a third story on the central part, divided into two rooms, the principal for the matron, or grand nurse of the establishment; the other for the apothecary.

As prevention is preferable to the cure of diseases, and many are contracted by exposure in the rainy season, the proprietor has erected thirty sheds scattered over the estate, to which the laborers may flee in case of sudden showers. In sickness, when necessary, wine is furnished.

In 1825 the small pox broke out on this estate, and ninety slaves had it the natural way, of which only one died. He had at the same time forty sick of other diseases.

The proprietor carefully avoids overworking his negroes, as tending to fill his infirmary. In the winter he gives them a recess from labor at noon of an hour and a half, and in summer of three hours, and no night work is permitted on the estate. The best comment on these humane arrangements is, that a more healthy, muscular, active set of negroes, as many have remarked, is not to be found on the island.

The bohea [*bohio*], or square of negro huts, is judiciously arranged on a hill, fifteen or twenty rods east from the principal building of the batey. Two families are accommodated under one roof, and a space of a few yards is left between each two buildings, fenced by a high open picket. In this manner the negro huts enclose a large square, which is entered by an iron gate. When the plantation becomes as populous as the proprietor hopes it will, this square will be a little negro city, with streets running at right angles.

The valley between the mansion and the bohea is to be an extensive garden; and at the head of this valley are forming immense tanks, to be filled with water from the well arranged coffee driers, from which every rod of the garden can almost without trouble be irrigated.

Other parts of his plan, less original, are omitted. I only add, that the 1st of January is the negro's red letter day on this estate. On this day no work whatever is done; it is entirely given up to mirth and festivity. All liberties, except crimes, are permitted. At three in the morning, they make a general rush upon their master, and wish him a happy new year. Each receives a handkerchief as a present. Pardons are distributed in all cases, except of crimes which the laws of the land proscribe; and for one day in the year the slaves are everything but master.

Mr. S. has a peculiarity in sending his coffee to market, to which he may be indebted for getting the highest price. Coffee he remarks, often suffers by rain, on its way to Havana, though covered with hides,—and afterwards by dampness in stores and at sea. To prevent this he packs his coffee in large casks, neatly made by his own coopers, of atage wood, and iron bound. By this means it arrives at Havana and the most distant market perfectly *dry*. In cleaning his coffee, he highly approves of Chartrand's divider, and has a half dozen of them in use.

His crop of corn this year was 3750 bushels. I saw in his loft many bags of dried plantain, saved in the abundant season for his negroes in that season when it yields less abundantly. A new species of corn, I saw also in sacks, which he called melio.

Mr. S. has prepared his last bed, or tomb, at the northern entrance into his estate; and the coffin, he remarked, was to be soon made of incorruptible wood.

He intends soon to hire a musician, to be employed in selecting and instructing a band of forty of his negroes, that they may amuse him in his declining years, and attend him with mournful airs to his grave.

Samuel Hazard
Cuba with Pen and Pencil
(Hartford: Hartford Publishing Company, 1871), 343–45, 532–42

The country-houses of Cuba are, as a general thing, on the sugar estates, very large and roomy mansions, built of stone, floored with tiles of either clay or marble, according to the wealth or taste of the owner; the doors and windows . . . . are immense, and the latter entirely without glass, while no provision is made for fire, and, from my experience of one or two northers, it is never needed, though it is said that in some seasons, when *los nortes* are particularly cold, a fire would be very comfortable indeed for a day or two, as long as these winds last.

The houses have generally piazzas front and back, which are very spacious, and frequently used as dining and sitting rooms, being enclosed by canvas curtains lowered from the edge of the roof. These houses are rarely more than one story high, built with the closest eye to a certain kind of lazy comfort and coolness; they have a large hall or room, generally as large as one of our public parlors, from which open on each side one or two suites of rooms, used by the family as bed-chambers and sitting-rooms. Beyond the hall there is, perhaps, a dining-room or the aforementioned piazza, curtained or closed in by blinds, and looking out upon one side of the court-yard, or *patio*; on each side of this extends back a wing, used on one side for offices, servants' quarters, etc., and, perhaps, on the other for stables,—the whole with a wall at the other side, forming an enclosed quadrangle, in which horses are fed, negro children play, and servants chatter.

This court-yard is varied in some of the more tasteful ingenios by beautiful gardens, laid out with orange, lemon, pomegranate, and other fruit trees, while the jessamine and heliotrope, and other bushes, add fragrance and beauty to the scene. The mention of these flowers reminds me that I was surprised to find so few on the island. Although some of them were intensely brilliant in color, yet it did not strike me that there was nearly such a variety of beautiful roses and smaller plants as there is in America. Even in the luxuriant vegetation of the Coffee Mountains of Guantanamo, there is a scarcity of handsome flowers; and I have upon my memorandum book several commissions to send seeds from the United States to Cuban ladies. . . .

In a district where these rural places are of a good class, and *potreros* are found, it is pleasant to mount one's horse, and ride round amongst them, as the owners, particularly of the better class, are quite intelligent about their own business, and always kind to the stranger; having, notwithstanding their rustic life, a certain air of easy politeness, peculiar, it seems to me, to the people of the Latin race. And almost the first thing you are asked, even in the humblest of these *finca* residences, is, "*Quiere café, Senor?*" (will you have coffee, sir), of which beverage these people are very fond. The houses are often very humble affairs indeed, as regards material, though they may be ample in number of rooms, with numerous outbuildings.

They are usually composed of one story affairs, roughly constructed of poles, palm-leaves, and thatch put together in such a way as to be impervious to rain, yet light enough to admit plenty of air, especially as the doors, if there are any, always stand open.

A living-room, with a sleeping-room or two, all on the same floor, which is often of earth, make up the main building, while a simple roof connects it with an outbuilding, where is the kitchen, in which are performed the household and other duties of the women.

Many of these women, be it said to their credit, are more industrious than the men, as they attend to their domestic duties, often weave cotton cloth for home consumption from the small amount of cotton raised, and have a general superintendence over the place. Cotton, by-the-by, though it cannot be said to be one of the products of the island, does grow in sufficient quantity to manufacture out of it a rough kind of cloth, used by the country people. Every attempt to cultivate it systematically, I was told, was a failure; and yet in the Coffee Mountains I saw beautiful cotton growing wild, in small lots, but the moment it was attended to and looked after, strange to say, it ceased to flourish.

It is upon these rural places also that the Cascarilla cosmetic powder, so great a favorite with Cuban ladies, is prepared from the egg-shells; and the extent to which this is used may be imagined, when it is estimated that there are over one hundred thousand pounds consumed every year.

The last of the rural places we are called upon to notice is the "Hacienda de Crianza," or *sitio*, as it is called,—an uncultivated, unenclosed place, where the cattle are allowed to run wild, unattended except by the *montero*, who goes about on foot, or the half-savage *sabanero*, who, being mounted, rides in amongst the herd. Their united business is to scour the fields every day, and pick out the new-born calves, with their mothers, and take care of them for fifteen or twenty days at the houses or sheds; to see if there are any dead animals, or to pick out those ready to send to market or kill for consumption.

"The rural population of the island," says a Cuban author, "has rusticity, but not that boasted simplicity of the European laborer. Our *guajiro* (countryman) is astute though frank, boastful though brave, and superstitious if not religious. His ruling passions are gambling (particularly at cock-fights, of which he is very fond), and coffee, that he drinks at all hours; his favorite food, pork and the platano, usually roasted." His costume consists of a pair of loose pantaloons, girdled at the waist by a bit of leather, a shirt of fancy-colored linen, a handkerchief of silk or cotton tied around his neck, or, more frequently, about his head, upon which is a broad-brimmed hat of *yarey*,—a species of common palm-leaf,—while his usually bare feet are thrust into common leather pumps or slippers. Rarely does he wear a coat, even if he owns one, and his shirt is worn *al fresco*, more generally outside than inside his pants.

He never works regularly, nor does much else than direct the cultivation of his property, look after the cattle, or, perhaps, act as carter or teamster. Sometimes he may plow, or sow a little grain, or even pick fruit; but if he owns any negroes, he makes them do the work. Some of them are, in fact, too lazy to help themselves; and I have seen one of these fellows, near a country railroad station, plant himself in a chair to be amused by the train, while he lolled back and had his hair *combed* by one of his negro-women.

Sometimes he does a little trading on his own account, and may, perhaps, keep a *tienda mista* a sort of country-store and tavern, if his *finca* is on a public road. He travels on horseback, armed invariably with the machete, and often carrying a sun-umbrella, taking care to stop at every tavern on the road, where he is ready to talk with any one he meets, or accept an invitation to "*beber.*"

La guajira (country woman), is not so talkative as the husband, particularly with strangers, to whom her partially Castilian blood makes her, at first, ceremonious and dignified, even rising to receive them. She can mount a horse, though she usually rides with her husband, sitting in front of him, upon the neck of the horse almost, while his right arm encircles her. She dresses in the most simple manner (often a little too much so) in a *camison*, or frock, with a kerchief around her neck; seldom wearing stockings, except on state occasions,—of a ball, visit, etc., her head often being covered with a huge straw hat when she moves about, but otherwise dressed with the utmost care to display to advantage her superb hair.

These country people all have manners and customs peculiar to themselves, even their food being different from that of the cities; and it is amongst them one can study *la cocina criolla* (the Cuban cuisine). They have but two meals a day, always accom-panied by coffee, which they also take on rising in the morning, at night-time, and at any hour of the day they fancy, or may have a guest.

Civilization has found its way even to the homes of these simple people; and, on the richer and larger places, English beer is now generally used, and to strangers even champagne is presented.

So natural a custom is it with these hospitable country people to entertain the guest, that, does he happen to be present when a meal is announced, he is not even honored with an invitation, but he is expected, as the most natural thing in world, to seat himself at the table and partake of their food, what it may be. To refuse to do so, unless he has the excuse to make that he has lately eaten, would be considered an offense.

As the service of the table, in most of the cities, at all the hotels, and many of the best private houses partakes of the nature of French cooking, it is only in the rural parts one can see the *bona fide* Cuban dishes.

The daily meals of the more humble farmers consist of fried pork and boiled rice in the morning, and, in lieu of bread, the roasted plantain. At dinner, they make use of cow-beef, jerked beef, birds, and roasted pig; but usually this meal consists of roasted plantains, and the national dish of *ajiaco*, or what we should call an Irish stew. This dish is to the island what *olla podrida* is to Spain. It is composed of fresh meat, either beef or pork,—dried meat of either,—all sorts of vegetables, young corn, and green plantains. It is made with plenty of broth, thickened with a farinaceous root known as *malanga*, and has also some lemon-juice squeezed into it. It is, I assure the reader, toothsome, cheap, and nutritious,—quite equal to the French *pot au feu*. Boiled rice is never dispensed with at any meal, and the cooking of it is understood to perfection. It is used mixed in all their stews, or with a simple sauce of tomatoes. *El aporreado* is made of half raw meat, dressed with water, vinegar, salt, etc., which operation is known as *perdigar* (or stewing in an earthen pan); then mashed and stirred together, it is fried slightly in a sauce (*mojo*) of lard, tomatoes, garlic, onions, and peppers. *Picadillos*, or hashes, are always good upon the island,—town or country,—even if one does not know who made them. The *tasajo brujo*, or jerked beef bewitched, so called from the fact that it grows so much larger in cooking, is the dish found almost everywhere, and cooked in many ways. It is almost always a savory dish the traveler need not be afraid of, particularly if he has had army experience. There are some other dishes, but with the knowledge of the above, the stranger will be safe to accept an invitation to dine with any of the *haciendados*, and it will also be seen that Cuban cookery is not such a fearful thing as we have been led to believe; for little or no oil is used, and the small quantity of garlic used is so disguised in other things that few people could tell it. . . .

Every village, or pueblo, has a patron saint, for whom there is a special *dia de fiesta*, which all the villagers and people in the vicinity celebrate with masses, etc., at the village church, and afterwards by games, dancing, and sports, the women taking part also as spectators if in no other way. But usually they are divided into two parties, each party being distinguished by the color of the ribbon it wears, and which gives its name to the band. Each party elects a queen, chosen for her grace, beauty, or good style, and the admirers of each are known as vassals, and they give their presence to the amusement going on. When the performers belonging to one party or the other are successful, the vanquished party with its queen and vassals has to render homage to the rival queen. The goose-fight, or *corrida de patos*, is another one of their sports, and a very cruel one it is; for in a plaza or smooth field two forked poles are set up, and from one to the other a rope is stretched; in the middle of this a live goose is hung, firmly tied by the feet. The place is now filled with spectators, while five, ten, or fifteen mounted *guajiros* pass at full gallop in front of the goose, and attempt to seize the head, which has been well greased, and separate it from the body in their full career. Of course many unsuccessful attempts are made, and the bird usually dies before the efforts are successful, but he who succeeds in this glorious attempt is declared victor.

Las loas (or prologues) are practiced in the country villages in their religious feasts and civil celebrations,—as processions of the Holy Virgin or the Patron Saint, etc. A little girl, dressed (or undressed) as an image, is conducted, publicly, in a small cart profusely decorated with banners, flowers, and branches; before her, march on horseback four or six men, in costumes of Indians, and behind, others clad as Moors. A band plays, and the procession, which is composed of almost all the people of the village, when arrived at the appointed place (plaza) stops, and the child stands up and recites or declaims her loa, a composition appropriate to the subject of the celebration.

Altares de Cruz,—the custom of forming altars in the houses in the first days of May, in order to celebrate the invention of the Holy Cross, is preserved very generally in the interior of the island, but with a character almost entirely profane. The altar is erected modestly in a sleeping-room of the house, on the 3d of May, or day of Santa Cruz, and on every day of the first nine, the guests gather before it, to dance, sing, play, and eat and drink at times. On the first night, the master of the house delivers a branch of flowers to the guest that he chooses, and the latter contracts, in receiving it, the obligation to re-form the altar, and pay the expenses of the next night's entertainment, he himself taking the name of the godfather or *mayordomo.* The second night arrived, the godfather or godmother renews this performance of the branch upon another victim, and it thus happens that each altar has a new mayordomo for each night, and as every one endeavors to do better than his predecessor, it happens that the last night winds up the festival with a superb supper and a full orchestra.

Mamarrachos is the name given to the individuals on horse-back, who, in a great part of the Vuelta Arriba, ride, masked and grotesquely costumed, through the streets, during the Carnival or other seasons of merry-making. Surprise parties, known as *asaltos*, are very numerous, not only amongst the country people but at the watering-places during the season.

The country dances, however, are something especially peculiar, many old-fashioned customs and figures being retained, although the usual waltzes and contra-dances are danced, too, under the name of *bailes de musica*, while the former are known as *changüis* or *guateques*, and are less formal, being the social meetings of intimate friends or neighbors.

The especial dance is the one known as the *zapateo*, and is peculiar to this island. It is danced to the music of the harp, the guitar, or the songs of the *guajiros*, by both women and men, and has good many peculiar figures, the principal object appearing to me, to be for the women to see how many men they can tire out, as they give every now and then a signal to their *vis à vis* "to leave," when he is replaced by another. A low humming or singing is kept up by those present, broken every now and then by the loud plaudits of the spectators at the success of some dancer.

In many sections of the country one still finds sugar estates, almost as they were originally, in the possession of owners of moderate means and little intelligence, who have not availed themselves of the advantages afforded by improved machinery and scientific modes of making sugar.

Some of the places, again, are so poor in soil and product, having been worked for so many years without intermission, that the owners do not deem it worth while, even if they can afford the outlay, to put up new mills and machinery,—much preferring to try new land.

Richard J. Levis
Diary of a Spring Holiday in Cuba
(Philadelphia: Porter and Coates, 1872), 61–63

The houses of the smaller farmers and the country people generally, even among some who are said to be wealthy, are of a character which we in the North would consider most wretched. But the wretchedness pertains to outward circumstances which do not exist in this tropical climate, where merely protection from sun and rain is desired. These houses are constructed of thin strips of the palm-tree or bamboo, with sometimes a fibrous material from the cocoanut tree packed in between them. The roof is thatched with palm leaves, and the floor merely bare ground, and that is worn into a rough, uneven condition. There may be partitions dividing the space into several rooms, which seem usually dark on account of closure of the window-shutter, if there be one. A few rough chairs and a table constitute the furniture, which with some enormous and ornamented saddles, some ox-yokes, and a piece of jerked beef, with small sheafs of unhulled rice, or bunches of herbs hanging from the rafters, make up the household property.

I rode this morning through the country beyond the sugar plantations, among the poorer orders of country people, who live in this style of houses. They are a humble class, of marked peculiarities; but their manners and courteous deportment in general are their best features. Their dress is primitive, being merely a linen shirt worn outside the pantaloons, which are of the same material, and a pair of low shoes or slippers on bare feet. They continually wear swords, either long or short, often ornamented with silver, and ride with large rattling spurs. It is impossible to be among them without being impressed with their kindness, and, even among the humblest, with a little polish of manner.

James Williams Steele
Cuban Sketches
(New York: G. P. Putnam's Sons, 1881), 26–29, 116–20

Nor is it the land of rural wealth and comfort, as we understand the term, notwithstanding the prolific soil and plentiful rains. The total want of the appearance of it is impressive. The farmer lives in a cabin of the rudest construction, and is himself as rude and poor as his dwelling. Those who are able to recall the cuts in the school geographies of twenty years ago, many possibly remember the representations of certain little thatched huts, whose roofs looked very much like the last year's hayrick. In front were depicted some naked little negroes, and in the background two or three palms. These were graphic pictures, and the very same may be seen to-day. They are the dwellings of the Cuban farmer and his family. White houses, hedges, blooming plants, green grass, smiling fields, are unknown. Any thing that looks like home is wanting in the landscape. I should conclude that farming in Cuba did not pay. If there is any money in it, it is not expended upon luxury. There are a few people around these wretched *sitios*, and they gave me the idea of serfs. Their hats are bad, their pantaloons are shabby, and their faces are seamed, worn, hard, and hopeless. In a land celebrated for its easily acquired fortunes, the farmer is universally ignorant, invariably poor. He may not be unhappy, for he is of a class to whom a condition of semi-wretchedness has been hard work and an unchanging condition. The reader will understand that I am not now speaking of the great sugar plantations, whose existence has helped to produce this state of things, and whose management can in no case be called farming.

These pictures of rural life must dwell in the memory of every one who has seen Cuba. The miserable little house, with its palm-leaf roof and earthen floor, is unfit for a cattle shed, and a degree worse than a Nevada "dugout." There is a piece of broken fence that never was whole, or oftener, a ragged and briar-covered cactus hedge. There are no outhouses or conveniences. The cocks and hens saunter in and out of the open door, and a lean goat or two stand in profound reverie. Pigs, lean and hairless, with their broken tethers adorning their necks, wander here and there in search of what a pig may fancy. Perhaps a bullock stands tethered by the nose amid plentiful stones and scant grass, and a sad-looking cow keeps him company. Naked children play beside the door, and squalid and half-clad women loaf promiscuously about the premises. Away in the fallow-ground the man of the place struggles to make a long scratch on the ground with his yoke of oxen and his Egyptian plow made of the crotch of a tree. As he walks beside its one handle, and urges his lean cattle with strange cries and a long stick, and creeps to the end of his inadequate furrow at a snail's pace, you wonder to think that the father and grandfather of this genius of famine did the same before him, and his son will do it after him, and probably none of them ever committed suicide.

You meet this man in the early morning on his way to sell his produce at the nearest town. It is green cornstalks, or melons, or, perhaps, two paniers of yellow oranges, or green grass, or milk in stone jugs stoppered with an ear of corn,—whatever it may be, it is always carried pack-fashion on horses. Wagons are not practicable on the Cuban roads, and a long and plodding string of animals, laden until only their tails and noses are visible, is the commonest of sights on the highway. Horse and man are stained alike by the deep-red mud of the country. Horse and man alike are lean in flesh, and intensely, ploddingly, laboriously occupied with the work in hand. They have daily gone the same paths for years bearing the same burdens, and seemingly without any reward. Life is not necessarily easy and indolent where the plantain grows, as we have so often heard it is.

This peasant, a son of the soil, and the man who, except the negro, has lived the longest and worked the hardest on it, has no connection with or interest in, the tall white chimneys that here and there appear across the landscape, and represent the great industry of the country. For hundreds of acres around them grows the cane. Hundreds of unpaid toilers feed their fires and caldrons from January to May. Hundreds of thousands of dollars are invested in the industry of which these monumental chimneys are the centres. These plantations grow nothing but cane. They do not generally so much as produce the corn eaten by the oxen and negroes. Every energy of every man and animal is concentrated upon the task of producing as many pounds as possible of the sugar which, for many years, has paid the largest profit of any known production of the soil, and paid it at the general cost of the whole country, in its morals, its education, its general happiness, its healthy growth, and the manhood and independence of its people. The decay of many, and the enriching of the few, is ever the direct result of the production of one great staple by slave labor. . . .

The Cuban village has been there some hundred or more years. Bayamo, Baracoa, and others were actually founded by the followers of Diego Velasquez [1465–1524, Spanish *conquistador*

of Cuba, 1511, and the island's first governor] somewhere about
1500, and the rest came stumbling along after. It would excite the
surprise and pity of the whole population if anybody were to
speak of founding a city now. The preposterousness of the idea
would send the projector to a lunatic asylum, if there were any
lunatic asylums. A Cuban Rip Van Winkle would have no difficulty
in recognizing his native place if he should unfortunately awake
and come back again. There is about them all a certain quality of
changelessness. I have passed through some of them at intervals
of two or three years, and while I beg pardon of their oldest
inhabitant for mentioning so trifling and unimportant an interval,
it seemed to me that the same untidy women were standing at the
doors in the same gowns. The same old men, with the same shirt
worn outside of their pantaloons, were, I fancied, still crying the
same lottery tickets. The same forlorn row of mosquito-bitten
horses, with the same old pack-saddles on their raw backs, were
still standing with closed eye and hanging lip, asleep under the
same shed, in front of the same old whitewashed, weather-beaten
grocery. I know they were the same goats, the same cocks and
hens, the same pigs; and the same incomparable, indescribable
sense of loneliness hung over all; the same as ever, the same for
always. The mystery of drowsiness, idleness, poverty, and content,
pervaded the air and possessed the people, and they were all
unchanged.

A peculiar feature of a Cuban village is a certain stickiness. It
is a sweetish mixture, largely composed of spilled molasses and
the drainage of sugar-hogsheds, with rain-water. The whole
country has a faint odor as of a molasses-cask. The natural article
of mud is red, brilliant brick color. Of the dust likewise. It rains
and is muddy seven months out of the twelve, and is dry and
dusty the remaining five months, so that the red color prevails
most of the time. It gets smeared in streaks and patches, or a
brilliant body-color, over every thing, and gives a distinctive
character to the region. There seems to be no good reason for
whitewashing, which always seems to have been done some
years previously, unless it be to show by more striking contrast
the gory streaks incarnadine. The mud is not of the kind that
comes off when it dries. It will wash, and every hairless and
vagrant pig who has slipped his tether and regaled himself with a
bath, and then has neatly dried himself against a warehouse or a

railway station, leaves there his indelible mark. Every old gray horse's tail is of a fine red that glistens in the sun, and his master's linen garments have a thick and polished coating of it.

All the houses of the place, inside and outside, and even the furniture, are stained and dried in this universal pigment. The sifting dust and tenacious mud of an age have produced a color that does not show dirt, and enables the people to avoid overmuch scrubbing and brooming. All the houses stand flat on the earth. They are not high, but they are endless sidewise and illimitable endwise. There is much door, and a great deal of window and shed-in-front, unless they are very small to comply with the humble tastes of the proprietor, in which case they remind one of the decayed out-buildings of a farm-house in Virginia. I have never seen a building in process of erection in one of these villages, and never met a person who had. They were made and finished long ago, and now they do not seem any more to be even repaired.

This is the railway hamlet, and one the traveller oftenest sees and that may be observed by anybody. It is, however, not a town made by the railway, as ours often are, but one the line happened to be built through. I must ask the reader to exercise his imagination upon the genuine inland country place, away from everywhere, where the steam-whistle is never heard. The age, the dulness, the infinite peace which broods over one of these, are nearly indescribable, and where these things come and abide I have observed that the inhabitants are happy. The roads that lead to them are, like the roads of Spain, impracticable for any thing greatly wider than a mule. Ambition has never entered here. The world is bounded by the sound of the church-bells. There is nothing more exciting in all their annals than the common accidents of every-day life. The thousand anxieties of the world poison no lives; there is no discontent. Even the climate is changeless, and cold and the driving blast can never make the straggling street more quiet than it is. The happy varlet whose lines have been cast here, is rich with a single pair of trousers and a speckled shirt, and an aristocrat when he goes abroad in his coat. Recall all the villages you ever visited, all the post-offices and cross-roads, all the mountain hamlets, and you will still lack something that only climate can make. This is of the tropics. Over all, the palm lifts its head, and the plaintain, like a huge cereal, shakes its wide, torn leaves in the idle wind. It is blood-warm. The fierce sunshine glares upon the scene every day, and the dew soaks it every night, and happy, half-clad, basking laziness abides forever.

I wonder is there a common kinship among all the tribes of toil and ignorance all over the world? For this villager's house, his life, his surroundings, remind me of something I have read of villages far enough away,—in Western Asia, perhaps, or in Japan. This Cuban has all he wants, and understands what he does want. Upon his floor of earth, the pigs, poultry, and dogs have as much place as he himself has. They pass in and out with a loafing, hands-in-the-pocket air. His table, when he has a table, is well supplied. He lives well, though a liking for his dishes is a matter of education. He has a great affection for the small-fry of domestic animals and the cock crows with impunity from the door-sill to celebrate the laying of an egg in the cupboard by the hen. He has no stable, no haystack, no crib. He does not need any of these things. The dense chaparral begins where his native village ends. Every one whom he knows, he has known always, and none of his acquaintances are aristocratic. When he dies, and the priest-fettered soul goes to find out the truth of all his unquestioned articles of faith, he is carried to the little desolate *Campo Santo* at the village-end, and perhaps talked of more and remembered longer than many a statesman is after he is dead.

There is another *Guajiro*, who is, even more than this villager, a rural specimen. His house is such as you see standing alone upon its hill-side, all over Cuba. It is the poorest of human habitations; four posts, with a roof of palm husks, and its wattled sides are a delusive refuge against a windy rain. It is only a local habitation, a place to go. Sometimes it is so poor in its surroundings that there is not even a goat. This man's days are spent in burning charcoal, or in raising a few vegetables for the nearest town, or he is a milkman, or a peddler of eggs. Whatever it is, he seems to toil all his life and gain nothing. You hear him pass by in the early morning, vociferating his unearthly ejaculations and horse-talk to his string of laden beasts. I have often wondered why he did not stop work, and defy fortune to do any worse for him than she had done. But he too seems happy enough, and the sum of his life is doubtless the same to him that the sum of ours is to us.

Yet all this is not the rural Cuba that most people care to see and write about. There is another view of the picture. There have been many magazine articles written, all more or less rose-colored, about life on the sugar-plantation. It is nearly all that a great majority of visitors see or care for, and all that any one they know cares for.

Maturin Murray Ballou
Due South; or, Cuba Past and Present
(Boston: Houghton Mifflin and Company, 1885), 230–32

The Monteros or yeomanry of the island inhabit the less cultivated and cheaper portions of the soil, entering the cities only to dispose of their surplus produce, and acting as the marketmen of the populous districts. When they stir abroad, in nearly all parts of the island, they are armed with sword, and in the eastern sections about Santiago, or even Cienfuegos, they also carry pistols in the holsters of their saddles. Formerly this was indispensable for self-protection, but at this time weapons are more rarely worn. Still the arming of the Monteros has always been encouraged by the authorities, as they form a sort of militia at all times available against negro insurrection, a calamity in fear of which such communities must always live. The Montero is rarely a slaveholder, but is frequently engaged on the sugar plantations during the busy season as an overseer, and, to his discredit be it said, he generally proves to be a hard taskmaster, entertaining an intuitive dislike to the negroes.

An evidence of the contagious character of cruelty was given in a circumstance coming under the author's observation on a certain plantation at Alquizar, where the manifest piece of severity led him to appeal to the proprietor in behalf of a female slave. The request for mercy was promptly granted, and acting overseer, himself a mulatto, was quietly reprimanded for his cruelty. "You will find," said our host, "that colored men always make the hardest masters when placed over their own race, but they have heretofore been much employed on the island in this capacity, because a sense of pride make them faithful to the proprietor's interest. That man is himself a slave," he added, pointing to the sub-overseer, who still stood among the negroes, whip in hand.

The Montero sometimes hires a free colored man to help him in the planting season on his little patch of vegetable garden, in such work as a Yankee would do for himself, but these small farmers trust mostly to the exuberant fertility of the soil, and spare themselves all manual labor, save that of gathering the produce and taking it to market. They form, nevertheless, a very important and interesting class of the population. They marry very young, the girls at thirteen and fifteen, the young men from sixteen to eighteen, and almost invariably rear large families. Pineapples and children are a remarkably sure crop in the tropics. The increase among them during the last half century has been very large, much more in proportion than in any other class of the community, and they seem to be approaching a degree of importance, at least numerically, which will render them eventually like the American farmers, the bone and sinew of the land. There is room enough for them and to spare, for hardly more than one tenth of the land is under actual cultivation, a vast portion being still covered by virgin forests and uncleared savannas. The great and glaring misfortune—next to that of living under a government permitting neither civil nor religious liberty, where church and state are alike debased as the tools of despotism,—is their want of educational facilities. Books and schools they have none. Barbarism itself is scarcely less cultured. We were told that the people had of late been somewhat aroused from this condition of lethargy concerning education, and some effort has recently been made among the more intelligent to afford their children opportunities for instruction. But at the present writing, the Egyptian fellah is not more ignorant than the rural population of Cuba, who as a mass possess all the indolence and few of the virtues of the aborigines.

There is one highly creditable characteristic evinced by the Monteros as a class, and that is their temperate habits in regard to indulgence in stimulating drinks. As a beverage they do not use ardent spirits, and seem to have no taste or desire for the article, though they drink the ordinary claret—rarely anything stronger. This applies to the country people, not to the residents of the cities. The latter quickly contract the habit of gin drinking, as already described. There is one prominent vice to which the Monteros are indisputably addicted; namely, that of gambling. It seems to be a natural as well as a national trait, the appliances for which are so constantly at hand in the form of lottery tickets and the cock-pits that they can hardly escape the baleful influences. There are some who possess sufficient strength of character and intelligence to avoid it altogether, but with the majority it is the regular resort for each leisure hour. One of their own statesmen, Castelar [Emilio Castelar, 1832–1899; leader of the rightist Republican Party and president of the Spanish republic, 1873–74], told the Spaniards, not long since, that gambling was the tax laid upon fools.

Perhaps the best place at which to study the appearance and character of the Monteros is at the Central Market, where they come daily by hundreds from the country in the early morning to sell their produce, accompanied by long lines of mules or horses with well-laden panniers. It is a motley crowd that one meets there, where purchasers and salesmen mingle promiscuously. From six to nine o'clock, A.M., it is the busiest place in all Havana. Negroes and mulattoes, Creoles and Spaniards, Chinamen and Monteros, men and women, beggars, purchasers, and slaves, all come to the market on the Calzada de la Reina. Here the display of fruits and vegetables is something marvelous, both in variety and in picturesqueness of arrangement. This locality is the natural resort of the mendicants, who pick up a trifle in the way of provisions from one and another, as people who do not feel disposed to bestow money will often give food to the indigent. This market was the only place in the city where it was possible to purchase flowers, but here one or two humble dealers came at early morn to dispose of such buds and blossoms as they found in demand.

VIII

Nineteenth-Century Society

Robert Francis Jameson
Letters from the Havana, during the Year 1820
(London: John Miller, 1821), 36–40

There are 370,000 people of colour in the island. Of these the *free* mulattoes and blacks rank first, more particularly in their own estimation. These beings (singular as it may seem to those ignorant of human nature) look down on those they are sprung from, if it be possible, with more contempt than the whites do, while they regard the latter with an envy, almost too natural to be condemned. Though tinted with the dye of slavery, they possess certain privileges, here called *freedom*, but which have little analogy to the European meaning of the word; they are unchained but the collar remains on their necks. They are subject to most of the restrictions imposed on the slave, such as respect carrying weapons, being out after dark without a lanthorn, etc. and they are equally deprived of information, their freedom by no means extending to their minds. Their condition is usually good, notwithstanding their extreme indolence. The high price of labour enables them to gain sufficient, by slight and discontinuous exertion, to pass nearly a third of their time in sleep or gambling. A free man of colour, who is a tolerable artificer, will make from *twelve reales* (6s.9d.) to *three dollars* (13s.6d.) per day, and this he earns rather by a sort of hysterical effort, than by *labour*. He will work half this day, a third of next, abandon his work the day after, and return as he feels the necessity. Perhaps in the middle of the work to be completed, he will leave his employer for another situated nearer his gaming haunts; no dependence is to be placed on him.

Those of this class who are domestics usually receive *six reales* (3s.4 1/2 d.) per day. If free from the vice of gaming they are generally honest, but a restlessness under any sort of restraint seems to characterize them. They consider themselves hired for some specific piece of service, as a *cook*, as a *calesero* (or coachman), as a *porter*, etc.; beyond the precise line of their duty, it is difficult to obtain their assistance, and they put their commentary on the contract of hiring. Two or three days after you have engaged them, they will tell you that you require too many dishes on your table—want your *volante* (carriage of the country) too often—or that you send too many messages. They quit you on the eve of a party, a drive out, or sealing a letter. Notwithstanding this, their service is preferable to that afforded by the gloomy slave, who knows he shall get nothing but harsh words and buffets for what he does, and who has no interest in exertion or prospect of its ending.

There are many coloured people whose freedom is the purchase of the extra earnings allowed them by law. These are the most valuable of their class and commonly continue in their course of industry as hawkers of market goods, and petty dealers in tobacco, etc. Those who reside in the country differ in little from the lower order of whites with whom they maintain a perfect fellowship. Both descriptions are frequently seen working together at the same trade, and I regret to say, still more frequently, gambling together. This vice and an immoderate love of dress are the bane of the labouring class. You would smile to see groups of black females with silk stockings, satten shoes, muslin gowns, French shawls, gold ear-rings and flowers in their woollen headdress, gallanted by black beaux, with white beaver hats, English coats and gold-headed canes, all smoking in concert like their superiors. These are your washerwomen and cobblers, festivalizing on a *"dias de dos cruces,"* or a church holiday. The next day you will have them at your door with some article of this finery, which they are seeking a sale for, to pay for the day's subsistence!

The distinction arising from holiday array is all this class of people can aspire to, or in which they can vie with the whites. The principle of depression, universally acted on with respect to them, keeps them down as a body, and puts them aside from the race of honourable emulation, excluding them from a course which the indolent whites are seen merely walking over. It is not to be wondered at, that the plant, which is prevented from rising, should grow crooked.

The number of free people of colour in this island is nearly equal to the total amount of that class in *all* the islands together. This is attributable to the mildness of the Spanish slave code which softens the rigour of their hard destiny, in a way very different from what would have been expected from a nation whose colonial enterprises have caused such waste of life and extent of misery amongst the Indian hordes.

John George F. Wurdemann
Notes on Cuba
(Boston: James Munroe and Company, 1844), 196–99

The Puerta de la Guira, near which Artemisa [Pinar del Rio] lies, contain 2610 whites, 378 free colored, and 8817 slaves; these are distributed as follows; 1021 on six sugar estates, 7225 on 73 coffee estates, and 2158 on 134 farms and other rural establishments. The whole partido of San Marcos has but two small sugar estates with 101 laborers, and 19 coffee estates with 1875; while its 168 farms are inhabited by 3078; its principal pueblo las Manjas contains a population of 183. Pendencias, in which is the Buena Esperanza, has 458 whites, 31 free colored, 3860 slaves. There is but one sugar estate in it with 190 laborers, 45 coffee estates, with 3861 blacks and whites, and 12 sitios [cattle ranches] with 298. The whole constitutes the most highly cultivated portion of the island, and although the prosperity of it has declined with the price of coffee, the scenery is so unique and lovely, that no one should neglect to visit it, even were the interested accounts of the difficulty of reaching it true.

One is struck by the number of estates here belonging to titled owners, some of whom have extensive landed possessions, that are rented out; paying a fixed annual tribute; so, that a large plantation may often be obtained for a yearly tax, without paying any purchase-money. Many wealthy persons have bought titles of nobility, not only on account of the rank they give possessors in society, but also for the exemption they confer from petty annoyances from captains of partidos, and other low officers of justice. The titled can only be tried by a high tribunal, and cannot be arrested for debt; military officers, also, can only be indicted before a military court, and priests before their ecclesiastical bodies.

There are 29 marquises and 30 counts on the island, more than half of whom have been created since 1816; Ferdinand VII, alone, made 11 marquises and 15 counts from 1816 to 1833. Most of them had acquired their wealth by sugar-plantations, and are jocosely called "sugar noblemen," often adopting the names of their estates, as the Marquis de Santa Lucia, the Conde de Casa-Romero. The Marquis del Real Socorro obtained his title from having presented a large sum of money to the government, when its coffers were exhausted, and a few others have had theirs conferred for military and other services to the State. The greatest number have, however, been bought, no considerations being paid to aught but the wealth of the individual; the mother country thus taxing the idle arrogance of her colonists. The prices vary from twenty to fifty thousand dollars, the purchaser being also compelled to entail a certain amount of property with the title.

The origin of many of this class of society, while it exposes them to the private derision of the untitled crowd, creates among themselves a clanish feeling, and presents an insuperable barrier to a general social spirit. The marquis of 1832 looks down with something like contempt on his younger brother of 1835, and those of the 17th or 18th century hold themselves quite aloof from the mushroom generation of the 19th. The tone of Cuba society is also eminently aristocratic, and certain circles are very exclusive. The native of old Spain does not conceal his hatred of foreigners and contempt of the Creole, and shields his own inferiority of intelligence and enterprise under a cloak of hauteur. The native of Cuba, on the other hand, sees himself almost entirely excluded from all offices under government, the army and the church, and regards with no favorable eye those who are thus sent to mend their fortunes at his expense, and to exact to the utmost from his gains. The Spaniard and the Creole thus form two distinct classes of society; and the foreigners from other countries, regarded with jealousy by one class for the liberal principles they insensibly instill in the people, and with envy by the other for dispossessing them of some of the branches of industry, constitute another class.

Then the untitled crowd is divided into the sugar-planter, the coffee-planter, and the merchant; the liberal professions and the literati; all below them forming a single class, with which the rest do not associate. The planter holds a scale above the merchant, whose genius directs the stream of wealth that flows into the land; and at whose nod the former beholds his fields covered with cane, his bohea [*bohios*] peopled with Africa's sons, and his costly sugar-works spread their extensive sheds, for which he pays a heavy interest. There is so much corruption at the bar and on the bench, that, as a class, the dispensers of *justicia* are not respected, how much soever individuals among them may attain a high rank in society. The medical profession here confers no honor in itself, for the doctor is frequently confounded with the barber-surgeon; and it is probably in revenge for thus being placed on a level with Strap, that the Spanish physicians forbid their patients to shave while indisposed, thus undermining their professional brethren. But wealth here breaks down all the barriers of distinct classes; the millionaire has a box-ticket in the theatre of Cuba life, and ranges at will from the pit to the galleries.

In polite life the manners resemble those of Paris, with the addition of a double proportion of empty compliments ingrafted on it. It is pleasant enough to acknowledge the introduction to a fine woman by the common phrase, *"a los pies de usted señora,"* "at the feet of your grace, my lady," while the action is almost suited to the words; but compliments to the other sex are on the same extravagant scale, and the half of one's visit is occupied in bandying them from one to another. One cannot express his admiration of a breast-pin, an article of dress, or anything else, without receiving an answer that it is at your command; with such sincerity of expression, that the stranger is half tempted to accept, merely to oblige the one who offers. The constant offer of the house and all its contents, on an introduction to a family, is well known. It is, however, extremely unpolite to accept the merest trifle thus tendered, and it is even considered a breach of good-breeding to express your admiration of things with which the owner can easily dispense.

William Henry Hurlbert
Gan-Eden; or, Picture of Cuba
(Boston: John P. Jewett and Company, 1854), 155–59,
163–66

The whites in Cuba numbering, I suppose, (for nobody exactly knows,) about four hundred thousand souls, are divided primarily into old Spaniards, or Peninsulars, and Creoles. The old Spaniards fill all the offices of the island, and transact by far the greater part of its commercial affairs.

The mother country has been in the habit of applying her sons, like leeches, to the bodies of her colonies, and the successive generations of old Spaniards have come upon the Indies, like those great waves of barbaric invasion which swept over the Roman Empire. Naturally enough the old Spaniard looks down upon the Creole with the contempt of a conqueror. Not less naturally the Creole regards his kinsmen of Castile with a sort of spiteful aversion. The bright-eyed boy at the cafe curls his full lip with scorn, when you ask him if he was born in Cuba, and his shrill treble grows a clarion in the reply, "No, Señor! Soy Asturiano!" The judge on the bench, the beaten soldier at the barracks, assume towards the native of the island, something of the port with which an Alvarado or a Sandoval [Pedro de Alvarado and Gonzalo de Sandoval, officers in the Cortes expedition to Mexico, 1519–21] imposed respect upon the defeated Aztec. But the Spanish superiority does not consume itself in sneers and airs. The old Spaniards monopolize the most profitable traffic. The Catalans, the yankees of old Spain, the hard-headed, shrewd Catalans, faithful to their motto of "five years of privations, and a fortune," are to be found in every town and hamlet, and in every state of social development, from the domestic grub, toilsomely outspinning the brilliant cocoon that is to be, up or down to the gay and gorgeous butterfly of the second generation, rejoicing in the sunshine of fashionable life. The Catalans are generally very loyal, for they enjoy a number of monopolies which, like all monopolists, they blindly and ignorantly cherish, to the serious injury of Cuba. Political economy in Spain seems to be just abreast with the wisdom of the age of Walpole. For instance, the flour monopoly so protects the exporters of Ferrol and Santander, that the wheat of northern Spain, originally very good, is forced upon the Cuban markets, after undergoing voyages of such a length, that one can only account for them, by supposing that each captain, on every trip, has to find the new world all over again, without reference to Columbus. . . .

More irreconcilably hostile than the merchants to the Creole population, are the old Spanish officials. It is really hard to exaggerate the extent to which bribery and corruption are carried among these persons, or the annoyances to which the unprotected natives are subjected at the hands of Dogberrys clothed with more or less authority. At Havana, it is notoriously impossible to procure any paper of importance at the government house, without employing an *agente* or general broker, a limited number of whom are licensed by the government. I tried to experiment myself of applying personally for a certain document, but after dancing attendance for nearly a week in the large and little rooms of the Palace, I gave it up and put the matter into the hands of an agente, who within the day brought me the required parchment stamped conspicuously with the word *gratis*, and demanded seven dollars as the price thereof! These fees are of course divided with the subordinates at the Palace. The whole thing is in the purest oriental taste, but one must be very immoral to enjoy it.

Throughout the country, the "paternal" government is as *affectionately watchful* over the people as a duenna aunt over a pretty niece, and as *judiciously* firm as an old-fashioned schoolmaster. Englishmen and Americans, more accustomed to worry than to be worried by their governments, can hardly bring themselves to believe in the reality of such an incessant, inquisitive, undignified tyranny as prevails wherever a "strong government" is "maintaining order."

No man can be trusted with irresponsible power, and the system which multiplies petty authorities beyond the reach of public opinion, must entail upon any country the curse which weighs on Cuba. To support the army which keeps this swarm of functionaries safe, the Cubans are taxed much more heavily than any other civilized people.

From the officials, who aptly enough supply the places of the venomous and annoying insects from which Cuba is singularly free, I pass to that great body of the natives on which they feed.

The first conquerors of Cuba, like Harrison at Naseby field, "did not their work negligently." The name of the second

commercial city of the island, Matanzas, or the Massacres, com-
memorates, it is said, the last of the great slaughters which
overtook the idolatrous Indians, who were so profane as to object
to the combined gift of slavery and salvation which the Christians
proffered them. The trooper's sword and the miner's spade
evangelized Cuba, and the present natives of the island, unlike
the hybrid peons of the continent, are of pure Spanish blood. The
twenty-two cities or towns of some size which exist in the island,
contain a fair proportion of these Creoles, a few more are scattered
over the great haciendas or estates of the sugar and coffee planters; but the great majority of the native born whites is to be found
on the vegas and tobacco farms, in the villages and hamlets of the
interior. These are the people who must give to Cuba its chief
national peculiarities. The planters, of course, give tone to the
highest ranks of Cuban society. To their number belong the
thirty or forty marquises and counts of Cuba, the "sugar nobles,"
as the old Spaniards call them in disdain, though one might
suppose that if blood may be used to clarify sugar, sugar may
reasonably enough be used to clarify blood, and it is hard to see
why a title honestly bought with good gold doubloons is not quite
as good a thing as a title taken by force of arms, or purchased by
worse than menial services rendered to some vulgar sensual
prince. Closely allied with the planters are the great Creole merchants. Often very opulent, these Creoles of the first rank are
almost always distinguished for the easy courtesy of their manners,
and for the genial hospitality of their households. Nor are they
wanting in enterprise. Cuba, in the matter of railways, may compare favorably with many of the American States, and the railways
are the result of Creole energy and enterprise. The Creole planters are indefatigable in their efforts to improve their estates, and
to develop the resources of their magnificent island. No one of
the southern States can show a finer, few can show so fine a body
of intelligent and well-bred gentlemen as the haciendas and the
cities of Cuba may be justly proud of possessing. The women of
this class generally exhibit those qualities of warm and devoted
affection which so universally adorn the female history of the
Spanish race. But the imperfection of their education, in many
cases, and in many more the absence of noble incitements to
mental and moral activity, condemns these fine natures to a life
which withers and wastes their best energies. From these higher
classes of Cuban society have come the most enlightened and

fervent advocates of Cuban liberty and independence. Were we to judge the intellectual and moral resources of the island, by the proofs, with which the poets, patriots, and orators of this class have furnished us, of cultivated powers and lofty aspirations, we should go far beyond the mark. With the exception of the extraordinary mulatto of Matanzas, Placido [Gabriel de la Concepción Valdéz, 1809–1844, a gifted poet implicated in the Escalera conspiracy of 1844 and executed by Spanish authorities], all those Cubans who have distinguished themselves generously, in literature or in life, belong to the planting or urbane classes.

W.M.L. Jay [Julia Louisa M. Woodruff]
My Winter in Cuba
(New York: E. P. Dutton and Company, 1871), 83–84

Juan and I rattle and swing to the depot in a *volante*. Then I am left in the waiting-room for some moments, while he attends to tickets, permits and checks. Here, I find myself, for once, the "observed of all observers,"—not so desirable a position, by any means, as it sounds! However, after returning as many of the glances levelled at me as I can, conveniently, I decide that my neighbors are justified in staring, if my travelling costume is as much of a queerity to them as theirs is to me! The ladies are all attired in silk or muslin, as if for an afternoon at home, without bonnets, gloves, or wraps; two only wear the Spanish mantilla of black lace which I have seen at church. Their long trains—which they never hold up—sweep the pavement. Their flitting, glistening, coquettish fans—always in motion, and now and then opened and shut with a sharp, sudden snap, only attainable by long practice— make the room as brilliant as if it were swarming with butterflies. They have no parasols; I have not seen such a thing in use since I came to this Land of the Sun, where it would seem to be almost a necessity. But Cuban ladies never go out in the middle of the day, while the sun is hottest, if it can be avoided. When they do, the overhanging volante top is a sufficient protection, or if they choose to ride with that thrown back, they face shine and wind "like a man." No, I do not mean *that*, either—for the men all wear hats! Such exposure has its legitimate effect on the complexion, and the "fair sex," in Cuba, is uncommonly dark.

On the floor of the room are squatted some half dozen negresses, in the capacity of ladies' maids. Their heads are gorgeously turbaned, of course; but their dress, in other particulars, seems designed for a broad caricature of that of their mistresses. Others, in a lower order of servitude, are clad in a single garment, a coarse sort of "baby-frock," slipping off the shoulders, and frequently gaping in the back enough to reveal the shining ebony skin and firm, strong muscle beneath. If, by any chance, one of these is so fortunate as to own an under-garment, it is sure to be "Isabella" color; and lest any of my friends should inquire forthwith for that new tint on Broadway, or Main street, I will just mention, *en passant*, that it gets its name from a certain Spanish Queen, who vowed to the Virgin that in consideration of some favor which she desired, she would not change her linen for a year. And she kept her vow! Isabella color is very common in Cuba.

There are two railway routes from Havana to Matanzas. One, known as the "Regla route," is very direct, and measures about sixty miles; and other winds through the interior of the island, to bring out the sugar crop, and lengthens the journey to nearly one hundred miles. Being offered my choice, I designated the latter, as it would give me a better opportunity of studying the country.

The cars are quite homelike in appearance bearing the name of a well-known Massachusetts firm; but so dingy, from long use, as to suggest the need of fresh importation. They differ from ours only in having cane backs and bottoms to the seats; upholstery being almost unknown in Cuba, as it is thought ill suited to the climate. They who know how long my existence vibrated between cushion and pillow, before I came hither, will wonder that I live to make the statement; and the recollection of our luxuriously stuffed furniture is infinitely aggravating to an invalid. Moreover, the Cuban race lounges so naturally and persistently, I marvel that it does not provide itself with the means to do it thoroughly. The comfort of a cane-seated sofa is not patent, to me!

Samuel Hazard
Cuba with Pen and Pencil
(Hartford: Hartford Publishing Company, 1871), 183–87

When there is an opera troupe in Havana, representations are given generally four times a week; and, as all the best troupes generally go there sometime during the winter, one is always sure of hearing some good music during the season,—particularly is this the case in the holiday season, and usually, Sunday nights, the house is crowded. Off-nights, they have sometimes excellent dramatic performances by native or Spanish troupes.

To enter the house, gentlemen simply buy their *boleta de entrada* (entrance ticket), and if they wish a seat, they need also to buy a *boleta de luneta* (a seat in the pit), which is that part of the house frequented almost exclusively by gentlemen in full dress.

If it is desired to be economical, a seat in the *tertulia*, which answers to our second tier, is quite comfortable, respectable, and much cheaper. The seats called *butacos* are armchairs. The part of the house containing these is divided into two portions, one of which is reserved exclusively for ladies unaccompanied by gentlemen, the other for ladies and gentlemen.

The *palcos* (boxes) are fashionable parts of the house, and these are known as *primer, segunda,* and *tercer* pisos (first, second and third stories), all of which are good, though preference is usually given to the first or second.

These boxes have no fixed seats, simply four or six chairs, and are all open, being divided from the lobbies by a simple movable blind, partition, and door, and in front, a light and graceful railing, surmounted by a velvet-covered balustrade.

At night, when there is a full house, it is a really beautiful sight to see the elegantly dressed women, *en grande toilette,* as they sit in the boxes in the different tiers, the light railing in from not preventing the full length figures of elegant material showing, which, with the bright and cheerful colors in which the house is painted, give a very brilliant appearance to the scene, the sombre-coated men in the *luneta* only serving to make an effective background or setting. . . .

Calling a passing volante, we will go out to "El Louvre." This is the best and largest cafe in Havana, and may be said to be "the club;" for here you see all the world (without his wife). It is a fine, large saloon, opposite the Tacon theatre, at the corner of the streets, and is a very cool and pleasant place in which to get your *refrescos,* or smoke your cigar with a friend.

The Tacon is a large, substantially-built theatre, capable of holding about three thousand persons, and was, until within the last few years, considered, with the exception of the Grand theatre at Milan, to be the largest and handsomest of the world. There is a colonnade in front that in bad weather the carriages are allowed to drive under, and discharge their occupants; also a fine, large hall, with refreshment-rooms on each side, into which open the entrances to the lobbies of the theatre. The interior of the theatre is very handsome and capacious, is five stories in height, and possesses a very large stage, to the right of which, looking from the auditorium, is the box of the Captain-General, with its state decorations, by whom of an opera night it is generally occupied.

There is always present, also, an official representative of the government, whose business it is to see that the performance goes on properly; and if anything happens by which it appears the public are trifled with, the manager or the singers at fault are arrested, and compelled to perform, under penalty of a heavy fine.

The Cubans, like all natives of warm climates, are very fond of music, and have exceedingly fine taste and a correct ear; and as a consequence they will stand no nonsense from the performers, condemning them with the noise of their feet, which they move in measured time. It is proper to applaud only with the hands.

Between the acts there is a good deal of visiting by the gentlemen upon the ladies, who usually remain in their boxes to receive their friends, seldom or never going into the lobbies.

The gentlemen, on the contrary, fill the main lobby during the acts, to chat together, smoke their cigarettes or the heavier "entre opera" cigar.

Some oddities will strike the stranger, even in the opera house, particularly that of the dandified, showily dressed little negro pages, most of them bright-eyed, sharp little fellows, who, in most "gorgeous array," stand outside the boxes of their beautiful mistresses, ready to obey and mandate or execute any commission they may entrust to them,—such as carrying messages from one box to another, or slipping a card or note into the hand of some gentleman admirer. The government, too, takes particular care to keep everything in order and propriety, to secure which there is a special force detailed from the Guardia Civil to keep order. Outside they even station the military on opera nights to prevent the carriages from going through the streets alongside of the theatre, since, as they are entirely open, the noise from them would drown out the performance. These sentries are perfect pictures, being mounted gens d'armes, on superb gray horses, and uniformed in white cloth coats, large boots, white tights and black chapeaux; looking altogether, as they sit immovable on their well packed saddles, and very models of *chasseurs à cheval*.

George Walton Williams
Sketches of Travel in the Old and New World
(Charleston, SC: Walker, Evans and Cogswell, 1871), 12–13

Before leaving Havana, I must speak of the ladies. I have looked in vain for the beautiful Spanish and Creole women, of who we hear and read so much. You seldom see a lady walking in the streets; their visiting and shopping, is done in the *volantes*— they drive in front of the stores, and the silks and satins are brought out to them. There are no King street promenaders here. If a display is to be made, it is in the ugliest of all carriages, the *volante.* You may see a few elegantly dressed ladies walking in the Plaza de Armas. There is no grace or elasticity in their movements; they drag themselves along very clumsily, not unlike the Chinese. The majority of the women seem to live an easy life; they do not appear to work either with their hands or heads. I have watched them from early morning till late at night, and coquetting with their fans is about all that I have been able to see them doing. Sitting in front of the tall, prison-barred windows, with chairs arranged to catch the breeze, looking at every passer by, is a favorite occupation—seldom do you see them reading. A characteristic anecdote is related of an American sailor, who saw several ladies looking out upon the street through their grated parlor windows, supposing them to be prisoners. He told them to keep a good heart; and then, after observing that he had been in limbo himself, he threw them a silver dollar, to the great amusement of the "prisoners," and the spectators who understood the position of the inmates. Young ladies are not permitted to be alone with gentlemen. I do not know whether this is due to a want of gallantry on the part of the men, or to the great caution of prudent mothers. You occasionally see the gentlemen talking to them through the iron bars. Ladies do not wear bonnets as with us; a thin veil is usually thrown over the head. I have been to church daily since I came to the Island, and I have not yet seen a lady accompanied to the house of worship by her husband. It may not be fashionable for them to do so—or I may say customary—

238 *Slaves, Sugar, and Colonial Society*

for never was there a people under the sun who cling with a stronger grasp to old customs than the inhabitants of Cuba.

James Williams Steele
Cuban Sketches
(New York: G. P. Putnam's Sons, 1881), 57–63

The first female I saw in Cuba, to particularly observe her, was such a being as one remembers ever after. I was not charmed with her. She wore a gown of faded stuff, and a dingy shawl over her head. I saw, without any obtrusive endeavor to see, that she wore shoes and no stockings. Her mouth considerably resembled a crack in a fallen cocoa-nut, and there was a mole, the size of a blackberry, beside her nose. She unhesitatingly opened a conversation with me upon the subject of lottery tickets. She was evidently not a *Cubana*, as the greenest of strangers might perceive, but as Spanish as about forty years in the back room of a bodega could make her.

The next I saw within speaking distance was seated in a landeau beneath the gas-lights in the Prado. She was a mature beauty, fair-haired, rosy, and vivacious. I caught the Spanish name, but was addressed by her in pure and unaccented English. She was an American as much as I was, and had been the heroine of a much bewritten "diamond wedding" in New York some years before.

I continued to look for the Cuban lady, and was assisted in my search by eyes equally as inquisitive as my own, belonging as they did to one of the sex that is at present under consideration, and that have ere now discovered things that I cannot say I had myself endeavored to place in a clear light before them. I finally saw my first Cubana one evening in the parlor of a friend's house. My hostess informed me that she had reached the mature age of fourteen years. She was of large size and quite mature. She is, as I sometimes see her now in the year 1879, rather past the days of her youth, having been thrown upon the market early and disappointed in love. Her eyes were big and very black, her hair a coarse and shining mass, her complexion dark, her hands long, and such a varied assortment of jewellery I have seldom seen at one time outside a shop window. I was never informed whether she had it all at that moment upon her person;—there was enough.

By and by this young woman laughed. If a peacock could indulge in merriment it would be such a note of gladness as hers was. There was that reedy quality in it that the voices of tropical birds and women are prone to have. She talked, and I thought of how beautiful an adaptation to nature it would be if her vocation had been to sell lottery tickets. She was very handsome, without dispute, but her adornment, her hair, her voice, somehow caused me to think *la hija del pais,*—the veritable Cubana, a type, though not an exact similitude of all her sisters—an exuberant production, even for Cuba.

I do not think there is a land in the list of civilized countries that produces women so generally comely as the daughter of Cuba is. As a rule, she has a round figure, not large, but inclined to dumpling-shape. Whatever else she may be, she is never what the Americans call "scrawny." But her face, while seldom wanting in intelligence, is hardly ever vivacious. A sameness, a desert-like monotony of expression, pervades the sex. Strong traits of individual character are rarely indicated. If the reader has ever seen a flock of ducklings on their way to the nearest water, he has a fair idea of this little woman's gait and general air. Her hair is often a "glory" to her, and is sometimes of that blue-black shade only possible with the daughters of southern Europe and their descendants, though occasionally the Cuban girl varies the program by being a blonde, and, to be plain, rather fat.

This lady is often a woman at twelve, and the mother of a large family at nineteen or twenty. So pretty in her youth, in age she becomes either lean and dried, or fat and unwieldy. She fades early, and, for want of strength of character, is apt to lose control of her husband, who, nevertheless, still continues to need such control as badly as any man of his times. But whatever she may grow to seem, her eyes never fade. To the last, through all vicissitudes, they are big and black.

The Spanish race is, in fact, remarkable for the beauty of that feature. Even the males possess eyes that often, though not always, set them apart as handsome men. But I have learned that it means nothing, not even great intelligence. It does not indicate character of any stronger or nobler kind than any squint-eyes person may possess, and is far from being an indication of either mental force or moral courage.

The Cuban woman is the victim of a peculiar education, acquired in the school, the family, and the church. She believes, as did her mother before her, that when she goes out alone, or is necessarily in any male haunts, all baggage is at the risk of the owner. She is sure that men pretend to great gallantry, and are fond of paying outside regard to the fair ones, and are civil and polite, all as a mere blind. She has no silly belief that a gentleman would not do so and so. If he catches her alone, she is a ruined female from that moment. She must always have somebody with her who is not of the dangerous sex. There is a procession formed when she wishes to go a few blocks, as follows: First, two or three young ladies, the more the better. Second, a mulatto or negro servant, or, if possible, two or three, the more the better. Sometimes there is only one young lady and one servant. This is a case of great emergency. Man is a roaring lion, seeking some unprotected female of his species continually. No little miss ever goes to school alone, and cannot and must not pass along the street without a guardian.

The Cuban woman is timid and guarded in the presence of every man. A foreigner, speaking the language, and ignorant of these peculiarities, sometimes ignorantly endeavors to be civil. He is lucky if, to all he may say, he gets any answer at all. She to whom he speaks regards him as by nature a designing wretch, whom she is to avoid, to never see, to ignore entirely. Ancient maidens, long since become a perfect guaranty in their own persons against any imaginable familiarity with them, act in the same way, and never get over it, and keep a keen eye upon the younger ones. Until one grows accustomed to it, it seems one of the most ridiculous of all the follies of the ancien regime. . . .

One pities the Cuban young man who is in love. He cannot see her alone, and cannot come regularly to the house until a fair understanding of his intentions is arrived at. And when at last he has attained a felicity of being daily expected, he must do all his courting in the presence of the family, and utter his sweetnesses across the critical ear of his future mother-in-law. Until they have been to church, they two are never left alone. The whole family take sly turns in watching them. There is a regular detail made, I think, from the older servants of the house, to keep an eye upon them.

But there is human nature everywhere, even in Cuba, and the two are always getting off to a window-seat or a distant pair of chairs, though, with equal certainty, somebody sidles off in that direction and mounts guard. The smitten pair do not walk together in the evening. He does not accompany her to the theatre or to mass. They enjoy all the bliss they can under great difficulty, and with all mankind looking on.

The indirect result of all this espionage, of course nobody in this land of custom has ever observed. There are a great many small intrigues and innocent endeavors to circumvent the detectives. There are eloquent glances, signals, fan-talk, and the sly interchange of notes. Then the iron-guarded window, instead of being a protection, becomes a great convenience. It is more than a front gate is with us. She knows when he will pass by, and stands inside with a fair hand clasping the bars of her cage, and waits for him. They stand there with the iron between them, and talk. Every day it is so, and if mamma wishes to stop it, she must come and stand in the window also.

There are other respects in which the young man has a hard time. He must come every day. He must, and she holds him to the strict letter of this law. He is bound to show by every means in his power, that he holds all other women in contempt and detestation. He must not dance with any other, and had better not be caught holding on to any other window bars, in any other street. He tells all his friends about it, and she all hers, and the matter is diligently discussed. If he should fail to come around regularly every day he has to tell a satisfactory story. I have known her to send her brother after him. He takes his revenge after marriage.

When the Cuban lady becomes a wife and mother, then all her traits develop. She is domestic, faithful, patient, and her lord's absolute property to an extent unknown among northern people. She thinks she ought to obey him, and he agrees with unanimity. She does not seem to know that she is oppressed, and has never made an effort toward emancipation. She does not know any thing about cooperative kitchens, or the Sorosis, or her inalienable right to serve on committees, edit newspapers, and lecture. There never was a woman's rights' convention in this happy land, or a Dorcas society, or even a crusade.

But she has a trait that enables her to make herself very uncomfortable at times; she is insanely jealous. When she suspects nothing and nobody, she still keeps a wary eye for a possible slip. She wishes her husband to come and sit by her, and follow her about, and mutely beg her to smile upon him. When he goes out, she wishes to know where he is going and when he will return. When he returns, she asks him where he has been. She does not like him to dance with other women, and would blindfold him, if she could, to keep him from looking at them.

Eliot Durand
A Week in Cuba
(Chicago: Belford and Chinks, 1891), 60–61

The courtships of Cuba are carried on in the most public manner. The suitor arrives in evening toilet, and is ushered into the outer reception-room. The shutters are thrown open and the gas turned on. The chairs are all placed vis-a-vis, which, by the way, is the habitual arrangement, the suitor and the *suitee* sitting on one side, with the mother and other members of the family opposite. One would naturally think that a young man would make slow progress in love-making after this fashion, and indeed he might, were it not for the balls.

Dancing seems to be a very popular amusement, and a Cuban waltz will be looked upon by an American with amazement. I am sure there never was any other thing like it. It matters little how large the crowd is in the ball-room; that does not hinder the dancers. The couple engaged to dance choose a place in the ball-room large enough to stand in, and there you may find them at the close of the waltz, possibly an hour later.

The mode of waltzing may best be described by calling attention to an American couple when getting their bearings and about to commence. It is simply a series of slow balances, first on one foot and then on the other. Occasionally the couple will turn part way around, and then stop and talk to each other awhile.

It is in these dances that the lover probably improves his opportunity, for, deep in the crowd, out of sight of the *duenna* (who is always present), the conditions are favorable to amorous conversation, and he may even press the girl of his choice to his vest pattern, to slow music.

At the balls the ladies exhibit the most delicious abandon, and treat their gentlemen friends with the utmost familiarity, although maintaining a cold reserve to strangers.

Maturin Murray Ballou
Due South; or, Cuba Past and Present
(Boston: Houghton Mifflin and Company, 1855), 276–77

There are said to be three hundred thousand free negroes on the island, of whom comparatively few are found inland upon the plantations; they are all inclined to congregate in the cities and large towns, where, truth compels us to say, they prove to be an idle and vicious class, and as a body useless both to themselves and to the public. There are believed to be at present in Cuba about one hundred and forty thousand male and about sixty thousand female slaves. To carry on the great industry of the island as systematized by the planters, this number of hands is entirely inadequate. It is sometimes asked how there came to be so many free negroes in the island. It should be clearly understood that the laws which govern Cuba are made by the home government, not by the planters or natives of Cuba, and that indirectly these laws have long favored emancipation of the blacks. For many years any slave has enjoyed the right to go to a magistrate and have himself appraised, and upon paying the price thus set upon himself he can receive his free papers. The valuation is made by three persons, of whom the master appoints one, and the magistrate two. The slave may pay by installments of fifty dollars at a time but he owes his full service to his master until the last and entire payment is made. If the valuation be twelve hundred dollars, after the slave has paid one hundred he owns one twelfth of himself, and the master eleven twelfths, and so on. Until all is paid, however, the master's dominion over the slave is complete. There has also long been another peculiar law in operation. A slave may on the same valuation compel his master to transfer him to any person who will pay the money in full, and this has often been done where slave and master disagree. This law, as will be seen, must have operated as it was designed to do, as a check upon masters, and as an inducement for them to remove special causes of complaint and dissatisfaction. It has also enabled slaveholders of the better class, in the case of ill-usage of blacks, to relieve them by paying down their appraised value and appropriating their services to themselves. All this relates to the past rather than the present, since, as we have explained, the relationship of slave and master is now so nearly at an end as to render such arrangements inoperative.

There was a law promulgated in 1870,—the outgrowth of the revolution of 1868, which dethroned Isabella II,—declaring every slave in Cuba to be free after reaching the age of sixty, and also freeing the children of all slaves born subsequent to that year. But that law has been ignored altogether, and was not permitted even to be announced officially upon the island. In the first place, few hard worked slaves survive to the age of sixty; and in the second place, the children have no one to look after or to enforce their rights. Spain never yet kept troth with her subjects, or with anybody else, and the passage of the law referred to was simply a piece of political finesse, designed for the eye of the European states.

Carolina L. Wallace
Santiago de Cuba before the War
(New York: F. T. Neely, 1899), 36–43

Cuban women, or, as they call themselves, Creoles, are usually very good looking. Indeed, among young women it is rare to see a homely one. With dark eyes and hair abundant and curling and pale complexions with regular features, they possess a type of beauty all their own. The children are little fat cherubs of the Murillo type, and run about untrammeled by clothing until they are seven or eight years old. Nothing prettier than a young girl just blooming into adolescence can be imagined; a little older they incline to embonpoint, and I will remark *en passant* that flesh is an important factor in beauty here. To be slender and thin is considered ugly and worthy of commiseration. Neither is color desirable. An additional whiteness is obtained by a free use of cascarilla, a cosmetic prepared here from fine white shells, ground up into an impalpable powder, which is abundantly and generously applied, and even if visible and thick enough to rub off upon a gentleman's coat sleeve nothing is thought of it, as it is in universal use. Rouge is never used.

Fine shoulders, beautifully molded arms, small hands and feet, with the typical high-arched Spanish instep, complete the ensemble. Easy, graceful manners, and fine voices, musical and trainante, with much vivacity and gesture, expressive features, emphasized by little movements of the hands and shoulder shrugs, render them charmingly piquant. There seems to be no awkward period in the life of a Creole girl, for from the opening bud to the full-blown flower, the interval is short.

At fourteen a girl is considered marriageable, and is never permitted to go out alone, and even after an engagement is declared, she never receives her *fiancé*, except in the presence of some older member of the family. He may accompany her to the theater, concert or bullfight, but always with the family.

If the parents oppose a marriage, the lover may *steal* her—of course the robbery is committed with her own consent—and deposit her in the house of a mutual friend, where he is allowed to visit her under the usual conditional etiquette, until the time necessary for taking all the preliminary steps preparatory for the marriage has expired. Once taken away from her parents' house parental authority cannot prevail against the marriage.

Large families are not considered objectionable, but, on the contrary, many children are the precious jewels in the crown of motherhood.

When quite a little girl the Cuban maid has a playmate among the colored children, chosen from the servants or slaves of her own age, who grows up with her in the double capacity of companion and servant, and who, when she marries, goes with her as her own attendant to her new abode.

Creole women are frank and affectionate by nature, and do not hesitate by word or glance to show their admiration—the concealment, skirmishing and flirtation practiced by Americans being quite unknown.

When a man falls in love with a girl he at once declares his sentiments to her parents and asks permission to visit her; thus all embarrassment is avoided.

A marriage in church often takes place at midnight or very early in the morning, avoiding publicity, and the newly-married pair go direct from the church to their own house, or perhaps into the country for a month or so to pass the honeymoon.

On moving into a neighborhood the newcomer is expected to send his card to all the residents on each side of the street in the block on which he lives, these being considered his neighbors.

It is not unusual if any one sees you pass wearing some article of dress which especially pleases them, to send a servant with their compliments bearing a tray and request you to send it for them to look at and probably to imitate. Should you express admiration for anything of theirs, it is at once placed at your disposition. Of course, this is merely a form of compliment which you are never expected to take in earnest.

Young girls are always conducted to and from school by an attendant, and no lady goes into the street unaccompanied, as it is not considered *comme il faut*, and she would, by so doing, expose herself to the possibility of being spoken to by any man who met her unaccompanied. Neither would a man be found visiting a lady alone (unless he were privileged by his great seniority of years), nor would he detain her in conversation in the parlor of a hotel, lest by so doing he should compromise not only her but himself as well. You cannot walk or ride out alone with a man—there is safety only in numbers, and a *tête-à-tête* is not admissible except when the opportunity presents itself in the midst of company. *Les convenances* are rigidly observed. Yet this is a country where love is in the air, and the winged god, ever watchful, has his shafts always ready, and with unerring aim plants them where he wills, despite the barriers that hedge about his divinity only to increase and stimulate his persistency.

Although a lady may go out into the street with nothing over her head or shoulder, either in a volante or walking, she would not lift up her trailing skirts to save them from the dust, lest by so doing she expose to view her pretty foot or ankle; yet a Spanish officer told me that he fell in love with the lady of his admiration at first sight of seeing her foot as she descended from a volante at El Caney. She, with her family, came to the hotel where we were both stopping, and although he did not understand a word of French, nor she a word of Spanish, I had the pleasure of seeing the rapid *dénouement* of their mutual infatuation, and by receiving from both their confidences, thus helping in bringing about the consumation of their betrothal. In a short time she with her family sailed for France, and the young comandante had masses said at the cathedral for their safe journey across the ocean. Although I cannot complete this little romance by saying he followed her to France and married her, as I left myself soon after, yet I have no doubt that the little foot that walked into his heart so emphatically, did not relinquish its possession, but kept him fast under its tiny weight, till not only the foot itself, but the whole of its possessor became the crowning joy of the soldier's life.

Creole women in general are not intellectual, though those who are sent away to be educated have many accomplishments. They have great artistic perceptions, are quick to learn, and having natural ability for music, they are fine musicians, but early marriages and many children soon fill up a woman's life with domestic duties, and a natural indolence does not conduce to study. They excel in all social graces—possessing charming affability, with cordial, affectionate manners, which render them very fascinating. Fond of dress and finery—the warm climate being conducive to many changes in the filmy fabrics, which are manufactured especially for the Cuban market—they require a large assortment of gowns; for no one who has any regard for her reputation for being well dressed would be seen at theater, ball or opera in a dress that had been worn before.

At the theater and opera ladies never occupy the orchestra chairs, but must always have a box. The chairs are reserved for the men, who engage them for the season, just as are the boxes.

The low, open-work gilded railing and partitions being all open, the whole toilette is displayed, back and sides as well as front. A constant movement of the beautiful fans that with a soft click of pearl on pearl and ivory on ivory, as their jeweled sticks are folded back and forth with a swinging motion peculiar only to Spanish women, is heard all over the house like the fluttering wings of a flock of birds or the rustle of the wind among the trees.

The beauty of the Cuban woman soon passes its meridian. She either becomes immensely stout or shrinks and shrivels like a piece of parchment. Her pale complexion becomes brown and dark, and she settles down into an old woman, unredeemed by intellect or intelligence; even as the gorgeous flowers of her own country which, after they have been gathered a few hours, wither and curl up into a blackened mass, devoid of all beauty and fragrance.

List of Sources

(Numbers in brackets refer to pages within this volume)

Abiel Abbot, *Letters Written in the Interior of Cuba* (Boston: Bowles and Dearborn, 1829) [102, 147, 179, 203]

James Edward C. B. Alexander, *Transatlantic Sketches*, 2 vols. (London: Richard Bentley, 1833) [133, 150, 181]

Robert Baird, *Impressions and Experiences of the West Indies and North America in 1849*, 2 vols. (Philadelphia: Lea and Blanchard, 1850) [112]

Maturin Murray Ballou, *Due South; or, Cuba Past and Present* (Boston: Houghton Mifflin and Company, 1885) [29, 88, 129, 221, 243]

————, *History of Cuba; or, Notes of a Traveller in the Tropics* (Boston: Phillip Samson and Company, 1854) [119]

Fredrika Bremer, *The Homes of the New World: Impressions of America* (New York: Harper and Brothers, 1853) [116]

Alexander Gilmore Cattell, *To Cuba and Back in 22 Days* (Philadelphia: Press of the Times, 1874) [172]

Richard Henry Dana, Jr., *To Cuba and Back: A Vacation Voyage* (Boston: Ticknor and Fields, 1859) [12, 59, 120, 142, 165, 198]

William Drysdale, *In Sunny Lands* (New York: Harper and Brothers, 1885) [90]

Eliot Durand, *A Week in Cuba* (Chicago: Belford and Chinks, 1891) [242]

Antonio C. N. Gallenga, *The Pearl of the Antilles* (London: Chapman and Hall, 1873) [78, 127, 171]

Joseph John Gurney, *A Winter in the West Indies* (London: John Murray, 1841) [105]

Samuel Hazard, *Cuba with Pen and Pencil* (Hartford: Hartford Publishing Company, 1871) [18, 74, 169, 208, 234]

Julia Ward Howe, *A Trip to Cuba* (Boston: Ticknor and Fields, 1860) [65, 123]

William Henry Hurlbert, *Gan-Eden; or, Picture of Cuba* (Boston: John P. Jewett and Company, 1854) [56, 109, 230]

Alexander von Humboldt, *The Island of Cuba*, translated by J. S. Thrasher (New York: Derby and Jackson, 1801, 1856) [1, 41, 97]

Robert Francis Jameson, *Letters from the Havana, during the Year 1820* (London: John Miller, 1821) [4, 100, 225]

W.M.L. Jay [Julia Louisa M. Woodruff], *My Winter in Cuba* (New York: E. P. Dutton and Company, 1871) [27, 69, 233]

Richard Burleigh Kimball, *Cuba and the Cubans* (New York: Samuel Hueston, 1850) [158]

Richard J. Levis, *Diary of a Spring Holiday in Cuba* (Philadelphia: Porter and Coates, 1872) [170, 215]

John Milton Mackie, *From Cape Cod to Dixie and the Tropics* (New York: G. P. Putnam, 1864) [167]

James McQuade, *The Cruise of the Montaukto Bermuda: The West Indies and Florida* (New York: Knox and Company, 1885) [33]

Richard Robert Madden, *The Island of Cuba* (London: C. Gilpin, 1849) [48, 157]

John Mark, *Diary of My Trip to America and Havana, in October and November 1884* (Manchester: A. Ireland and Company, 1885) [35]

Rachel Wilson Moore, *The Journal of Rachel Moore Kept during a Tour to the West Indies and South America in 1863–1864* (Philadelphia: T. Ellwood Zeil, 1867) [17, 125]

George Augustus Henry Sala, *Under the Sun* (London: Tinby Brothers, 1872) [24]

James Williams Steele, *Cuban Sketches* (New York: G. P. Putnam's Sons, 1881) [144, 174, 201, 215, 238]

John Glanville Taylor, *The United States and Cuba* (London: Richard Bentley, 1851) [53, 114, 163]

Frederick T. Townshend, *Wild Life in Florida with a Visit to Cuba* (London: Hurt and Blackett, 1875) [86]

Anthony Trollope, *The West Indies and the Spanish Main* (New York: Harper and Brothers, 1860) [15, 67]

Henry Tudor, *Narrative of a Tour in North America, Comprising Mexico, the Mines of Real del Monte, the United States, and the British Colonies with an Excursion to the Island of Cuba*, 2 vols. (London: James Duncan, 1834) [104]

David Turnbull, *Travels in the West: Cuba, with Notices of Porto Rico and the Slave Trade* (London: Longman, Orme, Brown, Greens, and Longman, 1840) [42, 182]

Carolina L. Wallace, *Santiago de Cuba before the War* (New York: F. T. Neely, 1899) [244]

George Walton Williams, *Sketches of Travel in the Old and New World* (Charleston, SC: Walker, Evans and Cogswell, 1871) [237]

John George F. Wurdemann, *Notes on Cuba* (Boston: James Munroe and Company, 1844) [7, 44, 107, 137, 152, 187, 227]

Bibliographical Essay: Selected Titles

The historical literature treating nineteenth-century Cuba is extensive and diverse, and is especially noteworthy for important historiographical advances in recent years. A number of general English-language historical surveys provide an overview of the nineteenth century, including Hugh Thomas, *Cuba: The Pursuit of Freedom* (New York, 1971); Jaime Suchlicki, *Cuba: From Columbus to Castro*, 2d ed. (Washington, DC, 1987); and Louis A. Pérez, Jr., *Cuba: Between Reform and Revolution* (New York, 1988). Several older Cuban surveys have been reprinted and are still of considerable use. Among the better ones are Fernando Portuondo, *Historia de Cuba*, 6th ed. (Havana, 1965); and Ramiro Guerra y Sánchez, *Manual de historia de Cuba*, 6th ed. (Havana, 1980). Some of the newer published surveys of Cuba include Fuerzas Armadas Revolucionarias, *Historia de Cuba* (Havana, 1971); and Oscar Pino Santos, *Historia de Cuba: aspectos fundamentales*, 2d ed. (Havana, 1964). Still valuable, and in some ways still unsurpassed, are the volumes dealing with the nineteenth century in Ramiro Guerra y Sánchez et al., *Historia de la nación cubana*, 10 vols. (Havana, 1952). In addition to the conventional historical narratives, the essays in Guerra y Sánchez treat music, literature, journalism, education, trade, and foreign relations.

Much of the historical literature dealing with nineteenth-century Cuba has developed around specific thematic issues. Especially noteworthy are the recent studies of slavery. The literature has rich antecedents, both in Cuba and outside, much of which remains useful and should be consulted. The older studies include Hubert H. S. Aimes, *A History of Slavery in Cuba, 1511–1868* (New York, 1907); and Fernando Ortiz, *Hampa afro-cubano: los negros esclavos* (Havana, 1916).

The historical literature on slavery in Cuba began anew during the 1960s and expanded rapidly thereafter. One early trend involved the treatment of slave themes that were explicitly comparative in approach. Representative of this development are Herbert S. Klein, *Slavery in the Americas: A Comparative Study of Cuba and Virginia* (Chicago, 1967); and Gwendolyn Midlo Hall, *Social Control in Slave Plantation Societies: A Comparison of St. Domingue and Cuba* (Baltimore, 1971). After the 1970s, slave studies began to focus much more specifically on Cuba, examining slavery in the larger context of the Cuban experience. Among the better treatments of the development of slavery in Cuba are Franklin W. Knight, *Slave Society in Cuba during the Nineteenth Century* (Madison, 1970); and "Slavery, Race, and Social Structure in Cuba during the Nineteenth Century," in Robert Brent Toplin, ed., *Slavery and Race in Latin America* (Westport, CT, 1974), 204–27. Cuban titles include Juan Pérez de la Riva, *El barracón y otros ensayos* (Havana, 1975); and Eduardo Torres-Cuevas and Eusebio Reyes, *Esclavitud y sociedad* (Havana, 1986). For a study of the illicit slave trade see José Luciano Franco, *Comercio clandestino de esclavos* (Havana, 1985). The suppression of the slave trade is well treated in David Murray, *Odious Commerce: Britain, Spain, and the Abolition of the Cuban Slave Trade* (London, 1980). Robert L. Paquette, *Sugar Is Made with Blood* (Middletown, CT, 1988), provides an extensive treatment of the circumstances and conditions of slavery with focus on the Escalera Conspiracy of 1843–44. Among the better treatments of the abolition of slavery are found in the works of Rebecca J. Scott, including "Gradual Abolition and the Dynamics of Slave Emancipation in Cuba, 1868–1886," *Hispanic American Historical Review* 63 (August 1983): 449–77; "Explaining Abolition: Contradiction, Adaptation, and Challenge in Cuban Slave Society, 1860–1886," *Comparative Studies in Society and History* 26 (January 1984): 83–111; and *Slave Emancipation in Cuba: The Transition to Free Labor, 1860–1899* (Princeton, 1985). Older but still useful are Arthur F. Corwin's *Spain and the Abolition of Slavery in Cuba, 1817–1886* (Austin, 1967); and Raúl Cepero Bonilla's *Azúcar y abolición* (Havana, 1971).

The study of slavery in nineteenth-century Cuba inevitably opened new lines of research dealing variously with labor systems, race relations, and social organization. These themes produced a rich literature on the nineteenth century. Pedro Deschamps Chapeaux, *Contribución a la historia de la gente sin historia* (Havana, 1974), deals variously with African slaves, free people of color, fugitive slave communities, and Chinese coolies. The Chinese presence in nineteenth-century Cuba is examined in Duvon C. Corbitt, *A Study of the Chinese in Cuba, 1847–1947* (Wilmore, KY, 1971); Denise Helly, *Idéologie et ethnicité: Les Chinois Macao à Cuba, 1847–1886* (Montreal, 1976); and Mary Turner, "Chinese Contract Labour in Cuba, 1847–1874," *Caribbean Studies* 14 (July 1974): 66–81. Juan Pérez de la Riva has written three important essays dealing with Chinese labor: "Aspectos economicos del trafico de culíes chinos a Cuba, 1853–1873," *Universidad de La Habana*, no. 173 (May-June 1965): 95–116; "Los culíes chinos y los comienzos de la inmigracion contratados en Cuba (1844–1847)," *Revista de la Biblioteca Nacional "José Martí"* 17 (May-August 1975): 74–88; and "El trafico de culíes chinos," *Revista de la Biblioteca Nacional "José Martí"* 6 (July-December 1964): 47–57.

The historical literature dealing with Afro-Cubans and race relations in the nineteenth century has also expanded rapidly in recent decades, and in many different directions. Older works still of value include José Fernández de Castro, "El aporte negro en las letras de Cuba en el siglo XIX," *Revista Bimestre Cubana* 38 (July-December 1936): 71–88; and Alberto Arredondo, *El negro en Cuba* (Havana, 1939). Among the more useful works of recent years dealing with race and race relations are Pedro Deschamps Chapeaux, *El negro en la economía habanera en el siglo XIX* (Havana, 1971); Verena Martínez-Alier, *Marriage, Class and Colour in Nineteenth Century Cuba* (Cambridge, 1974); Donna M. Wolf, "The Cuban 'Gente de Color' and the Independence Movement, 1879–1895," *Revista/Review Interamericana* 5 (Fall 1975): 403–42; and Ada Ferrer, "Social Aspects of Cuban Nationalism: Race, Slavery, and the Guerra Chiquita, 1879–1880," *Cuban Studies/Estudios Cubanos* 21 (in press).

An extensive historical literature also has made important contributions to the study of the nineteenth-century economy, and perhaps nowhere more than in the area of sugar production. Among the most important works are Manuel Moreno Fraginals, *El ingenio*, 3 vols. (Havana, 1978); Roland T. Ely, *Cuando reinaba su majestad el azúcar* (Buenos Aires, 1963); and Félix Goizueta-Mimó, *Bitter Cuban Sugar: Monoculture and Economic Dependence from 1825–1899* (New York, 1987). Also useful are Laird W. Bergad, *Cuban Rural Society in the Nineteenth Century: The Social and Economic History of Monoculture in Matanzas* (Princeton, 1990); Fe Iglesias, "The Development of Capitalism in Cuban Sugar Production, 1860–1900," in Manuel Moreno Fraginals et al., eds., *Between Slavery and Free Labor: The Spanish-Speaking Caribbean in the Nineteenth Century* (Baltimore, 1985):

54–75; and Franklin W. Knight, "Origins of Wealth and the Sugar Revolution in Cuba, 1750–1850," *Hispanic American Historical Review* 57 (May 1977): 231–53.

The literature dealing with Cuban emigration in the nineteenth century has antecedents early in the century. Some of the better older works are Manuel Deulofeu, *Héroes del destierro* (Cienfuegos, 1904); Juan José E. Casasús, *La emigración cubana y la independencia de la patria* (Havana, 1953); and José Rivero Muñiz, "Los cubanos en Tampa," *Revista Bimestre Cubana* 71 (1958): 5–140. More recent studies dealing with Cuban emigration include Rolando Alvarez Estévez, *La emigración cubana en Estados Unidos* (Havana, 1986); and Gerald E. Poyo, *"With All and For the Good of All"* (Durham, 1989).

Cuban commercial relations are examined in a number of specialized studies. A general treatment is found in Roland T. Ely, *Comerciantes cubanos del siglo XIX* (Havana, 1960). More narrowly focused essays treat nineteenth-century Cuban commercial relations with the United States. These include René Alvarez Ríos, "Cuba: desarrollo interno y relaciones con los Estados Unidos de Norteamérica," *Política Internacional* 2 (1964): 59–135; and Roland T. Ely, "The Old Cuba Trade: Highlights and Case Studies of Cuban-American Interdependence during the Nineteenth Century," *Business History Review* 39 (Winter 1964): 456–78.

Cuban relations with the United States account for the greater part of the literature dealing with Cuba's foreign relations. General surveys of these years include Herminio Portell Vilá, *Historia de Cuba en sus relaciones con los Estados Unidos y España*, 4 vols. (1938–41); Emilio Roig de Leuchsenring, *Cuba y los Estados Unidos, 1805–1898* (Havana, 1949); Philip S. Foner, *A History of Cuba and Its Relations with the United States*, 2 vols. (New York, 1962–65); Lester D. Langley, *The Cuban Policy of the United States* (New York, 1968); Michael J. Mazarr, *Semper Fidel: America and Cuba, 1776–1986* (Baltimore, 1988); and Louis A. Pérez, Jr., *Cuba and the United States: Ties of Singular Intimacy* (Athens, GA, 1990).

A particular emphasis of this Cuba-U.S. literature is on North American intervention in Cuba during the 1840s and 1850s and again in 1898. Literature of the first period is concerned principally with the rise of annexationist activity and the series of filibustering expeditions against Cuba. Although somewhat dated, the study by Basil Rauch, *American Interests in Cuba, 1848–1855* (New York, 1948), is still a useful point of departure. Emeterio S. Santovenia, *El Presidente Polk y Cuba* (Havana, 1936), provides a survey of midcentury U.S.

policy. Perhaps the most important work of scholarship for this period is the three-volume study by Herminio Portell Vilá, *Narciso López y su época* (Havana, 1930–1958). Of much more limited use is Robert G. Caldwell's *The Lopez Expedition to Cuba: 1845–1851* (Princeton, 1915).

Works dealing with the U.S. military intervention in 1898 are far more numerous and have involved larger numbers of historians from both the United States and Cuba. A representative listing of this vast literature includes Albert G. Robinson, *Cuba and the Intervention* (London, 1905); Philip S. Foner, *The Spanish-Cuban American War and the Birth of American Imperialism*, 2 vols. (New York, 1972); Alvaro Catá, *Cuba y la intervención* (Havana, 1899); Cosme de la Torriente, *Fin de la dominación de España en Cuba* (Havana, 1948); and Enrique Piñeyro, *Como acabó la dominación de España en América* (Paris, 1908).

The literature dealing with the three principal phases of the thirty years of the Cuban armed struggle for independence—the Ten Years' War (1868–78), "La Guerra Chiquita" (1879–80), and the war for independence (1895–98)—is voluminous. An obligatory point of departure is consultation with the appropriate bibliographical guides. For the Ten Years' War: Aleida Plasencia, ed., *Bibliografía de la Guerra de los Diez Años* (Havana, 1968). For "La Guerra Chiquita": Miriam Hernández Soler, ed., *Bibliografía de la Guerra Chiquita, 1879–1880* (Havana, 1975). For the war of independence: Araceli Garcia Carranza, ed., *Bibliografía de la guerra de independencia (1895–1898)* (Havana, 1976). Among the better works dealing with these years are Emilio Roig de Leuchsenring, *La guerra libertadora de los treinta años, 1868–1898* (Havana, 1952); Ramiro Guerra y Sánchez, *Guerra de los Diez Años, 1868–1878*, 2d ed., 2 vols. (Havana, 1952); Francisco J. Ponte Domínguez, *Historia de la guerra de los diez años* (Havana, 1958); Fernando Figueredo, *La revolucíon de Yara*, 2 vols. (Havana, 1902); and Enrique Collazo, *Desde Yara hasta el Zanjón*, 2d ed. (Havana, 1967).

Particularly useful for the Ten Years' War is the volume edited by Maria Cristina Llerena, *Sobre la guerra de los 10 años: 1868–1878* (Havana, 1973), which contains more than fifty essays dealing with various aspects of the war, including military strategy, politics, slavery, labor, culture, and sugar production. The war of 1879–80 is treated by Asela Artes de Lagueruela, *La Guerra Chiquita* (Havana, 1953); and Rebecca Rosell Planas, *Factores económicos, políticos y sociales de la Guerra Chiquita* (Havana, 1953). The better studies for the independence war of 1895–98 include Evelio Rodríguez Lendián,

La revolución de 1895 (Havana, 1926); Rafael Gutiérrez Fernández, *Los héroes del 24 de febrero* (Havana, 1932); Miguel Angel Varona Guerrero, *La guerra de independencia de Cuba*, 3 vols. (Havana, 1946); Herminio Portell Vilá, *Historia de la guerra de Cuba y los Estados Unidos contra España* (Havana, 1949); René E. Reyna Cossío, *Estudios histórico militares sobre la guerra de independencia de Cuba* (Havana, 1954); and Ramón de Armas, *La revolucion pospuesta* (Havana, 1975).

Index

Alvarado, Pedro de, 230
Arango y Parreño, Francisco de, 98–99
Architecture, 10–11, 15, 18, 25, 27, 30–31, 138
Artemisa, 227

Bahía Honda, 4
Baracoa, 217
Batabanó, 4
Bayamo, 217
Bejucal, 50, 51
Blacks (negroes): as coachmen, 31, 36, 226; as domestics, 100–101, 112, 226; as servants, 16, 49, 120. *See also* Free blacks; Slaves and slavery
Borges, Nicolás Estebes, 197

Calvo, Nicolás, 42
Canary Islands: labor from, 130–31
Cardenas, Joakin [*sic*], 52
Casa de Beneficencia, 180–81, 183–85, 186, 192–95, 198–200
Casa-Romero, Conde de, 228
Castelar, Emilio, 223
Census: of 1775, 98; of 1817, 99; of 1842, 152; of 1857, 120
Charities: sources of income, 186–87
Chartrand, Mr., 63, 64, 65
Chinese, 35, 37, 144, 223, 237; as sugar labor, 66, 69–70, 74, 85, 87
Cienfuegos, 67–68, 80, 90, 91, 94–95, 129, 171, 221
Coartado system, 97–98, 101–2, 110, 112–13, 121, 125. *See also* Manumission

Coffee production, 38, 57–58, 102, 103, 153, 209–10, 227; Augenora estate described, 203–8
Cojimar, 4
Country houses: *fincas* described, 208–9; rude *sitios* described, 210, 215, 216
Cournand, Antonio, 195
Courtship, 240–41, 242, 245–46
Creoles: 26, 43, 53, 83, 99, 121, 228, 232; in commerce, 9; women, 244–47
Crime, 144–45; executions, 137, 138; statistics, 139–41
Cuisine, 211–12

Day, Mr., 106
Del Monte, Domingo, 190
Del Pino, Felix, 161
Del Real Socorro, Marquis, 228
Diaz de Esplando, Juan, 148
Disease, 57, 199–200; in Havana, 5–6, 30, 32; among slaves, 57, 63, 120

Education, 182–87, 190–92, 193, 201–2, 222; statistics, 182–83, 190–91; trade schools, 142
El Louvre café (Havana), 34, 36, 235
Emancipation: of slaves, 121, 127, 132, 243–44. *See also* Manumission
England: 167; British plantation owners, 42–43; and slave trade, 111–12, 113, 124

Fincas: described, 208–9
Fortifications (Havana), 1, 3, 5

Free blacks: 121, 227, 243; as labor,
    94, 128–29; position of, 98, 225–
    27. *See also* Manumission

Gambling, 16, 53, 158, 210, 222–23,
    226; among clergy, 147, 152,
    156, 165
Gonzales, Jacinto, 65, 66, 67
Guanabacoa, 2, 20, 21, 152
Guantánamo, 209
Guardia Civil, 236
Güines, 41, 42, 48–50

Haiti, 57
Havana: described, 1–39
Hospitals, 142–43, 189–90, 197–98;
    for the insane, 179, 182, 183,
    185, 187–90, 192, 195, 198; for
    lepers, 179–80, 182, 183, 187;
    for the military, 195–97, 199
Howe, Dr., 142
Humboldt, Alexander von, 29
Hurricanes, 19, 197

Isle of Pines, 21

Jackson, Mr., 135, 181
Jagua, 4
Jamaica, 67, 85, 128, 132
Jaruco, 4
Jews, 9, 156

Las Casas, Luis de, 3, 180
Limonar, 45, 116
Lottery, 38, 186, 218, 223, 238, 239
Luz, Francisco de la, 51

Madden, Dr., 185
Manumission, 97–98, 110, 125, 130;
    of unborn, 128
Marianao, 21
Mariel, 4, 41
Matanzas, 4, 30, 38, 41, 43, 59, 79,
    111, 122, 138, 186, 232, 233, 234
Military, 20, 138–39, 236; hospitals
    for, 195–97, 199
Montalvo, Sr., 48
Monteros: life of, 221–23

Moret y Prendergast, Sr., 127
Moret Law (1870), 127–28, 244
Morro Castle, 1, 4–5, 30

Opera: described, 234–37, 247
O'Reilly, Conde de, 52
Orphanages, 198. *See also* Casa de
    Beneficencia

Palenques, 115–16
Patriotic Society of Havana, 182, 195
Petersen, Mr., 91, 92, 95
Pinar del Río, 191, 227
Plácido, 233
Poey, Juan, 78, 80, 82, 83–84, 129
Ponvert, E. and L., 91–92, 94
Population: classes, 228–29;
    nobility, 227–28; statistics, 227
Porto Rico: slavery in, 84, 114
Prisons: 140–42; Havana prison
    described, 133–37, 137–39,
    142–44
Puerto Príncipe, 183, 191

Railroads, 79, 219, 232; travel on,
    233–34
Regla, 3, 20, 79, 234
Roman Catholic church: bishop of
    Havana, 148, 151, 165; cathe-
    dral described, 154–55, 170–71,
    172–73; churches and services
    described, 148–50, 150–51,
    153–54, 173, 174–76; convents,
    152–53; corrupt clergy, 147–48,
    151–52, 156, 161–62, 165; effect
    of slaveholding on, 157–58;
    feast days, 177–78, 212–13;
    income, 157, 158, 170; Jesuits,
    158, 166, 170; low condition of
    religion, 158–63, 166–69, 172;
    managing schools, 201; as
    poor, 174, 176; and slaves, 68–
    69, 107, 108–9, 131, 160; village
    rituals, 212–14
Romay, Pedro Maria, 190

Sandoval, Gonzalo de, 230
San Felipe, Marquis, 52

Santa Clara, Count de, 3
Santa Lucia, Marquis de, 228
Santiago de Cuba, 30, 43, 169, 171, 183, 191, 221
Santo Domingo: 42; slave insurrection in, 85, 128, 132, 152
Slaves and slavery: disease among, 57, 63, 120; as labor on public works, 125; as labor on sugar estates, *see* Sugar production; laws regulating, 107–8, 110, 120–21, 124–25; mortality, 99–100, 104, 114; number imported, 100; runaways, 109, 114–16; sale of, 105, 106–7, 122–23, 127; suicide among, 116–17, 120, 160; tribes described, 119. *See also* Emancipation; Manumission
Slave trade, 111–12, 113, 114, 118, 132; slave ships described, 104–5, 126–27
Sociedad Económica, 142, 190–91
South Carolina: slavery in, 102–3, 107
Spaniards: Catalans, 230; contempt for Creoles, 228, 230, 231; influence of, 8, 9, 43, 53, 121, 230–33
Sugar: prices, 42, 88, 89, 93; profits from, 44, 63, 85, 92–93
Sugar estates, 54–56, 227; Alexandria, 52–53, Ariadne, 116, 118, Carlotta, 45, España, 79–80, 82, Hormiguero, 91–95, La Pita, 52, Las Canas, 80–83, Olanda, 48–50, Santa Anna, 51–52, Santa Sofía, 69–74, Saratoga, 45; hospitals on, 71–75, 76, 79, 87, 110; nurseries on, 76, 87–88, 110
Sugar production: danger of cane-field fires, 47, 63; engineers (*maquinistas*), 63, 66, 75–76, American, 89; equipment and machinery, 42, 54, 57, 58, 76–77, 86, 93, 94, 130; foremen (*mayorales*), 49–50, 51, 52–53, 63–64, 66, 75, 102; free labor, 94, 128–29; process described, 42, 44, 45–48, 58–59, 60–62, 78, 87; slave labor, 41–42, 44–45, 48, 50, 51, 53, 55–56, 62, 68–69, 82, 89, 103–4, 113, 116–19, of children, 86, of women, 62, 87, 110
Suicide, 160, 217; of Chinese, 70, 74; of slaves, 116–17, 120, 160

Tacón, Miguel, 7, 23, 137–38
Ten Years War, 85, 145, 244
Tobacco production, 2, 38, 86, 111, 195, 232; and slavery, 111
Torre, Marquis de la, 3
Trade: international, 38–39, 92, 93; retail, 8–9, 13, 21–23, 25–26, 29, 226
Trinidad, 4

United States, 21, 185, 209; perceptions of, 22; slavery in, 85, 110, 125

Valdés, Antonio José, 197–98
Valdéz, Gabriel de la Concepción, 233
Velásquez, Diego, 217–18
Village life: described, 212–14, 217–21
Vuelta Abajo, 111
Vuelta Arriba, 56–58, 214

Women, 7–8, 13, 21–22, 31; described, 237–42, 244–47; dress, 21, 34, 35, 233–34; in Havana, 13–14, 16, 34; and slavery, 52, 62, 87, 88, 98–100, 110, 131, 234. *See also* Courtship

Zulueta, Julián de, 78, 79, 80, 82–85

Latin American Silhouettes
Studies in History and Culture

William H. Beezley and
Judith Ewell
Editors

Volumes Published

William H. Beezley and Judith Ewell, eds., *The Human Tradition in Latin America: The Twentieth Century* (1987). Cloth ISBN 0-8420-2283-X Paper ISBN 0-8420-2284-8

Judith Ewell and William H. Beezley, eds., *The Human Tradition in Latin America: The Nineteenth Century* (1989). Cloth ISBN 0-8420-2331-3 Paper ISBN 0-8420-2332-1

David G. LaFrance, *The Mexican Revolution in Puebla, 1908–1913: The Maderista Movement and the Failure of Liberal Reform* (1989). ISBN 0-8420-2293-7

Mark A. Burkholder, *Politics of a Colonial Career: José Baquíjano and the Audiencia of Lima* (1990). Cloth ISBN 0-8420-2353-4 Paper ISBN 0-8420-2352-6

Kenneth M. Coleman and George C. Herring, eds. (with Foreword by Daniel Oduber), *Understanding the Central American Crisis: Sources of Conflict, U.S. Policy, and Options for Peace* (1991). Cloth ISBN 0-8420-2382-8   Paper ISBN 0-8420-2383-6

Carlos B. Gil, ed., *Hope and Frustration: Interviews with Leaders of Mexico's Political Opposition* (1991). Cloth ISBN 0-8420-2395-X Paper ISBN 0-8420-2396-8

Charles Bergquist, Gonzalo Sánchez, and Ricardo Peñaranda, eds., *Violence in Colombia: The Contemporary Crisis in Historical Perspective* (1991). Cloth ISBN 0-8420-2369-0   Paper ISBN 0-8420-2376-3

Heidi Zogbaum, *B. Traven: A Vision of Mexico* (1992). ISBN 0-8420-2392-5

Jaime E. Rodríguez O., ed., *Patterns of Contention in Mexican History* (1992). ISBN 0-8420-2399-2

Louis A. Pérez, Jr., ed., *Slaves, Sugar, and Colonial Society: Travel Accounts of Cuba, 1801–1899* (1992). Cloth ISBN 0-8420-2354-2 Paper ISBN 0-8420-2415-8